RT · LEO KOCESKI · JULIUS FRANKS · DON LU...

ELLIOTT · J. T. WHITE · JOHN GHINDIA · DICK KEMPTHORN · AL...

JIM MADDOCK · ED SHANNON · GEORGE GENYK · BILL FREEHA...

IM BETTS · MARTY HUFF · JIM BRANDSTATTER · DANA COIN · BI...

KENN · RUSSELL DAVIS · HARLAN HUCKLEBY · RICK LEACH · GEO...

NGLER · ALI HAJI-SHEIKH · JIM HERRMANN · STEVE SMITH · DA...

NS · MARK MESSNER · KEITH MITCHELL · JOHN DUERR · BOB A...

ERICK ANDERSON · J. D. CARLSON · BRIAN TOWNSEND · CORW...

FLOYD · BEN HUFF · KRAIG BAKER · JAY FEELY · JON JANSEN · D...

D · HERCULES RENDA · FOREST EVASHEVSKI · ALBERT WISTERT ·...

BURGER · PETE ELLIOTT · STU WILKINS · CHALMERS "BUMP" ELLI...

ROGER ZATKOFF · TED CACHEY · ED MEADS · RON KRAMER ·...

ACK · RICK VOLK · RON JOHNSON · TOM GOSS · CECIL PRYOR ·...

R · GORDON BELL · ROB LYTLE · LES MILES · CALVIN O'NEAL · M...

LJA · MIKE TRGOVAC · STAN EDWARDS · BUTCH WOOLFOLK · JO...

D HALL · ERIK CAMPBELL · JAMIE MORRIS · MONTE ROBBINS ·...

ND RICK STITES · CHRIS CALLOWAY · DEAN DINGMAN · YALE...

VIN BROWN · DERRICK ALEXANDER · MERCURY HAYES · ROD PA...

EW HENSON · DAVID BAAS · MARKUS CURRY · LLOYD CARR · GER...

Dad... michigan
...
greatest player...
michigan...
player ticket... got...
got m. merry christmas!
♡♡Dad♡♡

You are the greatest
Almost player but
also the greatest
wolverine fan!
I love you -
Jill

You are the BEST dad
anyone could ask
for! We are so LUCKY!
I Love you!!
chipmunk

Hail to the father named...
Hail to the greatest fat...
Hail, Hail to the greatest dad!! woo!
Merry Christmas dad
from
Spenser

WHAT IT MEANS TO BE A WOLVERINE

WHAT IT MEANS TO BE
A WOLVERINE

MICHIGAN'S GREATEST PLAYERS

TALK ABOUT MICHIGAN FOOTBALL

FOREWORD BY BO SCHEMBECHLER

KEVIN ALLEN, NATE BROWN, AND ART REGNER

TRIUMPH
BOOKS
CHICAGO

Library of Congress Cataloging-in-Publication Data

What it means to be a Wolverine / edited by Kevin Allen.
    p. cm.
  ISBN-13: 978-1-57243-661-9
  ISBN-10: 1-57243-661-1
   1. University of Michigan—Football—History. 2. Michigan
Wolverines (Football team)—History. I. Allen, Kevin, 1956–

  GV958.U5284W43 2005
  796.332′63′0977435—dc22

                                      2005048548

This book is available in quantity at special discounts for your group or
organization. For further information, contact:

Triumph Books
542 South Deaborn Street
Suite 750
Chicago, Illinois 60605
(312) 939-3330
Fax (312) 663-3557

Printed in U.S.A.
ISBN-13: 978-1-57243-661-9
ISBN-10: 1-57243-661-1
Design by Nick Panos; page production by Patricia Frey;
editorial production by Prologue Publishing Services, LLC.
All photos courtesy of Bob Kalmbach unless indicated otherwise.

CONTENTS

FOREWORD

What It Means to Be a Wolverine

In times of change, those brave enough to stay the course will be victors in the end.

There's no question that college football today is played on a landscape of radical change. Some is good. But some, I believe, undermines the very essence of what the game is all about.

All around the country, the word *tradition* is thrown around like a pocketful of dirty pennies.

That's a shame! *Tradition* is a precious word. It belongs only to the strongest who conduct themselves with honesty, integrity, and commitment to withstand every test of time.

That's Michigan football!

The legendary Fritz Crisler summed it up best more than 60 years ago:

> Tradition is something you can't bottle. You can't buy it at the corner store. But it is there to sustain you when you need it most. I've called upon it time and time again. And so have countless other Michigan athletes and coaches. There is nothing like it. I hope it never dies.

That was true before Fritz Crisler got to Michigan. It was true all the time he was here. And it's just as true today as the day he said it.

There are excellent football programs in every part of our country. Most conduct themselves honorably and contribute to the overall tradition of real college football.

Michigan football has always been and will always remain in a class by itself. Here the national championship team of 1997 gets fired up before the Ohio State game in Ann Arbor. *Photo courtesy of AP/Wide World Photos.*

But how can anyone come close to the tradition in Ann Arbor, where games have been played since 1879?

More victories than any school anywhere in the country; around 111,000 fans for each game at the Big House; the most distinct helmet in the country; the greatest fight song in the history of college sports; with Ohio State, the most celebrated rivalry in all of sports; New Year's Day bowl games; Big Ten championships; the tunnel; the Little Brown Jug; the marching band; the tailgate parties.

And always remember: the University of Michigan is one of the most academically acclaimed state institutions in the nation and sits on one of the most colorful campus settings anywhere.

The history is alive and endless. But the essence of tradition transcends victories, statistics, events, and all the other celebrated features that comprise college football.

The essence of tradition lies in the hearts of the people who protect and perpetuate the storied history that was handed down to them. And they carefully pass that legacy down to generations yet to come.

In the 126 years of Michigan football, only 16 men have been privileged to serve as head coach. And for the last 37 years, only three have been entrusted with that privilege.

The head coach serves as the guardian of that tradition. But it takes the combined efforts of the assistant coaches, administrative and medical staffs, and all of the dedicated people who work tirelessly behind the scenes to enhance that tradition and keep it so precious in the hearts of supporters sprinkled all over the world.

More than anything else, though, the great Michigan tradition is molded by the young men who are privileged to wear the winged helmet and unmistakable maize-and-blue uniform.

Think of some of the All-Americans who have represented the school so proudly. Bennie Oosterbaan. Tom Harmon. Francis, Albert, and Alvin Wistert. Len Ford. Pete and Bump Elliott. Ron Kramer. Tom Mack. Ron Johnson. Jim Mandich. Dan Dierdorf. Reggie McKenzie. Rob Lytle. Rick Leach. Anthony Carter. Jim Harbaugh. Desmond Howard. Ty Law. Jon Runyan. Tyrone Wheatley. Charles Woodson. Jon Jansen. Steve Hutchinson. Tom Brady. Stanley and Braylon Edwards.

And how about that center captain of the 1934 team? Gerald R. Ford is the only former president of the United States of America to have played on two (1932 and 1933) national championship teams.

That's just a handful of the many young men who have helped to mold that tradition. The list goes on and on.

But it takes more than All-Americans to sustain a tradition that only the University of Michigan enjoys. It takes the commitment of every player who puts on a helmet . . . even those who never set foot on the field. They do their sweating and bleeding all week long in practice so that the starters can do their jobs on Saturdays.

Recruiting young men to come to the University of Michigan is one of the special honors a coach enjoys. It's truly a privilege to offer a deserving youngster the opportunity to join the family and contribute to the tradition of Michigan.

I remember looking into the faces of those young men. I remember asking them: "Do you have what it takes to play for the University of Michigan? Can you meet the challenge of competing in the classroom at one of the finest institutions in the United States of America and then take everything you have in you onto the field and carry on the tradition that has been laid before you?"

It's the biggest challenge of their young lives. But I guarantee you—those who have the guts and determination to stick it out through graduation go on to become some of our nation's most successful people in every walk of life.

x

Two of the Wolverines' biggest legends, coach Fritz Crisler (right) and running back Tom Harmon (center), accept congratulations from Downtown Athletic Club president Walter P. Holcombe (left) upon Harmon's winning of the 1940 Heisman Trophy. *Photo courtesy of AP/Wide World Photos.*

The Michigan–Ohio State rivalry has stood as a symbol of college football for more than 100 years, and UM's Schembechler and OSU's Hayes epitomized the spirit of the game for a decade. *Photo courtesy of AP/Wide World Photos.*

They become "Michigan Men." They learn to succeed the right way. With honor, honesty, and integrity.

One of my most treasured memories occurred in May 2004. The university hosted a weekend reunion of all living former Michigan players. About seven hundred returned to their home. Some weren't walking so sprightly. And some may have put on a little more weight than they carried when they played at the Big House.

But they returned. They came from all points of the United States. And every decade was represented back to the forties. They exchanged stories about what it was like when they played in that grand stadium. They talked about that special camaraderie that only Michigan football can create.

I was asked to address this distinguished group. So was Lloyd Carr, Gary Moeller, and Bump Elliott, who preceded me as head coach.

I can speak for all of us. It was one of the greatest privileges any of us has had in our whole careers.

Some of these men were celebrated physicians. Some were attorneys. There were educators, captains of industry, and a wide spectrum of the whole American spirit.

Regardless of their professions, they are bonded for life through one very special commonality—each one is a "Michigan Man."

The discipline, the dedication, the integrity that they learned on the field became incorporated into their lives long after having played their final game.

For every one of those players and every coach who had the privilege of working with them, there is no greater reward. They know that tradition is as alive today as it was when they had the privilege of representing their school.

I remember when I was hired as head coach before the 1969 season as if it were yesterday. I brought several of my assistants from Miami of Ohio.

Back then, the locker rooms were in Yost Field House. The coaches' room was so small you could almost reach across the room and touch the opposite wall. One of the coaches said we had 10 times better facilities back at Miami.

That's when I stopped them.

"Did you ever sit in the same chair that Fielding H. Yost or Fritz Crisler did?" I asked.

No.

"Did you ever hang your clothes on the same spike that Bennie Oosterbaan did?" I continued.

No.

Not one more word was needed. The message was loud and clear.

Facilities have significantly improved since then. But the privilege remains the same.

It's the same feeling for the players. Every one of those storied All-Americans ran out the same tunnel as the players do today. And every ghost from all of their glories lives on that field to provide support, especially when the times are toughest.

It's an honor for me to introduce you to some of these legends from so many decades past. Savor the memories of these proven Michigan Men. And rest assured, there'll be a whole lot more to come.

—Bo Schembechler

ACKNOWLEDGMENTS

Detective skills were as vital as writing prowess in the production of this book. Many thanks are owed to those who provided leads, tips, or the last-known whereabouts of the Wolverines featured in this manuscript.

Special thanks go to John Ghindia Jr., the former Wolverines guard (Michigan, 1984) who helped us locate many of the featured players.

We thank all of the former players who contributed their stories to this book. However, an extra layer of gratitude goes to Rick Leach, Jamie Morris, Rick Volk, Aaron Shea, Kraig Baker, Yale Van Dyne, Bob Chappuis, Stan Edwards, Russell Davis, Billy Taylor, and Steve Smith, whose enthusiasm for our project made our work that much more enjoyable.

Mention has to be made of President Ford's participation in this project. There is no greater example of a Michigan Man than the 38th president of the United States. At 91, President Ford still keeps regular office hours. We hoped to get five minutes with him, and he gave us much more. His memory of events that happened 72 years ago was astounding. This is a man whose life has become a chapter in American political history, and yet he still speaks of his days on the Michigan gridiron as being among his most cherished memories.

Art Regner offers his particular gratitude to his WXYT radio colleagues Doug Karsch, Glen LaGrou, and Kevin Graham for giving him space to complete this project. He also thanks Sarah Zientarski for transcription. He dedicated his work to his mother, father, sister, his niece Jessica Regner, and

Michelle Dupue. "Without Michelle's belief in me and her support, this work would have never been completed," he said.

Newlywed Nate Brown thanks his wife, Sabrina, for quickly developing the patience of a writer's wife. That's a role that usually takes years to master. He is appreciative of her contributions, especially considering their wedding vows made no mention of editing of the spouse's prose. Mostly he thanks her "for being every man's dream wife." Nate dedicated his work to his brother, Pat, the only other person who understands how an Illinois State graduate could have such an obsession with Michigan football.

Thanks to the Allen clan, Terri, Erin, Kelsey, and Shane, for providing wit and wisdom for this project and many before it.

Finally, thanks must go to Triumph Books for providing us the opportunity to become voices for Michigan football tradition; and thanks to the Michigan fans whose passion for maize-and-blue football fueled the creation of this book.

—Kevin Allen

INTRODUCTION

Three weeks into Rick Leach's freshman season as Michigan's starting quarterback in 1975, he received his first taste of what it means to be a Wolverine when he was lampooned in an edition of the *Michigan Daily*.

"[It was] a picture of me as a blind man with sun glasses and a leader dog with a noose around my neck," Leach recalled. "That was in the student newspaper after two ties and a big victory."

Everywhere Leach went on campus, students were giggling at the cartoonish depiction, and his resentment grew by the hour. But later in the day his anger was washed away by the sudden realization that this was the level of accountability and pride that had attracted him to Ann Arbor. At Michigan, "B" work is unacceptable. "A" work is always expected, maybe even demanded. That's why the Wolverines haven't suffered a losing season since 1967. Since the program was launched in 1879, the Wolverines have only had 13 losing seasons. They haven't won fewer than eight games since 1984, and Michigan has been invited to a bowl game every year since 1975.

"Reality hit me—you know that you are in the big leagues," Leach remembered. "I thought, 'You better get it going and turn this thing around or you're not going to be here very long.'"

Many prestigious football programs boast winning traditions, but few can match the level of expectation that accompanies a Michigan scholarship offer. At Michigan, 7–4 is treated like a .500 record. That's the baseline. That's a "C" grade. A national ranking and a bowl appearance is treated as one of the basic rights of being a Michigan player. If Michigan slips into the second half of the national polls, fans began to wonder what's wrong with the Wolverines. If the Wolverines lose to Ohio State, it's a calamity on campus.

It's almost unforgivable to lose to in-state rival Michigan State. "I remember the first time [assistant coach] Les [Miles] described it to me when I was a redshirt," said former Michigan player Corwin Brown. "He said, 'This is like back in Chicago in an alley with your buddy about to have it out with some other guys.'"

Brown quickly understood what Miles was saying. "That's what that game was about because, bar none, Michigan State was always the most physical game that we played," Brown said. "I don't care how good or bad they were, it was always the toughest game."

Consistency of success is what defines the Michigan football program. The Wolverines have almost a tribal approach to winning. Each class of players passes the tradition along to underclassmen through stories and legends. Every man who has waited his turn to race through that Michigan tunnel before a game at Michigan State enjoys a bond with all others who have done the same for many decades. There is a closeness between all Michigan Men that is easy to see and difficult to describe. Former Michigan players from the thirties, forties, and fifties still make the trek to Ann Arbor to watch the Wolverines play in the fall, and they are looked upon with great reverence. When players were contacted to give their stories for this book, they were always curious about what other players would be involved. When the names were rattled off, no one ever had to ask who those players were, even though some of them hadn't suited up for the Maize and Blue in more than 60 years.

Clearly Michigan coaches have played a major role in maintaining the Michigan tradition over the last century. It's easier to maintain consistency when a school only has had 11 coaches over the past 105 years. In that period, the United States has elected more presidents than Michigan has hired football coaches. Each coach has brought a unique personality and different approach to their job, and yet there was a sameness in how they bonded with their players. Every player interviewed for this book viewed his coach as a memorable role model in his life. Some viewed their respective coaches as father figures.

Michigan coaches are generally portrayed as dictatorial, tough and gruff, but the truth that emerged from our interviews is that coaches such as Fritz Crisler, Bennie Oosterbaan, Bump Elliott, Bo Schembechler, Gary Moeller, and Lloyd Carr all had a caring side that wasn't frequently on public display.

The best illustration of the tough love approach that most Michigan coaches have embraced can be viewed in a speech that Schembechler gave to more than one player over the years.

"My door is always open to you if you have problems in school, with your family, with your girlfriend, or any issue you might have," Bo would say. "But where you play and how often you play is not open for discussion."

Several players reported that coaches, particularly Schembechler, would know more about their grades and even their family life than they did.

It's difficult to appreciate how close Michigan coaches become to their players. But former All-American running back Billy Taylor explains it this way: when his mother died while he was on the Michigan team, it was Bo Schembechler who delivered the news. When he got himself into some legal trouble after college, it was Bo who stood behind him.

Moeller, who replaced Schembechler, was only a head coach at Michigan for five years, but when many, many players and coaches were gathered in a banquet setting, Moeller, 44–13–3 during his tenure, was the one who received a standing ovation from his former players.

"There were great coaches that were back," said former Michigan linebacker Erick Anderson. "And Mo was the one who got the standing ovation because it's hard to follow a legend. He did it very successfully."

The most surprising truth uncovered in the research for this book is that most players believe that what it means to be a Wolverine extends well beyond what happens on the football field. It's really about camaraderie, relationships, and memories that are developed in their years on the Michigan campus.

"I loved the education that I received at Michigan," said former Michigan kicker Jay Feely. "Not just the textbook education, but education that expanded my mind. I took a Sport and Race Relations class. Many guys on the team were enrolled in that class. I wrote a paper for that class, and it made me realize something that I probably wouldn't have noticed if I wasn't looking for it—that a football team is a great study of race relations and the dynamics behind race. Michigan football takes the place as an identifying factor in your life when you're at the football building. You're not a black football player or a white football player; you're a Michigan football player. Because you have this identifying factor that is greater than race, you get into a team setting that is all intermixed. There's no black groups sitting here and white groups sitting there. But you take this same group of guys in their social setting, not in the football building going to meetings, and race reverts back to being the identifying factor."

Football is the players' identity, but it is the education that they seem to value most. That seems to be a theme throughout the generations.

When quarterback Drew Henson left Michigan in 2001 to play professional baseball after his third season, he was still 30 credits shy of graduating. He had been valedictorian of his high school class and he wanted his Michigan degree. While playing winter ball, he was enrolled at classes through the University of Michigan. Notes would be faxed to him. He would take tests at Arizona State University. When he went to Florida to play, he remembers writing essays and term papers between games. In the midst of his baseball season, he flew to Michigan, took his final exam, passed it, and walked across the stage with his graduating class. Then he hopped back on a plane and caught up with his minor league team on the fourth game of a road trip in Charlotte, North Carolina. That's how important his Michigan degree was to him.

"To get my degree, and more importantly to finish on time with the guys I came in with, I'm as proud of that as anything I've done," Henson said.

This book relies entirely on the memories of players. Their words were edited for length, accuracy, and literary style, but every effort was made to capture their true feelings on their Michigan experience. Sometimes the players told the stories better than we could write it. Such was the case of Russell Davis, now an athletic director in Jackson, Michigan, schools, who seemed to have one of the best grasps on what it means to be a Michigan football player.

When Davis was released by the Pittsburgh Steelers in 1983 he was, by his own admission, a man in need of an emotional compass.

"I was lost," Davis recalled, "I didn't have a clue of what I was going to do. I was struggling. My whole life had been football, and the applause and accolades that go with being a good football player weren't there anymore."

He dabbled in other professions for a couple of years before deciding that he really wanted to get back into football. He decided "to go see Bo." Davis figured he had been a captain and a MVP at Michigan, and he had owned a good relationship with his coaches. But as Schembechler is known, he didn't sugarcoat the issue when he met with Davis.

"Russell," he said, simply, "you didn't graduate."

Schembechler wasn't going to hire a coach without a college degree. He made that clear. "It was like he hit me with a ton of bricks," Davis recalled.

However, Schembechler wasn't through talking. "The first thing we are going to do, Russell, is to get you back into school and get your degree work finished up," he said.

"It was the turning point of my life," Davis said, clearly emotional about the memory. "If you asked me to say what it means to be a Wolverine, I would have to say it means a lifelong commitment going both ways."

WHAT IT MEANS TO BE
A WOLVERINE

The
THIRTIES

GERALD FORD
CENTER
1932–1934

In 1934 we were playing Illinois, and it rained and rained and rained. We would go into the huddle and, by the time we returned to the line of scrimmage, the water was high enough that the ball would be floating around in the water. We lost that game 7–6. That's why I was surprised when Fielding Yost came over to talk to me after the game. I never played under him—he was the athletic director during my career. But I will never forget that hat he wore, and the cigar in his mouth. He came into the locker room after that game and said, "Ford. You centered the ball many, many times in the worst weather I ever saw for a football game and you never made a bad pass. Good job."

It was a helluva compliment.

It's funny what you remember. I would have to say that my two proudest moments as a Michigan player came when the school retired my number—No. 48—and when my teammates voted me Most Valuable Player after my senior season in 1934.

We had won the national championship in 1932 and 1933 with Harry Kipke as the coach. I had been a substitute on those teams because Chuck Bernard was an All-American center in front of me. We had a lousy season in 1934, and it's not difficult to explain why that occurred. Coach Harry Kipke's offense relied on a passer and a kicker, and our passer, Bill Renner, broke an ankle and couldn't play. Our kicker, John Regeczi, who was the best college punter I ever saw, hurt his knee and couldn't play. We didn't have any offense in 1934.

Gerald Ford, the 38th president of the United States, poses at center during the 1934 season, the year he was voted the team's Most Valuable Player. Ford's Michigan teams won national titles in 1932 and 1933, and in January 1935 he played in the East-West College All-Star game.

But one game that season did have a dramatic impact on my life and my political career. Willis Ward and I came in as a freshman and we became very, very close friends. We rode together on the road trips. Willis was an exceptional athlete in football and track. To give you example of how talented he was, consider that at the Big Ten track meet in the spring of 1935, Jesse Owens broke or tied four world records in the 100–yard dash, the 220, the long jump, and the 220-hurdles. Willis won the high jump and was second to him in the 100. He did beat Owens in some races on other occasions, but I remember the two of them had more points than some schools at that Big Ten meet.

When we were preparing for a home game against Georgia Tech in 1934, we were told that the southern school wanted Willis dropped from our roster

because he was black. Georgia Tech's officials said their team would not take
the field if Willis was allowed to play. I was very upset, as were my classmates.
We wanted Willis to be allowed to suit up just as he always had. [On campus,
some students and faculty members held rallies in support of the idea that the
school should not give in to Georgia Tech's demands.] I considered not playing if Willis wasn't allowed to play. I really thought this was our chance to
establish a policy against racism. I consulted with my father, who said, "You
have an obligation to the team and the school." But I also thought I had an
obligation to my friend Willis Ward. In the end, it was Willis who urged me
to play.

Willis did not play against Georgia Tech, and we won 9–2. The game was
a long time ago, and I don't remember what was said on the football field, but
I know it impacted my thinking on civil rights issues. It was back then that I
began establishing criteria that was illustrative of my feelings about racism. I
was very proud of the fact that Willis and I were able to coordinate our feelings and views over the years. Willis went to law school, and I helped him
get a job as a prosecuting attorney and judge. He was a first-class fellow and
a good lawyer.

I always considered Kipke to be a first-class coach. I had been an all-state
player at South High School in Grand Rapids. I was named captain of the all-
state team, and Harry Kipke had actively recruited me. He even had me staying at his house on a weekend.

Harry always tried to help me. He helped me find a job when I got to
school. I only had $200, and $100 was for tuition. During my senior year I
remember going to Harry and telling him I wanted to go to Michigan law
school, but I needed a job and I asked Harry if he could hire me as a freshman coach or an assistant. I recall that he said that he could, but my pay
would only be $100 per year. "That," I told him, "doesn't solve my problem."

About a month later Harry Kipke called me and said that Yale coach
Raymond "Ducky" Pond was coming to town. Kipke wanted me to join
them for lunch. Ducky was looking for an assistant line coach. As a result of
Harry's recommendation, I got the job at Yale for $2,400 a year. My plan was
that I would coach and go to law school at Yale at the same time. Yale was
concerned initially about me being able to have the time to coach and attend
law school simultaneously, but eventually Yale officials allowed it.

There was no NFL when I graduated from Michigan, and if there had been
I might have considered playing. I played in the East-West Shrine Game on

January 1, 1935, and then in the following August I played against the Chicago Bears on Soldier Field in the *Chicago Tribune* game. Coach Potsy Clark offered me a chance to play for the Detroit Lions and [coach] Curley Lambeau wanted me to play at Green Bay, but they were offering me about $200 per game for only 14 games. It seemed like a better deal to go to Yale where I was getting $2,400 and the opportunity to go to law school.

I was always proud of my association with Michigan football. During my political career, I used to have a lot of trouble with my friends at Ohio State. We always had a bet, a buck or two, on the Michigan–Ohio State game. But I did pretty well.

Gerald Ford represented his Grand Rapids district as a member of the House of Representatives from January 3, 1949, to December 6, 1973. He was reelected 12 times, each time accumulating more than 60 percent of the vote. In 1973 President Richard Nixon appointed Ford as vice president to replace Spiro Agnew, who had resigned. Ten months later, the Watergate scandal forced Nixon to resign as well, and Ford became the 38th president of the United States. Ford had a strong civil rights record as an elected official, and in 1999 he mentioned Willis Ward when he wrote a guest editorial for the *New York Times* in support of the University of Michigan's affirmative-action policy. "[Ward's] sacrifice [in 1934] led me to question how educational administrators could capitulate to raw prejudice. A university, after all, is both a preserver of tradition and a hotbed of innovation. So long as books are kept open, we tell ourselves, minds can never be closed," Ford wrote. "Do we really want to risk turning back the clock to an era when the Willis Wards were isolated and penalized for the color of their skin, their economic standing, or national ancestry?"

HERCULES RENDA

HALFBACK

1937–1939

WHEN A UNIVERSITY OF MICHIGAN RECRUITER VENTURED into the hills of West Virginia to dig up football talent in 1935, he wasn't looking for me.

The Wolverines didn't come to mining country to unearth a 5'3", 140-pound right halfback. They were there to land my East Bank High School teammate Roland Savilla, a 6'4", 200-pound all-state tackle who was quick enough to run a leg of our school's state-caliber mile relay. As I've said for years, I was just the tagalong.

By the time we reached high school, Savilla and I had been friends for years. Our families had both emigrated from Italy in the early 1900s, and we grew up together. We lived close to one another until the third grade, when my family moved one hill over.

In junior high school, Savilla and I actually competed against each other. I was told that when our schools faced off, the coach of Savilla's team offered a simple message about how to defeat our team: shut down Renda.

"Coach," Savilla supposedly said, "don't worry about that little Italian. I'll take care of him."

Savilla shut me down, and his team won the game 7–0. He denied ever saying that, but that's the story I was told.

We reunited at East Bank, and with Savilla's help, I was able to score 30 touchdowns during my high school career. Maybe Savilla believed I could

Hercules Renda, shown practicing during his final season of 1939, played halfback for coaches Harry Kipke and Fritz Crisler.

play college football, because in my yearbook he wrote: "College classmates, I hope."

My dad and two brothers worked in the coal mine, and my two brothers gave their money back to the family. I worked in the tipple, the structure where coal is dumped and sorted by size. My parents allowed me to keep the money I earned for college, and I had $155 in my pocket when I came to Ann Arbor in 1936. The good news: out-of-state cost to attend Michigan in those years was $75 per semester. The cost for in-state students was $35.

Harry Kipke was my first coach at Michigan, and he gave me the opportunity to play quite a bit as a sophomore in 1937. No one was cut in those days, but you had to earn your playing time. That's what I've always loved about athletics. You decide whether you will play or not, based on how well you compete in practice. Before the first game of the 1937 season, a write-up in the newspaper suggested I would be a starter. But during the pregame warm-up I missed the first five or six punts that I tried to field. I remember thinking, "If Kipke was watching me, I'm surely not going to start." But I did start, and I definitely remember my first collegiate plays.

Every guy on the kickoff team was thinking he was going to make the tackle, and I was no exception. I was running down the field at full speed, and I saw the Michigan State player coming to block me. I moved to sidestep him, and he threw a body block. His heel caught me in the pit of my stomach and knocked the wind out of me. Meanwhile, the kick skipped out of bounds, and we got to do it all over again.

I'd recovered by the time we re-kicked and was more determined to make the tackle. Believe it or not, the exact same scenario happened again, and I was left trying to catch my breath.

We held Michigan State on downs, and the punter boomed the kick over my head. I was hit immediately as I scrambled back to retrieve the ball. That was my introduction to college football. As I was sprawled out, I was thinking, "This is nothing like high school football."

Kipke treated me very well on and off the field. He built a home on Geddes Road between Ann Arbor and Ypsilanti, and he hired me as a babysitter for his children and to clean up around the house. He paid me out of his own pocket. He was a good man.

But in their last four years under coach Kipke, the Wolverines never were above .500. Fritz Crisler was hired away from Princeton to replace him in 1938.

To change our outlook and our image, Crisler introduced the winged design for our headgear. It's the same design that's now become symbolic of Michigan tradition. To tell you the truth, the new design didn't create much attention back then. To us, it was just headgear.

Crisler was a disciplinarian, and even his coaches were subjected to his wrath if they didn't perform up to his expectations.

One day before practice, Crisler sent his line coach, Biggie Munn, on an errand. He returned while Crisler was talking to us before practice. Apparently, Crisler expected him to be back sooner, because he made him run to the brick wall that went around the field. It was startling to see an assistant coach being forced to run as punishment.

Right before Munn died in 1975, I ran into him coming up the aisle at a Michigan game and we talked about that incident.

"I have never been as mad at anyone as I was at Crisler when he made me do that," Munn told me.

Crisler liked to keep the opponents guessing. In those days, college teams would almost always run the ball on first and second downs and then pass on third. Going into the game against Ohio State in 1939, coach Crisler decided to reverse that plan. He wanted us to pass on first and second down. Ohio State kicked off, and on first down we threw a forward pass that the Buckeyes intercepted. They scored quickly to make it 7–0. On our second possession, we passed again and the Buckeyes picked it off again. The Wolverines were down 14–0 before the stands were filled up.

9

"Forget it," Crisler told us. "Just play ball."

When we went back to playing our traditional game, we ended up coming back to win that game 21–14.

In my junior year, Tom Harmon came up to the team, and he was even better than people say. He was 6'2", 190 pounds, and our squad only averaged 185 pounds per man. He was from Gary, Indiana, and he had won the state's 100-yard dash and hurdles titles in high school. He and Paul Kromer did much of the ball-carrying in 1938, and Paul probably played as well, if not better, than Harmon. Forest Evashevski was a tremendous blocker for both of them.

When I start talking about Michigan, I almost always digress because I met so many wonderful people associated with Michigan football.

Remember, I came from the hills of West Virginia. Think of a high school field in a coal mining town and think of coming to Michigan and playing in front of seventy-five thousand people sitting on wooden bleachers. How do you describe that?

Former Michigan coach Fielding Yost was such a genius. He originally wanted to construct 125,000 seats in the stadium, but the faculty was against the idea.

To me, it's like a dream that I played for Michigan. I've been blessed. I really don't have the words to describe the tradition, or how proud I am to have played for the Wolverines.

Often people have asked me to name my favorite moment as a Wolverine player, and I always tell them that "every moment I played was my favorite moment."

In my junior season, I picked off a pass late during an 18–0 win against Ohio State. I almost ran it back for a touchdown, and I wanted the ball as a keepsake.

Henry "Hank" Hatch was the equipment manager at the time, and he wouldn't go for it.

"I only give game balls to senior letter winners, and I will see that you get one next year," he said.

Sure enough, I scored a touchdown against Chicago in 1939, and I earned my game ball.

Arriving at Michigan weighing 140 pounds, I never pushed my weight over 160. The funny part is that I even played one full week at guard.

Crisler once made a comment that I "was the greatest football player among players of my height."

That probably doesn't say much, but I sure enjoyed playing. I have this photo that shows me returning a punt against Minnesota, and there are six Minnesota players either hanging from my waist or ready to converge on me. There isn't another Michigan player in sight. I think that photo says something about my ability. I had God-given speed and quickness that helped me get through those games.

Newspapermen had fun with my name. Hercules Powder Company made the dynamite that was used in coal mines, and that gave writers plenty of ideas. I have a *Michigan Daily* story in which a writer suggested that I "represent explosiveness."

When my mother was pregnant with me, she read the book about Hercules. She liked what she read and so gave me that name. With a name like Hercules, I've often wondered what life would have been like for me if I were a piccolo player instead of a football player.

In 1937 Hercules Renda started at right halfback for Michigan. He caught a touchdown pass from Stark Ritchie in his first collegiate game. Following graduation, Renda served as an assistant coach at Michigan for a year. He went on to become a high school coach, a position he held for more than 30 years.

FOREST EVASHEVSKI

QUARTERBACK

1938–1940

WHEN FOOTBALL TRAINING CAMP BEGAN IN 1938, I was a center. But 10 days before the season opener against Michigan State, coach Fritz Crisler said he wanted all the quarterbacks to stay after practice. "And Evashevski, you stay, too," he said.

We all ran wind sprints, and I beat them all. After we were finished, Crisler told me: "We are moving you to quarterback because we need speed ahead of Tom Harmon. We think you are fast enough to be his lead blocker." That's how I became a Michigan quarterback. I wasn't as fast as Tom, but I had more speed than any of the other blocking backs.

Tom was pleased by Crisler's decision. I think Tom also felt that the blockers were too slow. And he and I had become friends. My first day of practice as a freshman was spent watching Tom Harmon perform before the cameras. I didn't know who he was. He got a lot of notoriety coming out of Indiana. I soon found out who he was. He was a star. He could pass, run, and kick. He did the punting, kicked off, kicked extra points, and played defense. Tom made it fun for us. He used to drive Crisler crazy in practice. If he ran to the other side of the field, he'd roll around on the ground when he was tackled. He would grab his knee. Crisler would go running over there. He never noticed that Tom would be smiling. He scared Crisler to death.

Forest Evashevski (No. 69) leads the blocking for ball carrier Tom Harmon during a 1939 game in Chicago. Evashevski came to Ann Arbor as a lineman and left as a quarterback.

As a kid, I dreamed of playing Michigan football. I wasn't much sought-after when I graduated from Northwestern High School in Detroit because I only played a game and one-half of high school football. I had played sand-lot football. At Northwestern, there were three houses where you went every day for attendance and notices. After you went there, you would go to class. Northwestern had "house" football; the houses would play each other. Some of the guys asked me to fill in. Someone told the varsity coach about me, and they brought me out and put me in uniform for Northwestern High. The school was in a championship game. I didn't play. I sat on the bench, but the next year I came out for football and played as a center. During the second game, however, I was taken to Redford Receiving Hospital with a cerebral hemorrhage. That was my senior year. I was 16.

Then I read in the newspaper that Ford Dealers were going to have a team in the Michigan Amateur Football League. They were having tryouts, and if you made the team you got a job at Ford. So I went out and made the team in 1935. By that time I was 17. It was an industrial league, and I played two years there. Then I went to Michigan at 18. We had good teams when I was there. Ed Frutig was an end, and he became an All-American. He had great hands. He didn't have great speed, but if the pass was anywhere near him, he caught it. Paul Kromer came to Michigan as a heralded star from Ohio. Paul was a really good football player, but somehow he and Fritz clashed a bit. Paul wasn't as large as Harmon; he weighed only 165 or 170, but he played a lot for us. Bob Westfall was an Ann Arbor kid; he was younger than we were. He was a class behind us, but he was a very good offensive football player.

Harry Kipke was the varsity coach when I got there, but he was fired after the season and Fritz Crisler and his staff came in. They brought in the winged helmets, and the backs and ends were happy because it was easier to see your receiver downfield. That yellow stands out.

Fritz was a great teacher. I think there were coaches who equaled him in strategy, but Fritz had a manner of teaching that was precise and clear. I took a lot of his approach with me when I went off to be a coach. Many coaches ramble. But Fritz was concise and accurate. When he introduced a new play, he lined up every player and told them why the play was designed. Then he went through each position and explained what players were to do. When you were through hearing his explanation, you had the whole concept of the play. Many coaches just give you your assignment. But he gave you an assignment and told you why you needed to do it. He also spelled out the consequences if you didn't do it.

At Michigan, everyone started calling me "Evy" because there had been a Herman Everhardus who had played there [from 1931 to 1933] and he had been called Evy. People still call me that today.

Football in Ann Arbor when I played may have been a bigger event than it is today. Back then there weren't as many distractions as we have today. Today a fan can sit home and watch Notre Dame or Southern Cal play on television. Back when we played, football in Ann Arbor was the whole menu on Saturday afternoon.

I was pretty close to Fielding Yost. One day his secretary called and asked if I could have dinner on a Sunday evening. I was flattered. The other guy invited was Tom Harmon. Over dinner, he said to us, "Do you know why I asked you here? It's because we will graduate together." We didn't know what he meant. He explained that he was retiring [as athletic director] the year we graduated. We had a very nice evening, and Yost talked and talked and talked

14

about the famed Willie Heston teams in 1902 and 1903. [Yost coached running back Heston from 1901–1904 and never lost a game]. He cherished that team. He had great pride in their accomplishments.

The last game in which Tom Harmon and I played together was probably the most memorable. There was a lot of hype. Tom Harmon had a big game, and I scored a touchdown. We won 40–0. We went out in a blaze of glory.

After leaving Michigan, I was in the Navy, where I was taught hand-to-hand combat in Iowa Pre-Flight school. In 1942 Iowa Pre-Flight had a football team, and we beat Michigan 26–14. I scored a touchdown. Another former Michigan player, Bob Flora, was also on the team. It was quite strange to be playing against Michigan. Eventually, I moved out to the Pacific and was assigned to a carrier. As I got to San Francisco, V-J Day came. Then the Navy gave me a football team to coach. Servicemen were waiting to go home with nothing to do. They thought the best thing to do with them was have sports. I coached until I was discharged.

Coaching became my career. Eventually, I went to Iowa in 1952 and coached for nine seasons. I retired as athletic director in 1970. When you are coaching, the only loyalty is to your paycheck. But it was tough playing at Michigan. I had many friends in Michigan, and they were torn because they rooted for Michigan but they wanted me to do well. If anything, it hurt me, because I always put too much emphasis on the Michigan game. One year in particular, I scrimmaged my Iowa players too hard in a quest for a victory against Michigan. It was the wrong decision. I probably over-trained. That's why I didn't have much luck against Michigan.

While I was at Iowa, I was all-Hawkeyes; but when I retired from there, I became all-Michigan again.

At Iowa, Forest Evashevski won two Big Ten titles and tied for another. He won two Rose Bowls. The Hawkeyes were 37–8–2 in his last five seasons. When Evashevski retired, Ohio State coach Woody Hayes called him "the best offensive coach in the nation."

The

FORTIES

ALBERT WISTERT

TACKLE

1940–1942

Early in my Michigan career, a newspaperman interviewed me. He asked me what my goals were for my career. "I want to be an All-American like my brother, Whitey," I said.

"What are you talking about?" he said. "You never even played high school football."

"That's OK," I said. "That's my goal."

As it turned out, I became an All-American and was voted Michigan's Most Valuable Player in my senior year.

My dad had been a police sergeant in Chicago and he was shot and killed [in 1927]. I was six years old. My mother had six children to raise. She didn't have much money. "What if you get hurt playing high school football?" she said. "I couldn't pay the medical bills, so you can't play."

We were allowed to play baseball and basketball. But by the time I went to Michigan, my brother, Francis—we called him "Whitey"—was on the Michigan coaching staff. In 1930 Whitey had been working at the Majestic Radio factory in Chicago, and a high school friend had invited him to Michigan. Once he got a look at the campus, that was all he needed. He became an All-American there. He was a great athlete. He also played baseball. And it was only natural that his brothers would follow him to Michigan.

I certainly looked up to Whitey. I saw him pitch the one game he started in the majors for the Cincinnati Reds. It was in Chicago against the Cubs.

Albert Wistert (center) opens the hole for Tom Kuzma, who scores the Wolverines' first touchdown in a 20–20 tie with Ohio State in 1941. Wistert was a tackle at Michigan from 1940 to 1942 and then went on to play nine years in the NFL.
Photo courtesy of Ivory Photo.

He lost 1–0. He pitched a great game and almost won it himself with his bat. In the seventh inning, he drove a ball out toward the left field bleachers. The outfielder jumped up and speared the ball before it went into the stands. I also saw him play for the Cincinnati farm team in Nashville. The first baseman there was hit in the head with a baseball. He missed the season and Whitey replaced him at first. People started calling him Whitey "Wheatie" Wistert. Back then you received a box of Wheaties if you hit a home run and they gave him many boxes of Wheaties that season.

I was 6'1½", maybe 200 pounds when I got to Michigan. I was the smallest of the three Wistert brothers. I was pretty green as far as football was concerned. Chicago has a tremendous park system, and I could play football there without my mother's permission. I didn't have the benefit of great coaching there, but I learned about the game

The best coaching tip I received came from freshman coach Wally Weber. He took me aside one day and said, "I've been watching you run, and you are very fast, but you are too long in the same place."

He was right. I was taking short, choppy steps. I was not using my arms properly. He put me with the track coach to teach me how to run. After a month, when the track coach was done with me, I could really run. That was a big asset for me during my days in college and pro football.

Fritz Crisler was a tough coach. In 1939 we were scrimmaging, and I was hit from behind and broke my ankle. That day I wasn't wearing my ankle wraps—and that was a must, according to Crisler. He would always tell us that before we came to the field, we had better have our ankle wraps. And there should be tape over them to further protect the ankles. On that day, I was late for practice, and to save time I didn't put on the ankle wraps. When the trainer took off my shoe and sock and showed my bare injured ankle, Crisler was watching. "Where are your ankle wraps?" he asked, not too nicely.

I tried to explain that I was running late, but Crisler wasn't accepting my excuses. "Serves you right," he said. "Move the body or move the ball. We can't waste any more time here."

He certainly didn't give me any sympathy. I had a lot of interesting moments with Crisler. The first game I ever played for Michigan was September 28, 1940. I remember because it was Tom Harmon's 21st birthday. It was the first game of the season, and it was at the University of California-Berkley. My fiancée was from Glendale, California, and she had come up to Northern California for the game. I was paying attention to her and not paying attention to the fact that we were supposed to be on the bus going to practice after the luncheon at the Palace Hotel in San Francisco.

The bus left without me, but a trainer stayed behind to find me. We grabbed a taxi and caught the bus on the Golden Gate Bridge. We flagged it down so it would pull over and let us on.

At the luncheon, I had swiped a sterling silver coffee server. I had put it in my pocket, and when I climbed on the bus the guy sitting in the front seat with Crisler saw the bulge in my pocket. He shook my pocket, and the coffee server went "clank, clank, clank."

When we got out to practice, Crisler called the whole squad together and said they had gotten a call from the hotel, that some silverware was missing. I knew that was baloney. He said that if there was something that we want and we can't afford, we should come to the coaches. Of course, he was looking right at me when he said it.

All of this was rather upsetting for a guy who hadn't yet played his first game for Michigan.

But I did start and had a good game. However, I broke my breastbone in that game. I had a date afterward with this wonderful girl who would become my wife, and I couldn't even put up my arms to hug her. But I played the rest of the season.

In my sophomore season, I had a big day against Pittsburgh. Sportswriter Grantland Rice was there, and I got a lot of notoriety as the "blond kid from Chicago—Whitey Wistert's kid brother."

Two weeks later we played Minnesota. How we lost that game I will never know. We lost 7–6, and that one point cost us the Big Ten and national championships. I wanted that national championship because Whitey had won one. I wanted to duplicate what he did.

We scored right away against Minnesota, but missed the extra point. It was 6–0 and we kicked to them. Minnesota couldn't move. Then the Gophers punted, and our left end Ed Frutig blocked it. The ball squibbed out of bounds at Minnesota's 3-yard line. The game wasn't five minutes old. I repeat, how could we have lost this game?

But on our second down, Minnesota intercepted our pass. Right after that, I got conked in the head and suffered temporary amnesia. When we took over the ball, Forest Evashevski called the play for Bob Westfall to run off guard. I was supposed to trap a guy outside and knock him out of the way. But I didn't know what I was supposed to do. Guys knew then that something was wrong with me. The doctor was called out. I didn't know where I was or what I was doing. I had a concussion. I had to leave the game, and it was while I was out of the game that Minnesota's Bruce Smith ran 80 yards for a touchdown. They kicked the extra point. They took me out, sedated me, let me sleep, and I played in the second half. But we lost 7–6. That was a very tough defeat.

I only carried the ball one time in my college career—against Northwestern in 1941—and on that play I broke my wrist and nose. After that play, I decided no more of that. I preferred to block for the guys with the ball. I've had my wrist operated on twice, and it still isn't right to this day. It feels like a sprained wrist. I couldn't even pass my army physical because of it, so instead of going into the army during World War II, I played for the Philadelphia Eagles.

My older brother, Alvin, became the third Wistert brother to play for Michigan. He played after me, from 1947 to 1949. When Michigan played in the Rose Bowl after the 1947 season, I was living in California. Some guys came over to my house afterward, including my brother Alvin. When everyone left, Alvin and I were still having beers. Maybe it was 2:00 or 3:00 in the morning.

"What do you think your chances are of making All-America like your two brothers?" I asked him.

"No way," Alvin told me. "Remember when we were kids, how when you ran, you'd get short of breath and then you would get your second wind and you could run forever? Well, I can never get that second wind. I can't go beyond getting that shortness of breath. And these kids are all so young that I'm playing with and against, I don't think there is anyway that I'm going to be an All-American tackle."

"Really?" I answered. "With that attitude you don't have a snowball's chance in hell of making All-American."

"What do you mean?" he said.

"You talk yourself out of it before you ever get a chance to make it," I said. "Did you ever hear of a man named Norman Vincent Peale and his power of positive thinking? What you have to do is begin to think positively about making All-American. And say to yourself, 'I'm going to make it, regardless of anything.'"

He sat quietly for a while and then said: "You know, kid, you got something there. I do want to make All-American like you did, and Whitey did. By God, I'm going to make it, too, or it will be my dead body if I don't."

With his new attitude, Alvin became an All-American in 1948 and 1949.

Albert Wistert played nine years for the NFL's Philadelphia Eagles as a 215-pound tackle. He was All-Pro eight of those seasons. He was captain of the Eagles team from 1946–1950, and during those five years, the team played in the championship game three times. The Eagles won the NFL championship in 1948 and 1949. Michigan retired his No. 11 and Philadelphia retired his No. 70. It was the first number the Eagles ever retired.

LEO KOCESKI

HALFBACK

1948–1950

WHEN I WAS IN THE SIXTH GRADE IN CANONSBURG, PENNSYLVANIA, I said I was going to go to the University of Michigan. That's where I went. When I was in the eighth grade, I said when I get married I would go to Bermuda. When I married my wife Gloria, that's what we did.

Now I tell people that it's too bad I didn't say I was going to own my own company, because I probably would own my own company today. That's how good I was at setting goals at an early stage. That's just how I am.

Canonsburg is the home of Perry Como and Bobby Vinton. It's a popular little town. After high school, I probably had 20 or 30 offers, and a guy came up from South Carolina and started talking Polish to my mother. I remember thinking, "Uh-oh." I wasn't keen on going down there.

I remember Fritz Crisler was coming to Pittsburgh during my senior year in high school, and I was supposed to go meet him. But I made up some excuse, saying I had to study. Back then I was told that you needed a B average to play at Michigan, and I was an A- or B student in high school. I was in the 89–90 range, and I heard that college was harder and that I would drop one full grade. I was worried a bit. But in the spring I did go to Ann Arbor for a visit. The only words Crisler said to me were: "We will need backs."

Michigan was losing Jack Weisenburger, Bump Elliott, and Bob Chappuis, among others. I got my way and came to Michigan.

When I came to Michigan in 1947, the school had so many players that it had several different teams. The Wolverines had a freshman team, a J-V squad, and a 150-pound team in addition to the varsity team. I didn't even practice with the freshmen. The coaches took five or six of the freshmen—players they thought could make the grade—and scrimmaged them against the varsity. Before Michigan beat Stanford, we ran two plays against the varsity, and I broke them for pretty good yards. Coach Crisler never cursed at anyone, but he wasn't happy with his team at that point.

The other memory from those scrimmages against the 1947 team is that Dick Kempthorn hit me, and I think it's the hardest I've ever been hit.

In the spring of 1948, I was voted the outstanding player in spring practice. That puts the heat on you. Going into 1948, there was hope that Bump Elliott would get another year of eligibility. He had played two years in Purdue, and then played one season at Michigan. But either the NCAA or Big Ten declared him ineligible. Honestly, if he had been declared eligible, I don't

24

Leo Koceski runs with the ball during a 1949 game. Koceski's Michigan teams won three Big Ten championships and a national title, and he added two more Big Ten titles as a baseball player. *Photo courtesy of Ivory Photo.*

know if I would have played much in 1948. But even with Bump moving, I decided I had better switch positions. Gene Derricotte was going to be the left halfback, and either Pete Elliott or John Ghindia was going to be the quarterback. Walt Teninga was also a left halfback, and I figured he would move to right halfback. When I went home to Canonsburg on break, I remember practicing running from right to left. At left halfback you run from left to right.

That's what you did if you wanted to play. Another memory of playing for Michigan was the training table. I never ate so well as I did when I came to Michigan. Every day was steak or prime rib. We ate at the Michigan Union. This was no cafeteria. Tablecloths. Girls waited on us. In the preseason, you had three meals there a day. Once the season started, you got your evening meal. The Sunday dinner was always chicken or ham. Before we played Minnesota in 1948, I remember we had T-bone steaks.

Ernie McCoy was a scout for Michigan. Before the Minnesota game in 1948, he came in and said: "You had better be ready to play Minnesota, or you will get the living shit kicked right out of you, and you will be the sorriest bunch ever to wear the maize and blue."

Minnesota had a tough team. Former Minnesota [Vikings] coach Bud Grant was an end on that team, along with Leo Nomellini. We won that game 27–14, but I remember some interesting moments. Once, we were down on our own three, and we lost a yard, and then we lost another yard. It's third down, and Oosterbaan calls for a quick kick—only our punter Wally Teninga was on the bench next to Oosterbaan. He didn't realize that. They told me to kick. I said a Polish prayer and punted the ball about 50 yards to get us out of a jam. It was the only time I punted in my sophomore year.

Certainly, the 1950 "Snow Bowl" against Ohio State is a game everyone talks about. In those days, you took a bus to Toledo, stayed overnight, and then took a train to Columbus. I remember when the train pulled into the station, the snow covered everything. There was an icy spot near the train, and we all watched out the window as people would come by and hit that spot and fall right on their asses.

We didn't even know if the game would be played, but if the game was played, we were going to have to run in conditions like that.

I remember that assistant coach Dick Kempthorn had doe skin gloves, and he asked Chuck Ortmann to try them on. They fit him and the ball stuck to them. That helped because Ortmann set the record of 24 punts in a game. Chuck did a great job.

We didn't make a first down or complete a pass in that game. But I also don't think we lost the ball on a fumble. Carl Kreager was the real hero in that game because he was the center and he didn't make a bobble that game. That was a great feat. We blocked two punts—one from Tony Momsen and Al Wahl—and we won 9–3. Momsen fell on his for a touchdown.

What people forget is that, during the game, we heard that Illinois was upset by Northwestern. So we knew if we won, we would win the Big Ten championship and go to the Rose Bowl.

I mostly played defense in that game and intercepted a pass. [Don] Dufek was hurt in that game, and a sophomore named Dave Tinkham came in [at defensive back], and I can remember telling him, "Watch out for sleepers." I didn't want to get beat on the last play of the game.

My mother, brothers, and sisters came in from Canonsburg for that game, and they didn't get home until Monday or Tuesday.

The Rose Bowl was a great experience. At the Rose Bowl, we were down 6–0 going into the final five or six minutes of the game, and Chuck Ortmann completed a couple of crucial passes to Fred Pickard, who recently passed away. We got down close to the goal line, and on the fourth try, Don Dufek got the ball across the goal line. Harry Allis kicked the extra point, and we were up 7–6. We got another late touchdown, and we were Rose Bowl champions.

What else can I say about my Michigan experience? I played three years in football and won three Big Ten championships and one national championship. I never played baseball in high school, but I played three years of baseball at Michigan. I became the captain and won two championships. Six seasons of competition, and five championships. That's not too bad.

Leo Koceski had three catches for 100 yards in a game against Michigan State on October 23, 1948.

JULIUS FRANKS

GUARD

1941–1942

HARDLY ANY AFRICAN-AMERICAN PLAYERS WERE IN college football at the time that I played at the University of Michigan. I have to give all of the credit to coach Fritz Crisler for giving me the opportunity to play.

I was the second African-American player on the Michigan varsity in the modern era and the first African American from the school to make the All-America team. [According to the Michigan press guide, Ann Arbor native George Jewett became Michigan's first African-American football letter-winner in football as a sophomore in 1890.]

Willis Ward was an outstanding athlete who came out of Northwestern High School to join Michigan's football team in 1932. He was the first African American on varsity in the modern era. Willis, also a track man, played on the Michigan football team with Gerald Ford. By enduring the hardships that he did, Willis paved the way for me.

In 1934 Georgia Tech refused to play the University of Michigan in Ann Arbor if Willis was in the lineup. Athletic Director Fielding H. Yost made the decision to hold him out of the game, even in the face of protests by regents, students, and professors. After that episode, the regents instituted a bylaw that stipulated that if a player made the varsity team, he could not be held out of games because of his race.

Obviously, that's how I benefited by Willis Ward's experiences. In my time, Michigan played only Big Ten, Midwestern, or Eastern colleges. We couldn't go south, because we couldn't stay in a hotel together or eat together.

Throughout the Big Ten, there were few African-American football players. But following after Willis, I was treated very fairly at Michigan. Coach Crisler, the coaches, and the other players treated me wonderfully. The University of Michigan gave me the opportunity for an education, and without that, I wouldn't be where I am today.

I had never thought about going to the University of Michigan because my family was too poor. But playing at Hamtramck High School, I made the all-city team. That allowed me to attend a banquet at the Statler Hotel where Michigan would present "M" rings to all senior athletes. I sat there and listened to the seniors talking about the University of Michigan and what it meant to get an education there. That's when I decided to go there.

Soon I wrote a letter to coach Crisler and told him about myself, and then he passed the letter along to freshman coach Wally Weber.

College coaches weren't allowed to personally recruit in those days. The rule was that the student athlete had to contact the university and the school would send out boosters to make individual contact. Don Robinson played with me at Michigan, and it was his father who was assigned to me. Back then boosters would interview you, your coach, and your principle. Only then would they make their recommendation to the coaches. Coaches would determine if you qualified.

To me, the most important aspect of getting into Michigan was finding a job. Jobs were tough to find in those days. My hope was that through athletics I would be able to get a job. The school did take care of athletes. Half of the guys worked at Michigan Union, and others would work at sororities or other places. We would also clean the Michigan Stadium on Sunday morning.

When I met freshman coach Wally Weber, he scared the daylights out of me.

"Franks," he said. "If you came to the University of Michigan just to play football, we don't want you. You have to go to school and get good grades because we will check on you."

At Michigan, there was tremendous emphasis on education. Also, the freshman squad had 120 players, and every guy was "all-something." The competition was tremendous. But I received tremendous coaching at Michigan. Assistant coach Cliff Keen taught me how to play football. Line coach

Guard Julius Franks, shown during a 1942 game against Iowa Pre-Flight School, became the first African-American player from Michigan to earn All-America honors. His career ended prematurely after the 1942 season due to a bout with tuberculosis. *Photo courtesy of Ivory Photo.*

Biggie Munn had been an All-American guard. I was a guard. He helped me considerably.

The Michigan line at that time was "the Seven Oak Posts." They were some of the toughest players I ever played against. Elmer Madar was an All-American at end. Al[bert] Wistert was an All-American at tackle. Mervin Pregulman was an All-American center. Bob Kolesar and Bill Pritula were All–Big Ten linemen. We held our own. That line was developed by Munn. There was great leadership there. Guys like Wistert taught you a lot.

My teammates were great. At Michigan I never had any problems from a racial standpoint. They treated me fine. I met some great guys, went to their homes, and in some cases, to their weddings. A lot of the guys had come out of Detroit, and that's where I was from. For example, I had played against Don Lund in high school.

I thought Fritz Crisler was a genius, a true mastermind. If you played against a Crisler team, you knew you had competition. That man was brilliant. However, you couldn't get to know him because he was aloof. He was a strategist. He knew his football. He taught us how to win and play by the rules.

Our victory against Note Dame in 1942 in South Bend, Indiana, was the highlight of my career. Every one of the Seven Oak Posts had to play 60 minutes against one of the toughest opponents we ever played. Note Dame came out and did something that no team had done to us before. We kicked off the ball, and the Irish went down and scored on us. We had to play at our best to beat them. And I think the 32 points we scored against them were the most points a Notre Dame team had ever given up at the time. We beat them 32–20.

That turned out to be my final season. My last game was an all-star game in Chicago. When I came back, doctors determined I had tuberculosis. My career was over.

At that time, the war was going on. I think there was a letdown in health conditions because there were a lot of kids coming down with tuberculosis from the fraternity houses. Tom Kuzma, who had replaced Tom Harmon, was another player who came down with it.

But I'm very thankful for my Michigan days. When I said I wanted to go to Michigan to play, some people thought it was crazy.

It had been news when Willis Ward went to Michigan. However, there still weren't many African-American players in football. You certainly didn't read about too many of them. I admired men like Paul Robeson, who played at Rutgers and was the first black All-American in 1918; or Fritz Pollard, who had played at Brown [and became the first black player in the Rose Bowl in 1916]; or Jerome "Brud" Holland. He became Cornell's first black football player in 1939.

There weren't many black athletes in football, but there were more African-American track men at Michigan, going back to Eddie Tolan, who was in the 1932 Olympics. In 1938 Bill Watson became captain of the Michigan track team. Those were Detroit athletes, and we all knew about them. The track team broke down barriers earlier than the football team. We read about those athletes in the paper.

If Willis Ward would not have attended Michigan, I still may have gone there. Even today, even if there is discrimination some place, it won't hold me back from pursuing something I want.

Julius Franks became a dentist. In 1982 he was enshrined in Michigan's Hall of Honor, which recognizes persons who have made significant contributions to the Michigan program and enhanced the school's image.

DON LUND

FULLBACK

1942–1944

A UNIVERSITY OF MICHIGAN VICE PRESIDENT ONCE TOLD ME, "The one thing you don't do at Michigan is screw around with Michigan tradition."

How do you define tradition? When I was in the world of professional baseball for a lot of years, other players would ask me what I got from Michigan. I would tell them that what I got from Michigan was a feeling that everything was great there. There is camaraderie at Michigan that is difficult to describe.

Not that long ago, there was a banquet held in Ann Arbor and many players and coaches were there. Captains spoke. Coaches spoke. Bo Schembechler. Gary Moeller. Lloyd Carr. Bump Elliott. You could hear a pin drop when they spoke. And when it was done, everyone just stood up and applauded. It was an unbelievable feeling in that room. If you were in that room, you knew what it meant to be a Wolverine.

Coach Fritz Crisler always said, "You can block, tackle, and run as hard as you want, but remember you are Michigan Men. None of the extra stuff." He was on the NCAA rules committee, and he just didn't like if we would hit a player when he wasn't looking. I'm not saying everyone was perfect, but that's what Crisler preached. He just believed in sportsmanship. Crisler wasn't a Michigan guy, either. He was a Chicago graduate. He played for Alonzo Stagg there. But he would always tell us we were so lucky to be at Michigan. Crisler taught tradition. He preached it and preached it.

Don Lund (No. 33) poses with teammate Joe Ponsetto after they were named cocaptains by team captain Bob Wiese before Lund had to leave for military training in 1943. *Photo courtesy of Ivory Photo.*

And he had Bennie Oosterbaan on his staff, who was raised in Michigan tradition.

Also, people forget that Fielding Yost once came back to coach because he was unhappy that Red Grange ran wild against Michigan [in 1924]. What people don't know is what happened that following year. If you take a shovel and dig a small hole—that's the amount of yardage that Grange gained against Michigan the next year when Yost was coaching again.

Schembechler came out of Ohio, and the philosophy in that state is football, religion, and family. I think family and religion are tied for second. When boys are born in certain towns, a football is placed in their bassinet. In Ohio, people love their football. When Bo got here, he realized that it was just a different circumstance here. He learned what Michigan was about and then he preached it and believed in it. He was a great man to represent Michigan football.

I made Michigan's varsity team as a sophomore in 1942. Our season opener was against Great Lakes [Naval Base]. That team had all of these former All-Americans, ex-pros, and experienced college players. Great Lakes was favored to beat us. The week before, we had our last scrimmage. Kuzma ran a play, and a guy named George Kiesel hit him. Kuzma hurt his knee a bit. Crisler had an expression he used when guys would go down—"move the body or move the ball"—and this is where he may have started using it. When Kuzma went down, the trainer Ray Roberts was there, and Crisler came over and said, "move the player or move the team." As I look back, I realize that he was using psychology. He didn't want us to get down by thinking, "What are we doing to do without Kuzma?"

Bob Chappuis replaced Kuzma against Great Lakes, and he played a great game. We beat Great Lakes 9–0. We caught that team before it was organized. It was a good win for a bunch of young guys playing old-timers. It also launched Chappuis' career.

In my sophomore season of 1942, we beat Notre Dame in South Bend. That was a big game for us, and we had spent time preparing for that game. This is why Crisler never wanted to schedule Notre Dame unless it was the first or second game of the season. The week after beating Notre Dame, we had to play Ohio State. We lost and we weren't sharp. Tom Kuzma was a terrific halfback, but he couldn't do anything that day.

The next year, we came back and played in Ann Arbor, and the Fighting Irish beat us. They had a real good halfback named Creighton Miller. On one play, they ran a quick hitter and Miller got the ball. I was playing defensive halfback. He came up and faked to the inside and I took the fake. He did a "whoop, whoop." He was gone. He went all the way for the touchdown. I would run into him at golf tournaments, and I would tell him, "If you look on the 40-yard line of the north end zone of Michigan Stadium, you will find my jockstrap."

34

I was from the East Side of Detroit, and I saw Tom Harmon play when I was in high school. He had great speed and was deceptive. He did the kicking. He did the passing. He did the punting. He did the running. He did it all. Now, granted, my judgment as a high school player may have not been the best, but I believe he was the best player I ever saw.

He was just finishing up his last classes when I came to Michigan, and there were great stories about him. On Tom Harmon's 21st birthday, September 28, 1940, the team was playing at California, and Tom ran the opening kickoff all the way back for a touchdown. That's where the drunk came out of the stands to try to tackle him. He saw the drunk at the last minute and dodged him. The drunk supposedly said, "No one else could tackle him, so I thought I would give it a try." The funny part of that story is that supposedly Harmon became friends with that guy. The other note about that game was that Michigan flew to that game and the school was one of the first to fly its teams.

Running the single wing, Michigan would line up in an unbalanced line, and everyone would shift left or right. On one play, everyone would shift to right like the play would be run that way, but the ball would go to Harmon, and he would be on his own going to the left. He would have no blockers.

Supposedly, when Crisler was discussing that play with the team, Harmon said, "Coach, who blocks the end?"

Crisler responded; "Tom, you mean you can't lick one defensive end?"

Some people don't realize that Tom started out as a wingback for a couple of games. I found out later that Bennie Oosterbaan, who was an assistant then, was the person who lobbied to move him to tailback.

Crisler asked, "Who would we play at wingback then?"

"Anybody," Oosterbaan said, clearly making the point that the tailback was the position they needed to worry about.

Ever since I was a little boy I wanted to go to Michigan. I don't know what it was. Recruiting wasn't like it is now. Notre Dame had talked to me. Yale talked to me. Northwestern, Michigan State. But to me, Michigan was the place to go.

When I played at Michigan, Julius Franks was the only black player on the team. He was a really good player. He would line up like it was the last play and couldn't move. Then he would shoot across the line and devastate his opponent with a block. The fact that he was black wasn't a big issue. To me that's interesting now, because I was also on the Brooklyn Dodgers when Jackie Robinson came up. The Dodgers bought my contract and his contract on the same day.

Baseball Hall of Famer George Sisler was the scout who found me for the Dodgers. By the way, he was a Michigan guy. He had an engineering degree from Michigan and never used it. He went into baseball. Branch Rickey was the general manager who signed me, and he's well known for bringing in Robinson. Rickey had gone to Michigan law school and had coached the Michigan baseball team.

Don Lund played seven seasons of major league baseball with the Brooklyn Dodgers, St. Louis Browns, and Detroit Tigers. He eventually became an assistant athletic director and then an associate athletic director at the University of Michigan.

BOB CHAPPUIS

HALFBACK

1942, 1946–1947

WHEN MY B-25 BOMBER WAS SHOT DOWN OVER ITALY during World War II, I was wearing my Michigan letterman ring, and I was determined not to surrender it.

We all managed to bail out safely, and we were rescued by partisans. They represented the Italian underground resistance movement against the Germans. Their leader told us that he had to take all of our personal belongings. The partisans' leader took our flight jackets, dog tags, jewelry, and papers.

"You can have everything, but you can't have my Michigan ring," I said.

"Well," he said, "if you are seen with that ring, it will identify you as an American, and the Germans will probably shoot you."

That got my attention. I still didn't want to give up the ring, but I told the guy that when the war was over I had better receive the ring back "or someone was going to be in deep trouble."

Our plane was shot down over the Po Valley on February 13, 1945, and when the war ended a few months later, we said good-bye to the partisans. I asked for my ring, and believe it or not, they returned it to me. The ring was the only personal item that I got back.

That ring was very meaningful to me then, and still is today. After the 1942 Michigan football season, all of the letter winners were given a letterman ring. Usually it was given only to seniors, but many sophomores and juniors were going overseas to fight in World War II, and the coaches decided to give the rings to them as well.

The ring and I had a rough ride on my 21st bomber mission as an aerial gunner. The crew was forced to bail out when our plane was hit by antiaircraft fire. After previous missions, the crew would get back to our tent at our base on Corsica and talk about what we might do if we got into trouble. We all agreed that we wouldn't jump. We would ride the plane down. But that was a joke, because when you have two engines, and one is on fire and you are losing altitude fast, you say, "Where is the way out of here?" We bailed out.

The partisans rescued us and moved us around to keep us one jump ahead of the Germans, because they were looking for us. The Germans came to the farmhouse we were staying at and asked the people if they had seen the parachutes come down. They said they hadn't. We were in the barn, hiding in the hay.

After that, you wouldn't think I would be worried about my ring, but it was a symbol of achievement. And when you win a letter at Michigan, it's an important part of your life.

Actually, the ring was almost lost a couple of other times. Bump Elliott and his wife Barb had come to visit us in Fort Wayne, Indiana, and Bump and I were playing golf at the country club. I always take off my ring before I play. I gave it to Barb to hold. She put it on her finger. After the tournament, we were driving back and Barb was smoking. She threw her cigarette out the window, and my ring, which had been on her finger, went out the window with the cigarette butt. Bump was as upset as I was, although I tried not to show it. We searched for the better part of an hour and finally found the ring, although it had been run over by a truck or a car. Bump had the ring repaired for me.

Much later after the war, it was lost for several months at my home in Fort Wayne. I thought that was the end of that. I figured I had to move on. But one day, I was out filling the bottom of the bird feeder, I reached in, and there was my ring in the bottom of the bird feeder. I never did figure out what happened.

I've retired the ring now. I have it in a special spot in my house. I have another ring that I wear. I'm equally proud of that ring because it's our 1947 national championship ring.

The funny aspect about my Michigan career was I didn't even know if I was going out for football in 1946 when I came back from the war. There

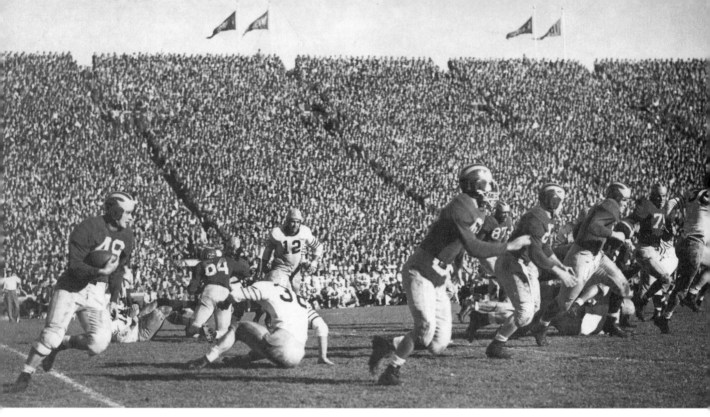

Bob Chappuis carries the ball during a 1946 game against Illinois. Regarded as one of the finest running backs in Michigan history, Chappuis was a star player on the 1947 national championship team known as the Mad Magicians. He was the Heisman Trophy runner-up that season and is also a member of the College Football Hall of Fame. *Photo courtesy of Ivory Photo.*

were seven people at the tailback position, and I wondered whether I would even make the team. Really, it was a tough decision for me. But I'm certainly happy I decided to play.

Once the players all became acquainted, we had a remarkable relationship. We liked each other so well that we didn't want to let each other down. We had a very skillful team. It was, however, a very small team. One of the guards, Stu Wilkins, was 5'11", 180 pounds, and Dominic Tomasi was even smaller. But the offense that the coaches developed at Michigan was designed for a small, quick team.

We had a lot of ball handling and misdirection, for the purpose of getting the defense to move. All our little guards had to do was keep the defense going in a certain direction. The backs would go the other way. That's a simplification of our offense.

They called us the Mad Magicians, and sometimes even the coaches didn't know where the ball was going. We ran a single wing. Occasionally, we ran from the T formation, but not very often. The quarterback called the plays, and he was the major blocking back in the backfield. Our quarterback, Howard Yerges, was a wonderful field general. When Yerges called a play, you knew it would work.

Michigan's offense was complex. For example, we had one play where seven different people handled the ball. The center J. T. White would center the ball to our fullback, Jack Weisenburger. It wasn't just a snap where he took it from the center. It was an actual center through the air. Weisenburger would run straight ahead and hand the ball to Yerges. He would lateral it to me, and I would hand it to Bump Elliott going the other way. Bump would hand the ball to an end going the opposite direction, and that end would pass the ball to the other end.

It probably helped me that I had run a single wing at DeVilbiss High School in Toledo, but we didn't have all the tomfoolery that Michigan had. In high school, I was known as the Tom Harmon of the single wing, and Bob Vernier was known as the Forest Evashevski because he was the blocking back, as Evashevski had been for Harmon. Michigan freshman Wally Weber had actually come to Toledo to look at Vernier, but we both ended up at Michigan.

39

In our unbeaten 1947 season, we didn't have many close games. But one came against Minnesota. That team wasn't very good that season, but it had some good linemen, namely Clayton Tonnemaker and Leo Nomellini. For most of the first half, Weisenburger would spin and give the ball to me, and I would look up and see Nomellini and Tonnemaker on me immediately. They were on my back all day long, or I should say *I* was on my back all day.

One of our rules was that once we were in the huddle, no one could say anything except Yerges. We were behind 6–0 to Minnesota, and we had the ball on our 40-yard line, with 20 seconds to play in the first half. Yerges came in the huddle and called a pass play. When he called it, no one said a word, but I'm sure we all wondered whether I could get the pass off. Maybe Yerges sensed that apprehension, because he said something after calling the play.

"We haven't been behind at halftime all season, and you better not be behind here," he said. "You guys are going to do it."

As we left the huddle, I said: "Bump, you are the key guy. Do you have any idea where you will be? I won't have time to look."

"I'll be down by the goal line," he said. "Throw it as far as you can."

That's what happened. Nomellini was on me quickly, and I threw the ball, not knowing at all if Bump was anywhere near that area. I was down on the ground with my face in the turf, and all of a sudden I heard a roar from our side of the field. I was thinking, "The little guy got down there," and sure enough he did. It turned out to be the play of the week, and I never saw it until we watched game film on Monday.

We kicked an extra point to give us a 7–6 lead going into halftime. We won the game 13–6.

Crisler's strength was his ability to motivate his team.

"If you are going to win this game you are going to have to play better than you know how," Crisler would say.

That's what we did. We often played better than we knew how. He always stressed motivating each individual player to get the best out of him. He did that in a straightforward manner.

Two days before the 1948 Rose Bowl, we were running through players just to work up a sweat. I was running around end when I got a terrible pain in my thigh. I went down on the ground, and I was hurting. Our trainer Jim Hunt came over, and started to fool around with my leg.

Coach Crisler walked over to investigate.

"What happened here, Jim?" coach Crisler said in a stern tone.

"Bob has pulled a hamstring," Hunt said.

Crisler looked at me and then at Hunt and said, "It's a good thing it didn't happen to someone who could run."

Talk about motivation. I got off the ground so fast. I was never really noted for great speed, and that always bothered me. Coach Crisler brought that home to me, and I was ready to play in the Rose Bowl. I was lucky enough to be the bowl's Most Valuable Player. I'm proud of that.

We never thought of coach Crisler as our best friend, but certainly we thought he was the best coach we ever had. We discovered later that he was very sentimental.

When we celebrated our 25th reunion in Ann Arbor, Crisler had been hospitalized with cancer. He was weak and yet he got out of the hospital bed to attend the reunion. But he could not speak.

But he wrote us all a very, very moving letter. I have it framed on my wall. It is impossible to describe what he said. Every time I read it, I begin to cry.

Because players were coming home from the war in 1946, Crisler had a roster that included players of all ages. He had 17-year-olds, 18-year-olds, 23-year-olds, 24-year olds, and Alvin Wistert, who was 31. He was the old man. Crisler's genius was that he worked all of these people into his system and made them a team. That was a remarkable accomplishment.

When people ask me what the highlight was of that 1947 season, I say that when you play for an undefeated football team, a national championship team, and a Rose Bowl winner, what else is there to say?

Bob Chappuis rushed for 91 yards and passed for 188 yards and 2 touchdowns in Michigan's 49–0 win against Southern California at the Rose Bowl on January 1, 1948. Chappuis was runner-up for the Heisman Trophy that season.

JACK WEISENBURGER

FULLBACK

1944–1947

I DON'T THINK "SHOCKED" IS THE CORRECT TERM to use about my recruitment to the University of Michigan. I think "flabbergasted" is the better choice. I had luck on my side because Bennie Oosterbaan was my primary recruiter. He was a Saginaw High graduate and decided to return a favor to his alma mater. The thought of attending the University of Michigan was exciting. What made it even more appealing was the opportunity to play both baseball and football as a Wolverine.

Knowing Michigan's reputation, I had no doubt about where I wanted to go. Helping the decision process was my knowledge of Tom Harmon. I had followed him very closely during his playing days at Michigan and was amazed by what he could do on the football field. The ability to play two sports, coupled with Bennie's persuasive recruiting, made my signing decision simple.

At the time, Ray Fisher was the head coach for Michigan baseball. I knew that he had played for the New York Yankees and Cincinnati Reds [1910–1920]. He'd also pitched for the Reds in a World Series in 1919. I was very aware that being on the baseball diamond at Michigan would be a good opportunity.

Football was a different story. I didn't know much of Fritz Crisler. But I became very well acquainted with him in my four years at Michigan.

Behind a block from Dom Tomasi, Jack Weisenburger scores his third touchdown of the 1948 Rose Bowl against Southern California, good enough for a modern Rose Bowl scoring record. Weisenburger was part of the Mad Magicians backfield that included All-Americans Bob Chappuis and Bump Elliott. *Photo courtesy of Ivory Photo.*

Playing for Mr. Crisler was a great experience. I would only call him Mr. Crisler, never "Fritz." Only later, after graduation, did I ever refer to him as "coach Crisler." He had an aura about him that demanded respect.

I came out of high school originally as a tailback, but I was not much of a passer because I had small hands. At Michigan, I started as a tailback, and was lucky enough to play some during my freshman year. But during my sophomore year in a game against Northwestern, there was a substitution problem. Several fellows on offense were struggling to make the substitutions in time after playing defense, since we all were playing both sides of the ball at that time. Our disorganization in executing the plays prompted Mr. Crisler to move me to fullback. His plan was for me to learn several plays at fullback until we figured everything out. But what ended up playing out was a surprise to both Mr. Crisler and me.

As it would go, I had a great day at fullback. The following week, I started at fullback against Army in New York City at Yankee Stadium. For the rest of my career at Michigan, I would be the starting fullback. It was probably the best thing that ever happened to me.

Understandably, it took time for me to grow accustomed to my new position. After we worked through some of the kinks, we ran like clockwork. When we executed our plays, I tried to be as deceptive as I could be when I would hand off the ball. Even though my hands were small, I could handle it well and hide it. It would be beneficial for our team, and Mr. Crisler was a genius for making the change.

My most memorable moment at Michigan was the final game of my collegiate career. To have the opportunity to play at the Rose Bowl is really unmatched. We went into the stadium at Pasadena. The Rose Bowl was larger than Michigan Stadium at the time, holding around one hundred thousand. Michigan's capacity was a bit over eighty-five thousand. To climax my career with an undefeated team, to win the game in a blowout against USC, and to score three touchdowns in that game was a great way to close out my collegiate career.

Being a member of the backfield called the "Mad Magicians" was special. Mr. Crisler explained that the timing and the wing system were very intricate. If a new person would come in, I would have to adjust my position and my spin. We were very fortunate to have the guys that we did. There was a game against Minnesota where we took in the winning drive during a hard-fought game.

We were playing in Ann Arbor against two All-Americans: Leo Nomellini and Clayton Tonnemaker. They were both murdering our line up front. Both were extremely strong and were just barreling through our line. But we continued to battle, and on defense, I intercepted a pass and dashed to the Minnesota 33-yard line. The Mad Magicians took it from there. We drove the rest of the way and sealed the victory against a very good Gophers squad.

Although I loved football more than baseball, my future in baseball was far more promising due to my smaller stature. Coach Fisher was wonderful and was one of the finest human beings I had ever been around. I had my most enjoyable years in sports with Michigan.

I'm as proud of Michigan today as I was then. To this day, there are people who can pinpoint the years I played and roll off teammates I played alongside. For them to remember that far back is amazing, but that's the essence of Michigan football. When I make it to a game, I still get a thrill when the band comes out and plays the fight song. Chills still go up and down my spine when the players emerge from the tunnel and jump to touch the *M* banner. Even though I'm watching the game and not on the field, I still have great pride for Michigan football. It's something you never lose.

Jack Weisenburger scored the first touchdown during Michigan's 49–0 rout of USC in the 1948 Rose Bowl. He also rushed for 91 yeards durning the same contest.

PETE ELLIOTT

HALFBACK/QUARTERBACK

1945–1948

I T WAS UNCLE SAM RATHER THAN COACH FRITZ CRISLER who brought me to Ann Arbor to play football in 1945. The U.S. Navy essentially ordered me to the University of Michigan.

Graduating from Bloomington [Illinois] High School in 1944, I attended Park College in Missouri and was a cadet in the Naval Reserve Officer Training Corps (NROTC). I was really in the Naval Air Force, but at that point in the war, there was no need for more people in flight training. After one year, the Navy divided our unit of four hundred cadets into three groups to be sent off for Navy officer training. The first group was sent to Northwestern; the second group was assigned to Notre Dame; and the third group was told to go to Michigan. I was in that third group.

Talk about how events change your life. Those were all great schools, but can you imagine how my life would have changed had I been placed in either of the other two groups?

I met my wife Joan while at Michigan. She was an Ann Arbor girl and her parents owned a bookstore on campus. Her dad died when she was very young, and her mother managed the store. Several Michigan football players, including Tom Harmon, worked at the store to pay for their books. My wife said Tom Harmon was one of her favorite people. They became friends.

Quarterback Pete Elliott (No. 45), whose brother Bump was in the same backfield, carries for six yards against Army during a 1945 game. Both brothers played on the 1947 national championship team that went 9–0 in the regular season and beat USC 49–0 in the Rose Bowl. *Photo courtesy of Ivory Photo.*

Football was important at Michigan in those days, as it was at all the Big Ten schools. If not for the television coverage, I would say that college football was as big then as it is today.

Michigan has always been outstanding in football—at least in most seasons—and everybody has always had tremendous respect for the school. The university has always ranked high in terms of the education students receive. Back then you were very proud of your Michigan degree, as you are today.

Certainly, there were differences. Back then, schools didn't usually provide football scholarships, and athletes would work for their education if they couldn't afford it.

In those days, Crisler had a huge impact on the football program. We respected him and we feared him. He was a bit aloof when he coached, but he was a great friend when you were through playing for him. I don't know of a better coach than Crisler, and I had the privilege to work five years as an assistant coach under Oklahoma legend Bud Wilkinson. Those two coaches were entirely different, and yet both were extremely successful.

Crisler introduced two-platoon football. I was playing for him in that game against Army in 1945. At Yankee Stadium, Crisler switched five or six guys on offense and defense. That was the first time that was done as part of a game plan. Before then, players generally stayed on the field for most of the game.

Crisler always made his points in dramatic fashion. Once during a practice, I made a mistake, and when I returned to the huddle I accepted responsibility for the botched play.

"My fault. My fault, sorry guys," I said.

Crisler wasn't accepting my apology.

"Everyone knows it's your fault," he said. "I don't want to see any more of those 'my fault' plays."

Crisler didn't want you apologizing for mistakes. He wanted you not to make them.

Everyone talks about our 1947 national championship team because we were 9–0 in the regular season and then defeated USC 49–0 in the Rose Bowl. We were known for our point-per-minute offense, but giving up "nothing" in the Rose Bowl wasn't bad, either. We were fortunate to have had a strong defense.

I'm prejudiced, certainly, but I've not seen anyone much better at right halfback than my brother, Bump, was in 1947. He wasn't a track runner, but he had plenty of speed and he made plays. He was also a strong defensive player—a great tackler.

Our left halfback, Bob Chappuis, was probably the greatest competitor I've ever known. He was a tough athlete, and when the chips were down, that's when he was at his best. If we were practicing and there was no defense, he would hit 6 out of every 10 passes he attempted. If we were playing in a game, and a receiver was open, Chappuis would find him 9 times out of 10.

Howard Yerges was an excellent quarterback, very smart and sharp at calling the plays. The quarterback called all of the plays back then, and coaches rarely second-guessed their decisions. That's because in practice all week they had prepared the quarterback for what needed to be called.

That trip to the Rose Bowl after the great 1947 regular season was certainly a highlight. People are surprised when I tell them we traveled west by train. We took a train from Ann Arbor to Chicago and then transferred to the 20th Century Limited for the ride to Pasadena. The trip lasted a couple of days, and we had a few meetings with coaches on the trip, but mostly we relaxed. It was a great bonding exercise.

In Pasadena, the Michigan players were invited to a live viewing of the Bob Hope television show, and we had the opportunity to meet actor Ronald Reagan, who was filming a movie. Who could have guessed he would be elected president 32 years later? Michigan players also were able to meet actress Marlene Dietrich, and Bump and I had the pleasure of playing a round of golf with Bing Crosby. It was quite a road trip.

Today it's forgotten that our 1947 national title was very much a disputed national championship. Notre Dame was actually listed as the national champ because the Fighting Irish were ranked No. 1 in the Associated Press poll after the regular season.

But another vote was taken for the AP poll after Michigan's Rose Bowl victory, and we were ranked No. 1.

Officially, we didn't win the national championship, but we believe we did win it. The next year we did win it again without any dispute. When you win a national championship, you feel like a lucky guy. We feel like we had exceptional people, and without any doubt, exceptional coaching.

It's also sometimes forgotten that Bennie Oosterbaan had replaced Crisler as head coach for the 1948 season. Bennie's approach was entirely different than Fritz's style. Bennie was closer to the players, more friendly. He talked to players more often. You could kid around with Bennie.

But it doesn't matter what kind of style a coach utilizes. The only question is: Do the players respect and believe in a coach? We did believe in both Fritz and Bennie. There was another assistant named Ernie McCoy who was also was a wonderful coach.

Personally, I was ready for the 1948 football season. I played other sports at Michigan, and in the spring of 1948, my Wolverines' basketball squad won the Big Ten championship and advanced to the NCAA tournament. At the tourney, my assignment was to guard Holy Cross standout Bob Cousy in the East Regional semifinals. He would go on to become a great star of the Boston Celtics. I did OK, but no one could shut down Cousy. We lost that game, but by the fall, I was ready to replace the graduated Yerges as quarterback of the football team.

It was a big thrill to go undefeated again and win the national championship. Maybe it was a bigger thrill because we had graduated several key players from the 1947 squad, and yet we were able to repeat. And this one was undisputed.

Pete Elliott is the only Michigan athlete to win 12 varsity letters. He won four each in football, basketball, and golf.

STU WILKINS

GUARD

1945–1948

WHEN YOU PLAYED FOOTBALL FOR FRITZ CRISLER or Bennie Oosterbaan at Michigan, you embraced an army mentality. The idea was that you held up the guy next to you, even if you were being shot at.

Obviously, football wasn't quite as serious as combat, but when you came to Michigan you realized you were always playing for the other guys on the team.

Players from the thirties and early forties, particularly Tom Harmon and Forest Evashevski, would frequently be on campus talking about the pride that goes into being a Michigan player. It was awesome to hear them speak. These guys set high standards for themselves, and you would tell yourself that you had to meet the standards. Your objective was always to play better than you had ever played before.

We had plenty of star players on our rosters in those years, but the stars were not stars in their own minds. Everyone understood that we all had to work together to be successful. We all knew that if the line didn't block, the passer wasn't going to complete the pass or the halfback wasn't going to get through the line. We never relied on one player.

Maybe we were big men on campus, but Fritz Crisler never allowed us to believe that we were.

It was actually an older brother who helped me find my way to Michigan. He was not an athlete. But we were at war, and he joined the Naval Reserve

Guard Stu Wilkins, posing for a photo in 1946, became a Michigan starter at age 17, and held his position for four straight years from 1945 to 1948. *Photo courtesy of Ivory Photo.*

Officers Training Corps (NROTC). He was given the choice of attending either Michigan or Georgia Tech. He chose Michigan because it was much closer to our home in Canton, Ohio. While he was at college, I would join my mother and dad to visit him in Ann Arbor. At the time, I was playing high school football, and when we would make the trip on weekends we would attend a Michigan football game. Quickly, I became thrilled with Michigan Stadium and the ambiance. When we returned to Ohio, I remember telling my dad: "I would like to go to Michigan, play Big Ten football, and go to law school there."

At the time I had no idea what a major step that would be.

Coach Crisler believed in tradition and discipline. The first speech he gave me after I joined the squad was about academics, not athletics.

"The first thing you have to do to play on this team is to go to school," Crisler said. "You have to keep your grades up. You have to have better than the campus average or you won't play for me."

The campus grade-point average was 2.25, and if you couldn't better that, Crisler really wouldn't let you play. That set a tone for me to be a better student. Really, it set a tone for all of us. In the years I played at Michigan, every letterman graduated on time, and I'm sure that wasn't the case at other schools.

53

During the war years, schools allowed freshman to play varsity. They were forced to change the rules or schools wouldn't have had enough players to compete every week. That was a break for me because it allowed me to become a Michigan starter at age 17. There were a few of us who were able to start four seasons at Michigan.

When I showed up on the Michigan campus, my hope was that I would be able to enjoy one semester before I was drafted into the army. I took my draft physical, and two weeks later, lo and behold, we had peace all over the world. The draft was no longer needed.

That made the 1946 season quite interesting because all the war veterans were back, and we had four or five players competing at every position. All you could do then was run 40-yard wind sprints faster than everybody and hang in when everyone else wanted to go home. You had to make yourself different than everyone else to impress Michigan coaches.

By my sophomore season, I felt like a veteran player. I believed I had come of age during my freshman season when we played Army at Yankee Stadium.

That Army team featured Doc Blanchard and Glenn Davis. Blanchard won the Heisman Trophy that season and Davis won it in 1946. In 1945 No. 1 Army posted a 9–0 record, which included a 28–7 win against us in New York.

There was always plenty of noise at Michigan, Ohio State, and other Big Ten stadiums, but when you are in a double-deck baseball stadium, the noise seems to hang there. Plus the cadet corps was there in full force. They have orchestrated cheers. It was quite an atmosphere in Yankee Stadium that day. I grew up during that game. We gave Army a game until the third quarter, when some of our players simply became tired.

Football was a special event on Michigan's campus. During my junior season, I remember walking to an 8:00 A.M. class on Monday after beating Pittsburgh 69–0 the previous Saturday. A fellow I didn't know stopped me on the street and said that I had let him down because "you didn't get the right score."

Apparently, he had bet on the game and we didn't score enough points.

The camaraderie in Michigan athletics extended beyond the football program. The campus seemed like a magical place to be. If you had earned an "M," regardless of the sport, you were supported. We would all go to the swimming and track meets, basketball, or other sports. We were always reaching out to some other team. That was just expected from a Michigan athlete.

You did what you could to help the Michigan program. Even after I graduated and became a lawyer, I would help with recruiting in the Canton area. I helped recruit Dan Dierdorf [1968–1970] and Roger Bettis [1977], who both came from the area.

It's certainly interesting being an Ohio resident and a Michigan alumnus.

One of my favorite memories came during my junior season in 1947 when we beat a good Ohio State team 21–0. When I came home to Ohio that summer, I was in enemy territory.

Stu Wilkins started every game at Michigan from 1945 to1948. He continues to work for his law firm to this day.

CHALMERS "BUMP" ELLIOTT

HALFBACK

1946–1947

W̲HEN I TALKED TO COACHES ABOUT PLAYING FOOTBALL at Michigan in 1946, they didn't exactly roll out the red carpet. They didn't discourage me from coming. But they also didn't say, "Oh, yeah, c'mon. We need you."

Michigan had so many players coming home from the war that they didn't really need reinforcements. I had lettered two years at Purdue before going overseas. But when I went out for Michigan's team, coaches put me at left half-back. Michigan had seven of those, and two had been starters, including Bob Chappuis.

After a week, coaches switched me to right halfback. Paul White, one of the former Michigan captains, was there. I was fifth-string at right halfback when I started.

But I got a chance to play in my first game on defense, and by midseason I was starting on offense and defense.

As an example of how strong Michigan was at that time, every back, first- and second-team, on offense and defense, had been a left halfback at one time. The left halfback was the primary running back. Weisenburger weighed 178 pounds and coach Fritz Crisler moved him to fullback. I had been a left half-back at Purdue. Our quarterback, Howard Yerges, had also been a left halfback. Pete Elliott, Walt Teninga, and Gene Derricotte—who started on defense—were all left halfbacks. They could play any of the backfield positions, and in fact, Pete did play quite a bit at quarterback in 1947.

We had plenty of talented athletes who could play anywhere and yet there was absolutely no ego on our team. That was the beauty of our team. We were a group of guys that wanted to play together and have fun. And the spinning single wing offense was fun to play.

It wasn't a power offense, although we ran some power plays. It's a lot of deception. That's why they called us the Mad Magicians. It's a lot of spinning, trapping, and pulling of the linemen. We came out in a T formation and shifted to a single wing with an unbalanced line.

The backfield had so much fun running this offense that we would come out early to practice to work with assistant coach Bennie Oosterbaan. Weisenburger would spin and fake to Chappuis or me, and then give to Yerges. Then Bennie would yell, "Stop!" And then he would yell, "Go!" And everyone would reverse themselves, moving backwards in slow motion, until they returned to their original positions. Our backfield was talented enough to be able to accomplish that.

We weren't very big. Our guards, Stu Wilkins and Dominic Tomasi, were 180 pounds. J. T. White was 200 pounds, but he was very tall. He might have been 6'7". Does that sound like a center to you? The biggest guys on our team were Alvin Wistert and Lenny Ford at about 220 pounds. But we had lots of team speed on offense and defense.

The teams that gave us the most trouble were the teams that shot linebackers through the gaps and didn't play conventional defense. That's why you don't see the single wing anymore, because defenses caught up with it.

We've had a reunion every fifth year since we graduated. That's more than 10 we've had now. We are all good friends. We always talk about how much fun we had playing for Michigan.

Probably my most memorable moment came when I ran back a punt for a touchdown at Illinois. We won 14–7, and that wasn't the deciding touchdown. But Pete and I were from Bloomington, Illinois. We had a lot of family and friends there, and that made it special

Truthfully, the reason I went to Michigan was Pete, and not necessarily Michigan. Yet I now appreciate the opportunity that Michigan gave me. When you meet such good people and have the success we had, you have pleasant memories. The guys coming back from the war knew why they were

Bump Elliott, shown here in the open field in a game against Pitt during the unbeaten 1947 season, was Michigan's only two-way player that season and was named the Big Ten's Most Valuable Player after leading the league in scoring.
Photo courtesy of Ivory Photo.

in school. Some were married and that was meaningful, too. Many guys had already made some serious choices in life. As a result, the guys were serious about what they were doing, although we all had a great time.

In August of 1946, I was still with my U.S. Marines unit in China, stationed 60 miles east of Beijing. Pete had enjoyed himself playing at Michigan in 1945, and right after I returned home from China, he was heading to Ann Arbor to report for football practice. I went with him and my mother to talk to Michigan coaches. Actually, practice had already started by the time I joined the team. Technically, I was still in the Marine Corps, on terminal leave, and after the second or third game, I had to travel to the Great Lakes base to get discharged.

When you go unbeaten, as we did in 1947, there are many highlights. But we all enjoyed our trip to the Rose Bowl. There were many events for the team, and Pete and I had the pleasure of playing a round of golf with Bing Crosby.

We didn't even have a friendly bet on the first nine holes. Bing then said he had somewhere he needed to be. So he said he could only play four more holes. He suggested that we play for a little money, maybe a dollar or two, over those final four holes. Bing had watched us play the first nine, and was generous enough to give us a couple of strokes.

Now remember, Pete was a collegiate golfer and hadn't played at his best in the first nine. Over the final four holes, Pete beat Bing to death. Bing later joked that Pete had set him up.

As much as we had, I learned much from coach Fritz Crisler. I like to believe I tried to pattern my coaching after him when I coached at Michigan. He was a unique character, a very intelligent man. He looked like a chief executive officer at Ford Motor Company. He was a great speaker. He could inspire people. He made sure every aspect was done the right way.

Coach Crisler certainly showed us what it means to be at Michigan and to graduate from there. Michigan always had respect for its opponents. Notre Dame's Johnny Lujack became one of my good friends. That's the responsible way to view an opponent. We never carried any grudges.

Back then it was highly emphasized that you were at Michigan to get the education. There was never any question why you were at Michigan. It wasn't just to play football. It was about education. Everyone had big objectives academically.

When I was coaching Michigan, we won the Big Ten championship and the Rose Bowl in 1964, and we only had one player on the team who didn't graduate in four or five years.

Michigan tradition is academics and being honest with the student-athlete. Fritz Crisler never promised anything to anyone. Oosterbaan was the same way. Everyone else that I knew at Michigan also tried to follow that ideal.

One of my proudest moments as a Michigan coach came when players voted to elect Ron Johnson as captain of the 1968 team. He was the school's first black captain. He was a great leader. His election came around the time that Martin Luther King Jr. was assassinated. Ron was one of my favorite players. He was a great example of what we were all about.

You always get involved with Michigan tradition. I wouldn't say I preached it. But you feel strong about it, and it just feels natural to talk about it.

Michigan coach Fritz Crisler called Bump Elliott the greatest right halfback he ever saw. As the head coach at Michigan from 1959 to 1968, he compiled an overall record of 51–42–2. Michigan won a Big Ten championship during Bump's 10 seasons.

J. T. WHITE
CENTER
1946–1947

WHEN IT COMES TO MICHIGAN STADIUM, I like to believe that I helped fill it and build it.

Actually, I helped upgrade the Michigan Stadium in the summer of 1949 after my first season as a Michigan assistant coach. In those days, you had to work in the summer to support yourself if you were an assistant coach. A Michigan man was awarded the contract to refurbish the stadium, and he hired some former players as bricklayers.

Eighteen months before that, I had helped Michigan go undefeated and beat Southern Cal 49–0 in the Rose Bowl.

I played center on the offense and linebacker on defense. I always say the most important person on the football team is the center because he handles the ball on every offensive play. I started every play with my head between my knees. The quarterback would be behind me and then he would say, "Let's go, one, two, three," and everyone would shift. Then the tailback would be directly behind me and the fullback would be offset. Jack Weisenburger was the fullback, and he was key to the offense. Sometimes I would center the ball to his left knee because he would have to spin in one direction; sometimes I would have to center the ball to his right knee if he was spinning in the other direction; and then other times I had to put it in the middle because he was going to lateral to the quarterback.

60

Center J. T. White takes his stance before the 1946 game against Illinois. Also a linebacker during his two-year career, White went into coaching and spent seven seasons on the Wolverines staff before going to Penn State for nearly three decades. *Photo courtesy of Ivory Photo.*

As center I had my hands full. Usually, the linebackers were on me, trying to give me what I call "the forearm lift." They were always trying to push me back to make me the fifth man in the Michigan backfield.

Coach Fritz Crisler more or less developed the spinning single wing. He was a great coach, and he was like legendary coach Paul Brown. They both looked right through you. They were tough coaches.

Once we were playing in Champaign, Illinois, and before the game, Crisler came up to Joe Soboleski and said: "Soboleski, I don't know about you, but I know J.T. will be all right." It was a nice tribute for me, but not so good for Soboleski. Apparently, the week before he didn't do quite as well as Crisler would have liked.

I know Crisler shared some traits with Brown because I played for Brown at Ohio State in 1942. After my dad died, I had to help take care of the family, and I had to get a job at Great Lakes steel mill in River Rouge, Michigan. I didn't have enough credits to qualify for Michigan at the time. But when I earned enough money for a car and out-of-state tuition, I went down to Columbus. In my sophomore season, I was an end on the team's national championship team. I never lost an Ohio State–Michigan game because I was playing for the Buckeyes when they beat Michigan in 1942. My brother Paul was on that Michigan team. Back then, when you beat Michigan, the coaches gave you a pair of gold football pants.

61

After the national championship, most of us went into the military. I was in a field artillery unit and never made it overseas. I played some sports at Fort Bragg. When I got out of the military, I worked a bit and then headed back to Ohio State in 1946. Carroll Widdoes had replaced Brown, and Paul Bixler had replaced him in 1946. After I got there, they didn't pay too much attention to me, so I transferred to Michigan to play with my brother. He was a fine left halfback. He had been captain of the 1943 team and actually played with the Pittsburgh Steelers briefly after he left Michigan. I made a great decision coming to Michigan. I played a lot of football over the next two seasons. I started in both 1946 and 1947. The 1947 team went undefeated, and it's probably more memorable because we went to the Rose Bowl. We probably had more incentive to get to the Rose Bowl than USC did, considering the players out there knew about Hollywood and movie stars since they lived there. We really wanted to go out there. We were very impressed with Hollywood.

Before we left, the Michigan players were all given Stetson hats to wear. My wife, Verna, was able to make the trip with me. Organizers had cars painted gold for us to take anywhere within a hundred-mile radius. They had a driver. One night we all got $15 to see the girls dance at Earl Carroll Vanities. For Christmas, they gave us all ties and dried fruit.

We took the train to Santa Fe and stopped at Albuquerque. Native Americans danced for us and made coach Crisler and Bob Chappuis chiefs. They even got headdresses.

At that Albuquerque stop, one of our ends, Dick Rifenburg, bought a turquoise ornament and then raffled it off to the team. He pulled his own name out as the winner. I will never forget that.

When I left Michigan, I had the opportunity to play for the Detroit Lions or the Brooklyn Dodgers of the All-American Football Conference. But I was 28 when I left Michigan, and I didn't think I could take it. I decided to go into coaching. I was at Michigan from 1948 to 1954, and then I went to Penn State where I worked from 1954 to 1982.

Back when I was coaching Penn State, people would ask me whom I would root for when my various schools were playing. "Flip a coin," I would say.

But my bachelor's and master's degrees are both from Michigan, and I have great allegiance to the school.

People would always ask me what "J.T." stood for, and I tell them it's "John Tecumseh Troublemaker Juan Blanca Super Knuck." John Tecumseh was an Indian in the army. Juan Blanca is "John White" in Spanish. Super Knuck comes from the fact that I used to call everyone "Knucklehead."

The truth is, my real name is John Thomas White. But I don't like the "John Thomas" because, when I was young, I saw a picture in the paper of a dog named "John Thomas." That's when I had everyone start calling me "J.T."

At one of the games in 1947, the Michigan band even spelled my name, "J.T.," with one of their marching formations. Now that's Michigan tradition.

J. T. White is believed to be the only player to win national championships on two different collegiate football teams. He played for the champion Ohio State and Michigan teams. He also won a national championship while working on Joe Paterno's coaching staff at Penn State.

JOHN GHINDIA

QUARTERBACK

1947–1949

Players used to call coach Fritz Crisler "the Lord" because he wouldn't allow it to rain when he held a practice. I thought he was a genius, a strong taskmaster, and a real smart man. He knew his business. And he was such a classy person. He never used a vulgarity. The worst he ever called a guy was a "jackass."

Crisler would say, "We take winning for granted at Michigan. We are going to win, and if we don't win, something is wrong." That was his philosophy.

When I showed up to play football at Michigan in 1946, I looked out on the field and saw that there were almost 60 lettermen returning. At that time, college teams were only carrying 50 guys on a traveling squad. I had played end, linebacker, and other positions in high school. I didn't know what position I wanted to play at Michigan because I could see All-Americans everywhere. Finally, I noticed that the smallest guy out there was quarterback Howard Yerges, so I told Crisler I was a quarterback, even though I wasn't really a quarterback. But Yerges was a small guy like me.

What I remember Crisler telling me is: "See that guy over there at left halfback? That's an All-American [Bob Chappuis], and he's going to pass on this team, not you."

Before the 1947 season, we had a scrimmage, and I fumbled the ball. I picked it up, ran through center, and ended up going about 75 yards for a

John Ghindia (No. 23) gets ready to block a Minnesota defender to pave the way for ball carrier Wally Teninga during a 1949 game. Ghindia's son John also played football at Michigan, going to four Bowl games in the early and mideighties.
Photo courtesy of Ivory Photo.

touchdown. The next week, before the season opener, coach Crisler said he was moving me to halfback. I was a sophomore, and I didn't play all that much. I played more in the first three games than I played the rest of the year. Once the Big Ten season started, I didn't play much at all. But I busted my tail and eventually ended up starting at Michigan. In 1948 Gene Derricotte and I both got hurt, and we spent the season in the whirlpool. But in 1949 I started eight games at quarterback.

I had two years with Fritz and two more years with Bennie Oosterbaan as coach. Bennie was a great guy, more fun than Fritz. He would come by, pat you on the back, and tell you to throw the ball to him. He taught us how to make one-handed catches. "Throw it anywhere you want and I will catch it," he would say.

We actually had a lot of plays with the quarterback throwing the ball, but coaches really wouldn't let me call those plays. As quarterback, I called all of

the plays. But I didn't call many where I passed. I didn't want to get kicked
out of the lineup.

In 1949 Stanford was supposed to be a good team, but we beat the pants
off that team. The next week we played Army, and [Michigan lineman] Alvin
Wistert was hurt. We had other injuries. I remember we were down 14–7,
but we were marching. We marched 50 yards, down to Army's 10-yard line.
It was second and 1, and I called a pass. It was intercepted. We were running
right through Army before then. The guy had to hurry the pass. That was
the game. I couldn't live that play down my whole life. After we lost to Army,
we went to Northwestern and lost our first Big Ten game that season. We
played Minnesota the following week, and the Gophers were undefeated.
They concerned us because they were like a pro team. They were so big. The
Gophers were ranked No. 3 in the country. We beat their tails. We still ended
up winning the Big Ten championship.

I'm very proud to have played at Michigan. People don't realize how tough
it is to play at Michigan. Other than me, how many people from my hometown played at Michigan? There weren't any. Take a couple of other cities
around here, and it was only one or two guys.

I thought our style of football at Michigan was the best, and it proved to
be the best. It seemed that everyone who used our system had success.
Michigan assistant coach Biggie Munn went to Michigan State and used the
same plays. Davey Nelson went to Delaware and used the same stuff. Forest
Evashevski went to Iowa and had success. They all had great years.

I had two roommates, and both ended up coaches. I thought I was a better coach than either of them. Tubby Raymond coached at Delaware and
Bob Hollway ended up coach of the St. Louis Cardinals. Kidding aside,
those guys did a good job, and I was proud of them. I remember when we
got out of school they got jobs coaching at Maine, they wanted me to go
with them. I ended up coaching high school, and I ended up making more
money. I always said I didn't want to be a coach. It was a thankless job. It just
didn't pay very well. When I quit coaching at St. Pat's, there was as an assistant's job open at Michigan. Bump Elliott was coach. He wanted to get former Michigan player Terry Barr who had played for the Detroit Lions. But
he wanted to offer him $9,000. I don't know how much Terry made with
the Lions, but $9,000 wasn't enough. That's why you have to admire the
quality of coaching that Michigan had.

In 1950 I was still around Michigan taking extra classes, and I went down to the famous "Snow Bowl" game at Columbus. It wasn't cold. It was a light snow, but it kept snowing. You just couldn't run the ball. We punted every time and won it on two blocked kicks. There were five of us who drove down to that game, and it took us 12 hours to get home. We pushed the car through Marion, Ohio. Cars were all off the side of the road. We pushed the car through snowdrifts for a mile or two until we got through.

I've had football tickets at Michigan for almost 60 years. My son John also played at Michigan. To have both of us play for Michigan . . . that tops everything, really. Ohio State wanted him. Michigan State wanted him very badly. Kentucky wanted him. But he wanted to go to Michigan. Michigan didn't offer him anything, however, until the week before signing day. We were all really happy that he ended up at Michigan. It was special to have him there. He was president of Detroit's U-M Club a couple of years ago, and he's very involved in Michigan activities.

The only negative for me is that I didn't get to play in a Bowl Game. I went to the Rose Bowl after the 1947 season, but I didn't get to play. My only complaint about Crisler was that he didn't play anyone even though we wiped out USC in the Rose Bowl. The next two years, we were Big Ten champions. However, we couldn't go again to the Rose Bowl. I didn't get to go when I was playing a lot more. Meanwhile, my son went to the Rose Bowl, Bluebonnet Bowl, and Sugar Bowl. He went to four Bowl Games.

I played with a great bunch of guys. We have a reunion every year and have a great time. The only bad thing is we keep getting older, and the reunions keep getting smaller.

John Ghindia won more than 600 games as a high school coach in various sports, including football. He was considered instrumental in launching the sport of hockey in Michigan.

DICK KEMPTHORN

LINEBACKER

1947–1949

WHEN COACH FRITZ CRISLER AND HIS ASSISTANT Bennie Oosterbaan recruited players to play football at Michigan in the forties, they made no promises and told no lies.

"Either you want to come to Michigan or you don't," Bennie would say. "If you do come, we are happy to have you, but there will be no $5,000 check for you."

One of Bennie's failures as a coach was that he wasn't a good recruiter. He just expected you to come to Ann Arbor because you loved Michigan, and he wouldn't lie for any reason.

"I won't promise you that you will play right away at Michigan," he would tell recruits.

My journey from my hometown of Canton, Ohio, to Michigan had a different twist. I had been in the Merchant Marine Academy, serving a tour of sea duty during World War II. I was really a member of the U.S. Naval Reserve, and we were stationed on cargo vessels. We would run between New Guinea and the Philippines. While I was at sea, two players from Canton— Stu Wilkins and Norm Jackson—were accepted at Michigan. Wilkins, a year younger than me, had played football as a freshman in 1945.

While I was home on leave that summer, Wilkins and Jackson kept telling me that I should leave the academy and come to Michigan to play football.

My dad convinced me to travel to Ann Arbor to take a look at the program, and Michigan coaches wouldn't let me come home. An assistant coach Art Valpey wrote my letter of recommendation to the academy.

There was no tryout. *The Saturday Evening Post* had published a story on the Canton McKinley High School football team in 1944, and the article had featured me. Apparently, the Michigan coaches had read it.

It felt good to be wanted because Michigan wasn't anxious to bring in more players that summer. The war had just ended and, as I recall, seven former captains came back to Michigan to play. In 1946 there were about a hundred guys who came out for football, and that was unprecedented.

Michigan was a classy football school. Before serving in the war, I had attended Miami of Ohio and played a couple of football games for coach Sid Gilman. I thought Michigan coaches would not pay any attention to those two games. But they did, and I was declared ineligible for the 1946 season.

The coaches ran a clean program. None of us ever heard a coach swear at practice or during a game.

"You can't block your way out of a paper sack," Crisler would say.

He might say you made a "stupid play," but he would never cuss at you. He would never hound-dog you. That wasn't the Michigan way to coach.

This was a special group of guys that came together to play at Michigan after the war. Many attended college on the GI Bill, and all of us were there because we admired Crisler and Oosterbaan.

We were proud to be at Michigan. The Michigan tradition that Fielding Yost established, and which Fritz and Bennie furthered, was difficult to beat. We were just a family. And on the field, our record speaks for itself.

Fritz Crisler understood how to bring our team to its peak performance. Remember, many of our players had been through World War II. Our halfback Bob Chappuis had been an aerial gunner and his plane had been shot down over Italy. We had guys who were happy to be playing college football. Pro football wasn't very popular back then, and we viewed this as our last opportunity to compete on the playing field.

The team concept was also stressed at Michigan because Fritz introduced the platoon system. He was a real innovator. He tried to get us playing like they play today. He wanted specialists. Dan Dworsky had been a center in 1945, but he became a linebacker. I played a little bit at fullback, but primarily I was a linebacker. He tried to allow players to do what they did best.

Dick Kempthorn (on ground) makes the lead block for Wally Teninga (No. 42) during a 1949 game. Probably best remembered for his defensive skills, the linebacker/fullback was named the team's Most Valuable Player that season.
Photo courtesy of Ivory Photo.

Jack Weisenburger was a great spinner and was very nimble at fullback. Bob Chappuis was an all-around gutty guy. He could run. He could pass. He could do it all. Howard Yerges was the field general. He called his own plays. He made sure players did what they rehearsed in practice. Bump Elliott was a quick, fabulous game-breaker.

Fritz left all of those guys in the backfield, and then he set up a defense. Bump was one of the few players who went both ways on that 1947 national championship team.

"If those guys on offense don't score, we are still going to win," Crisler would say.

I always say that our center, J. T. White, was the unsung hero of that 1947 team because opposing teams would try to stop our "Mad Magician" back-field by pummeling him. The idea was that if the center was worried about getting hit on every play we wouldn't have clean snaps and our backfield's deception plays would be disrupted before they started. Minnesota might have been the most physical team in the country at that point, and I remember J.T. had to play against Leo Nomellini, who became a Hall of Famer. White would get pummeled, but our plays were never disrupted. He didn't get enough credit.

Winning that Rose Bowl 49–0 over USC after going undefeated in 1947 was probably the highlight of my career. We went to Southern California for a couple of weeks and had a fun time—the climate, the atmosphere, it was all great. We met Hollywood stars and visited movie studios. I even posed for a photo with actress Loretta Young. Fritz had to work to get our minds back on football.

Michigan tradition was established before our group arrived. Fritz Crisler made sure we understood that. We talked about Michigan tradition at all of our team meetings. Fritz believed he had to carry on Fielding Yost's tradition. That was part of his job.

Linebacker Dick Kempthorn was named MVP of the 1949 Michigan team. Michigan was 25–2–1 in his three years on varsity.

ALVIN WISTERT

TACKLE

1947–1949

W HEN I PLAYED FOOTBALL FOR MICHIGAN IN 1947, opponents would say, "Here comes Pappy and his kids again." I was a 30-year-old college freshman. I was 13 years older than some of the other players on the Michigan team.

Coach [Fritz] Crisler just seemed happy to have the third Wistert brother to play at Michigan. And what did we do in my freshman year? We won the Big Ten title and the national championship. Crisler told us afterward that he was retiring as a coach. "This is the best team I've ever coached," he said. "If I kept coaching, no other team could live up to this team."

Then Bennie Oosterbaan became head coach, and damn if we didn't win the national championship again in 1948.

I was proud to be a part of that success, particularly when you consider that I had originally dropped out of high school many years before.

When I was at Carl Schurz High School in Chicago, Michigan baseball coach Ray Fisher said, "I can't wait until you get in college because you are a better pitcher now than your brother [Francis] was when he graduated from Michigan."

That's when I decided to leave school and turn pro.

Baseball was foremost in my mind. I ate, slept, and dreamt baseball. I wanted to play professional baseball. Coach Fisher had played in the majors, and when he told me I was better than my brother, that was good enough for me. Francis had signed with the Cincinnati Reds and pitched for them in 1934.

Also, my older brother had told me that my grades weren't good enough to get into Michigan. He said that I would probably have to spend a year in a high school in Ann Arbor and then get a principal's recommendation to get into Michigan.

I called the Reds, and they signed me to a baseball contract when I was 17. But in the spring of 1935, I slipped on ice, put out my hands to break my fall, and landed hard on my right hand. I jammed my elbow; I had bone chips. I couldn't pitch again. My career was over before it began.

Ultimately, I joined the U.S. Marine Corps, and I remember telling a fellow in the service that maybe I would go back to high school and then get a college degree from Michigan like my brothers. During the war, I served mostly stateside, but I did go to Guam in the Pacific. We were reserves, ready to go to Iwo Jima if called.

When I arrived at Michigan, there were so many guys out for football that practice and scrimmages forced you to work that much harder. Michigan practices, in a lot of instances, were tougher than the games.

To me, the Minnesota games were the most memorable of my career. We had to win those games. Here's why: when my older brother [Francis] was at Michigan, he never lost to Minnesota. But Michigan only managed to score 9 points total against Minnesota in 1931, 1932, and 1933. The scores were 6–0, 3–0, and 0–0.

Then my younger brother, Albert, came to Michigan, and he never beat Minnesota. When he was in college, I was living and working in Chicago, and I called him after his first loss to Minnesota. I was crying in Chicago, and he was crying in Ann Arbor. After that first loss, I said, "Get 'em next year." But Michigan didn't get 'em the next year or the year after that.

That's why, when I arrived at Michigan, I vowed "over my dead body" was I going to allow Minnesota to beat us. I felt I had to make up for Minnesota beating Albert those three years. That's why the Minnesota games were the most important. Minnesota had behemoths on its team then. Minnesota had giants, big darn Scandinavians. But we beat them three years in a row.

Crisler was tough, but he was fair. You had to respect him. In preparing the players for the game, he would tell us what the other team was going to do and

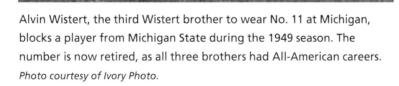

Alvin Wistert, the third Wistert brother to wear No. 11 at Michigan, blocks a player from Michigan State during the 1949 season. The number is now retired, as all three brothers had All-American careers.
Photo courtesy of Ivory Photo.

then explain what we needed to do to overcome it. It was like reading a book. Everything in the game would happen just the way he said it would.

He never left anything to chance. If he heard from a counselor that some player was not working hard in class, he would call them into the office for a talk. At my age, it was difficult to get back into a routine of study, especially when you consider that I had not been a great student before. But I had to be a good student to qualify to play. That's just the way it was.

I thought the unsung hero on the team was Joe Soboleski, a Polish kid from Grand Rapids. He played guard and tackle, and he was a hell of a player. He had great desire. He wanted to win. He was tough in practice and tough against opponents. He never got enough credit for being a great player

It meant so much to me to play for Michigan. To play Ohio State and beat them three years in a row, and to beat Minnesota three years in a row, was important to me. Players have such great pride in being Michigan players. Other schools have great traditions, but not when they are playing Michigan.

The Wisterts all wore No. 11, and I was very proud when the school retired that number. Here's the reason: it's the only time in a hundred years of college football history that all three brothers have gone to the same school, worn the same number, made All-America, had their number retired, and then all gone into the College Football Hall of Fame. I'm extremely proud of that accomplishment.

Alvin "Moose" Wistert was 32 when he graduated from Michigan, and he was the oldest player ever to play for the Wolverines. He made All-America teams in 1948 and 1949, and then worked in the insurance industry for many years before becoming a manufacturer's rep.

The

FIFTIES

ROGER ZATKOFF

LINEBACKER

1950–1952

I HAD OPPORTUNITIES TO GO ELSEWHERE; Michigan State, Illinois, and some others; but it was Michigan, and I was home. Actually, I had a girlfriend in Hamtramck, and I wanted to be close by. I ended up marrying her. She's still my bride 54 years later.

Back in my era, there wasn't the recruiting that there is today. In the forties, it was essentially the high school coach saying, "These are the schools that have an interest in you," because they had already contacted the coach. One day I was asked, "Would you like to go see a Michigan football game?" The answer was "Yes!" The rules said they couldn't pick you up or drop you off. I had to find my own way there.

I got out to Ann Arbor, stood by the tunnel, and waited. Finally, I was told to go in and find myself a seat. I wandered in and ended up sitting in the south end zone. It was absolutely wonderful watching Fritz Crisler's "Mad Magicians." Michigan was doing those spinning moves with the spinning fullback. It was phenomenal to sit up in the south end zone watching how Michigan was running those spinning plays while the opposing defense tried to stop them. It was very exciting. Michigan beat Pittsburgh 69–0.

After the game, you found your own way home. Nobody bought you a hamburger or took you into see the coach or the football team; it was just kind of like, "You're here." I hitchhiked in and I hitchhiked home down Plymouth Road. I hosted myself on my recruiting trip.

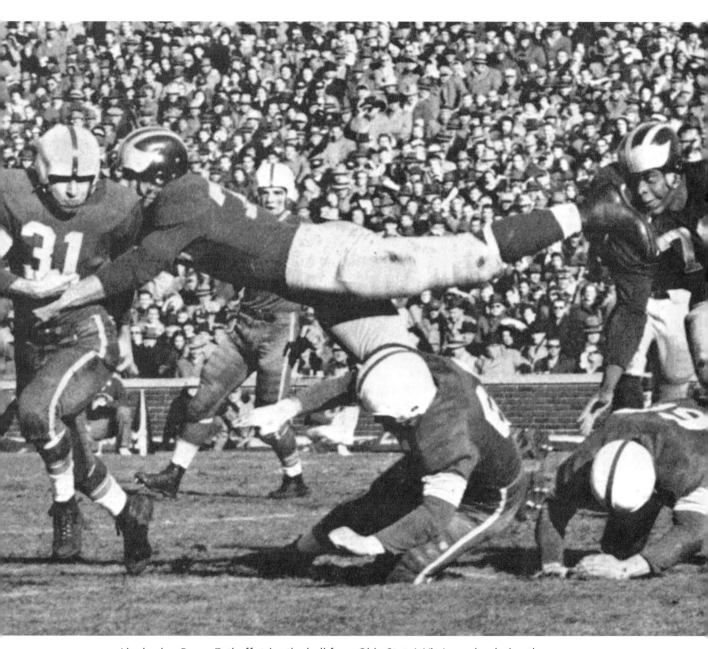

Linebacker Roger Zatkoff strips the ball from Ohio State's Vic Janowicz during the 1951 match-up. Zatkoff was one of Michigan's most celebrated linebackers in the early fifties and played in three straight Pro Bowls for the Green Bay Packers. *Photo courtesy of UM News and Information Service.*

Athletic scholarships weren't available in those days. The Detroit alumni club had a group of scholarships that they gave to potential athletes. Your local alumni club in different cities—Chicago, Detroit, Bay City, Grand Rapids, and all throughout the nation—gave these out. They couldn't give you a scholarship just because you were an athlete. But if you were an athlete, they had some money for you to "study" at the university. That was acceptable. My $145 per year came from the University of Michigan Alumni Club of Detroit. That was for both semesters, $75 for one semester and $70 for the other.

As a freshman in 1949, I wasn't allowed to play. As a sophomore, we were never sure who was going to start. There wasn't any big to-do about whom the starting quarterback was or who replaced whom. I played linebacker. Our linebackers at the time were Dick Kempthorn and Paul Palmer. I knew that there was a slot open, I knew there was competition for this slot, but being a young kid I figured it was mine. As practices went on, I became a starter. Our first game was against Michigan State. The Spartans had their "pony" backfield. I thought I had a pretty good–to-outstanding game for a sophomore in his first game.

The following week, I was standing in the training room getting taped. Crisler walked by the door. He looked at me, said, "Pretty good game," and walked away. I turned to Jim Hunt, the head trainer, and said, "Pretty good game? I thought I had one hell of a game!" Jim said that I didn't understand that "pretty good" was a very high compliment from him. Fritz never gave compliments!

Bennie Oosterbaan, my coach, was very quiet and reserved. I had very little interaction with him. The only time I got to see Bennie was when I didn't do well in class. He'd call me in and say, "You're not doing well in class. You better get your act together if you want to play football here." Bennie was the kind of guy who would say, "We may be outmanned, we might not have the staff to compete. But we are Michigan Men and we shall persevere." I would think to myself, "Yeah, Bennie, sure! We're going to get our ass whipped!" Bennie was not a great motivator in that respect; not like Schembechler, Yost, or Crisler.

My part was very small in the famous "Snow Bowl." I had hurt my knee the week before and couldn't play. I stood on the sidelines handing out hand warmers to the guys coming back to the bench. There were times in that game when you could not see across the field to the Ohio State bench; it was snowing and blowing that hard.

On Friday we took a bus to Toledo and spent the night. The next morning we took a train down to Columbus. The train parked alongside the stadium. The wind was blowing, it was cold, and people were slipping on this patch of ice. We thought it was really funny watching these people fall; now I don't think it's funny because I'm one of those old people who'd be slipping and falling.

The game was delayed to get the snow off the tarp and get the field opened up. While we were waiting for the game to start, we were still watching these people fall on the ice. One of the coaches was yelling at us, telling us to get our minds on the game. We would be serious when he was in there, but the minute he'd leave, we'd be laughing again. We were very fortunate to win that game and go to the Rose Bowl. There were blocked punts that brought that game to a head with Carl Kreager and Tony Momsen, falling on the ball to put us ahead. In the Snow Bowl, you got the ball, punted it, and hoped the other guys screwed up.

It was an experience to travel out to Pasadena for the Rose Bowl. For a guy from Hamtramck, who hitchhiked out to Ann Arbor, flying on an airplane was a big deal. It took forever to get there! There was a sense of tradition playing in the Rose Bowl. We knew we were the underdogs, playing Cal in front of a home crowd. We were determined to come out on top.

79

Since I had hurt my knee and didn't play against Ohio State, I didn't practice until two or three days before the Rose Bowl. In the first half, I reinjured my knee. I went to the coach at halftime and said, "I'll play, but my knee is not as good as it should be. I don't have the speed to cut or cover like I should." The game was too crucial. We were behind at halftime. I thought that we might be better with Ted Topor, my substitute, playing instead of me. Ted was healthy, and he went in. We ended up winning 14–6.

It was very important for me to go to the coach and realize my inadequacies based on my injury. It was more important for us to win that game than it was for me to play. After we won the game, it was an experience in itself. The Rose Bowl is a huge stadium of one hundred thousand people, and that's a big thrill.

I was very lucky. I got a chance to play in the Rose Bowl. I got a chance to play in the East-West game, the College All-Star Game, some Pro Bowl games, and an NFL Championship game. I was very fortunate to make it with the right teams, the right coaching staffs, and the right group of players that could jell together. The players' jelling together is the key to making it work.

Having played football for Michigan, I really have to attribute the success and the aura of Michigan to the coaching. I did not know Yost; I'm a little young for that. I'm only 74. But I did know Kipke, Crisler, Oosterbaan, Elliott, Schembechler, Moeller, and now coach Carr. It's their coaches that have maintained Michigan's tradition, work ethic, integrity, and dedication.

Regardless of whether it's winning years or losing years, and I've been on both, it's just an honor to play for Michigan. When you sit back and look at it 50 years later, you think, "Wow, what a wonderful time I had!"

Growing up in Hamtramck, my old high school coach, Joe Rosdeck, rode the hell out of me. I hated his guts, but later when I realized what he was doing in college and in the NFL, I'd go back to Hamtramck to hug him and thank him. It was his dedication and motivation that pushed me to become a better athlete. I've always had the desire to play. I loved playing; I loved hitting.

In 1991 Michigan established the Roger Zatkoff Award, given to the outstanding linebacker at the conclusion of each football season.

TED CACHEY

GUARD

1952–1954

YOU WOULD GET OBJECTIONS FROM OTHER HIGH SCHOOLS, but our Mount Carmel High School team in Chicago was proclaimed the "best there ever was" in one newspaper ad. Our team was highly recruited. Off our high school team, Dan Shannon and Paul Matz became co-captains at Notre Dame. Paul Leoni went to Kansas and became a captain. Bob Danklau went to Lewis College and was a captain of his team. And I ended up captain at Michigan.

Many excellent colleges recruited my teammates and me. Due to the wise guidance of my high school coach, Terry Brennan, who had recalled the famous Michigan guard Dominic Tomasi, and my principal, Rev. David Murphy O'Carm, who heralded Michigan's academic merits, I began to look toward Ann Arbor. I became receptive to the voices of the Chicago Club Alumni. Edward Madigan, Frank Mackey, Erwin Gunther, and William Lampe generously extended wise counsel. The late Mr. Lampe, a general manager of Oldsmobile, was once characterized by one of his daughters as having four main interests in life: God, family, the University of Michigan, and Oldsmobile. His daughter wittily said family members would not dare to list Mr. Lampe's order of priority for those interests. He was indeed an exceptional gentleman, the epitome of the best that Michigan can proudly claim. He introduced such athletes as Norm Canty, Fred Baer, Jim Maddock, Ed

Shannon, and myself to Michigan. All held him in high esteem and are better men today for having known Bill Lampe.

My arrival on campus lacked luster in 1951. When I reported for football at Michigan, I was a 172-pound guard. Every night after practice, you were supposed to weigh in and write it down on the weight chart. I told our trainer, Jim Hunt, "I'm not going write down 172 pounds. If I do, our line coach Jack Blott is going to kick me off the team."

That's when I decided to always add eight or nine pounds to my weight.

I was made painfully aware of my small size when I roomed with Fred Caffrey, a 6'3", 200-pound tackle. Both Fred and I were sidelined with injuries early that first season. A broken arm was the only injury I suffered in my four years. However, Fred suffered repeated knee injures, which prevented him from playing. I'm proud to say the university continued his scholarship through the Engineering School. I missed the extraordinary and eloquent coaching of freshman coach Wally Weber. But Wally's humor was a source of hilarity among the boys at Fletcher Hall. Anguish over my injury overshadowed the football season. I kept busy by selling programs outside the stadium and waiting tables at the Parrot Restaurant. In hindsight, time spent away from football allowed me to acclimate my mind and schedule to the heavy academic demands at Michigan. I learned that, if I were to profit in the classroom, I had to work twice as hard as I had anticipated. I learned post-graduation that the value of a Michigan degree is far higher and more prestigious than anyone could have convinced me at age 17.

My sophomore year brought me into contact with assistant coaches Jack Blott and Cliff Keen. They preached that athletes who were willing to sacrifice and work at 100-percent capacity would prevail. I had disappointments and letdowns, such as not making the traveling squad for the Stanford game. But through it all, my unwavering perseverance was sustained. This is not an uncommon feeling among Michigan athletes. As a result, I began as the last guard on the team, but eventually obtained my goal of securing a starting position. My desire for achievement on the athletic field spilled over into my scholastic life. Through hard work, I was able to reach my goals in the classroom.

If Michigan means great people, then Michigan means Bennie Oosterbaan. He was a man who mastered the sport privately and shared his vast knowledge of the game with everyone. Coach Oosterbaan made sure we knew the goals.

Ted Cachey played guard
for three seasons under
coach Bennie Oosterbaan
in the early fifties. He's
shown here during his
senior season of 1954.
*Photo courtesy of UM News
and Information Service.*

We were imbued with Michigan tradition and desire to win; once achieved, he made sure the happiness of success was shared.

One of my greatest thrills came September 25, 1954, in our opening game of the season. It was against the University of Washington in Seattle. It was my 21st birthday, and this would be my first game as captain. My parents surprised me by being at the airport when we landed. They were with the loyal Michigan Alumni from the Washington area. They greeted us with a chorus of "Hail to the Victors." University President Hatcher was exceptionally cordial to my parents and included them in all alumni festivities.

The highlight of the 1954 season was the final game against Ohio State at Columbus. Preseason ratings of our team forecast a .500 season. Our great sophomores, Lou Baldacci, Ron Kramer, Jim Maddock, Ed Shannon, and Tom Maentz were just beginning to show their considerable talents. However, we surprised many experts that season. We arrived in Columbus with the idea of winning. We wanted to tie for the Big Ten championship and earn a trip to the Rose Bowl. We moved the ball 68 yards after the opening kickoff to score. Many fans in the capacity crowd wondered if the two teams hadn't put on the wrong uniforms. At halftime, the score was 7–7.

In the second half, our goal-line charge was stopped three times. I've seen the movies and heard the calls rehashed many times. But the fact is we lost 21–7. A blizzard of torn programs hit us from the celebrating fans. However, Woody Hayes said after the game that Michigan was the toughest foe the Buckeyes had faced all season. We tied Wisconsin for second place that season. It was Michigan's highest finish since 1950.

My last appearance in the Michigan Stadium was at my graduation. But that, too, I remember well. As any aspiring young law student would have been, I was impressed by the remarks of Chief Justice Earl Warren. Dr. Jonas Salk, the recipient of an honorary degree that day, was kind enough to autograph my program. The honors of those days are history. Yet today I feel an overwhelming sense of gratitude to those persons who influenced me to choose the University of Michigan.

Ted Cachey is now an attorney in Orland Park, Illinois.

ED MEADS

GUARD

1953–1955

M Y DAD WAS A MICHIGAN GRADUATE IN DENTISTRY IN 1927, and he was on the wrestling team there. There was no question about where I was going to go to school. I wasn't all-state in high school. When I started at Michigan, I was 9th- or 10th-string. As a sophomore, I was 3rd-string. Then I became a starter as a junior. And when I became a captain as a senior, it surpassed my wildest expectations and dreams.

The captain is announced before the team picture because the captain was in a specific place in the photo. Before the announcement, you wouldn't even dare think that you might be the captain. You are just happy to be a regular. I was flabbergasted when they announced that I would be the captain.

I'm proud and grateful for the friends I've made from my association with Michigan. Some of my dearest friends are those I played football with on those teams. Without patting ourselves on the back, we have to say that it was just a good group that we had on those teams. Our coach, Bennie Oosterbaan, was a wonderful human being. He had a belief that if you were going to play for Michigan, you came because you loved Michigan. It wasn't about money or scholarships to him. You had to love Michigan. In all the speeches he gave, that message came through loud and clear. He bled blue. He was laid back, and he didn't drive us quite as hard as he could have. We had good teams. But there was only one Rose Bowl. And back then, if you didn't go to the Rose Bowl, you didn't go to a bowl game.

The two games that are indelible in my mind are the 1954 and 1955 games against Ohio State. Unfortunately, we lost both of those games. And there isn't a week that goes by that I don't think about that.

The most exciting game I ever played was against Iowa my senior year. We were down by two touchdowns, and then the Hawkeyes scored again to go up by three touchdowns. But it was called back by a penalty. We went on to win, going away. In my three years at Michigan, Iowa coach Forest Evashevski—who had been a Michigan player—never beat us. In 1954 we beat Michigan State 14–7, and the Spartans had been at the 1954 Rose Bowl. Also in 1955 our team became the first Michigan team to defeat Army.

Back then, you only sold out Michigan Stadium for the Ohio State and Michigan State games. But to go from Oxford, Michigan, to play football in that big stadium was overwhelming initially. But after you play there once or twice, you tune that out.

The other unique experience in my career is that I ended up going to medical school in Canada. And I was able to play two more seasons of collegiate football at the University of Western Ontario because you could still compete as long as you were working toward a degree. I played middle linebacker at Western Ontario. At Michigan, I had just played guard.

Although I live in a country where hockey is the sport, I still get pumped up about football in the fall. I have had Michigan season tickets since I graduated. We often go in groups of eight or ten to the home games, and make one or two away games during the season. In the past five or six years, I've been to every bowl game.

I played with Ron Kramer, and he's still one of my best friends. He's certainly one of the best athletes I ever played with. One Saturday, he played in the spring football game and then went over to the track meet, won a couple of events, and placed in two others. He played basketball. He could do it all. My best story about Ron Kramer involves another one of my teammates, Terry Barr. At that time, they were already both in the NFL.

They were playing in the NFL golf tournament. It was Terry's turn to hit, and he was waiting for the green to clear. "Terry, hit the damn ball," Kramer said.

"I can't, because I will hit it on the green, and there's people there," Barr said.

Kramer kept insisting that Barr hit. So finally Barr hit, and he put the ball up on the green, and it rolled through the guys who were putting.

Ed Meads, a guard during the early fifties, was selected as a team captain in his senior season of 1955. *Photo courtesy of UM News and Information Service.*

Perturbed, one of the golfers on the green yelled: "Who in the hell hit that ball?"

Thinking fast, Barr yelled back: "Ron Kramer."

The guy on the green simply stepped back and said: "Nice shot."

I played with a lot of tremendous athletes and great people on those Michigan teams. Barr and Tom Maentz fit that description. Lou Baldacci was an extremely good player and played a year or two with the Pittsburgh Steelers. John Morrow was a good friend, and he played with the Cleveland Browns and Los Angeles Rams for 10 years.

By coincidence, I have a house in Florida, one-half mile from Tom and a mile from another teammate, Ted Cachey. Another former Michigan player, Jim Conlin, who played in the early fifties, lives even closer to me than Tom.

You never lose your connection to the University of Michigan. I appreciate the feelings that people have for Michigan.

Ed Meads is a physician living in London, Ontario. He also served a tour of duty as a combat doctor during the Vietnam War.

RON KRAMER
END
1954–1956

THE FOOTBALL TRADITION AT MICHIGAN DIDN'T START in the thirties and forties. It started in 1901 when Fielding H. Yost came to Ann Arbor. He had more tradition in one finger than anyone who has come since him.

Michigan still has his buildings. Michigan still has the fields. Michigan still has all of the ideas that this guy brought to the school. Those ideas coincide with what's going on today at Michigan. We are building on his tradition. He built a stadium that now holds 100,000 people, and even back then it held 88,000. He really wanted it to hold 200,000. He had footings put in for another deck.

All of what we see at Michigan is what Yost had in mind. He built the stadium to pay for everything else. Football was the only money-maker. It wasn't just about the athletes. It was about everyone on campus. That's why he built the intramural building. People shouldn't forget him.

I'm a wacko traditionalist. Back when I was playing for coach Bennie Oosterbaan in the fifties, I used to go to the athletic department and watch Bennie Oosterbaan and Benny Friedman Michigan game films from the twenties. Friedman was the passer and Oosterbaan was the receiver. The films were so grainy that you could barely tell what was happening.

Fielding H. Yost died in 1945, but his wife was living when I was playing for Michigan. I can remember sitting with her for hours talking about her husband. She told me they traveled to Michigan from West Virginia on a horse and buggy. What a lot of people don't know is that Yost didn't stay year-round in Ann Arbor in the early years. He would go back to West Virginia after the football season.

As we talked, his wife would go to a chest and pull out old articles by famous sportswriters like Grantland Rice and Walter Camp. It was as if I were in the middle of a Damon Runyon story.

People don't know that Fielding Yost put in the golf course. He was going to buy even more land, but the cost was $2 per acre, so the school's regents wouldn't let him. The tradition at Michigan is all his, and the rest is just add-on.

Coming out of East Detroit High School, I considered other colleges. But my mother and dad loved to go to my ballgames and Michigan was close. They wouldn't have to drive far. That made my decision easy.

My current seats for Michigan football games are still the same two seats that my mother had in 1953. I put a plaque on one that says: "To Adeline, 1953–1987, 241 games in a row." Even after I was in the NFL, she continued to attend Michigan games. She stopped going in 1987, and No. 87 is the number I wore at Michigan. She died in 1988. That's the number [88] I wore in the pros. The last digits of my telephone number are 8788.

When Michigan retired my number, I cherished that mostly because my coach, Bennie Oosterbaan, was like a father to me. For him to think that strongly of my contributions, even though we didn't win any championships, meant a lot to me. It disturbed me that we didn't win any championships, although we were close. We had some good players and some great players, but we just couldn't quit get there.

Bennie Oosterbaan was tradition. Bo Schembechler is tradition. But they have built on what Fielding H. Yost started. And another contributor to the tradition who is often overlooked is the band. Band members work just as hard as anyone to prepare for those halftime shows. If you ever watch their workouts, you would be shocked at how hard they work on that quickstep march. Dr. William Revelli was band director for many years [1931–1971], and he brought in the quickstep march. My understanding was that before him, they would just march like the army. I knew him, and he was a great guy.

One of the great traditions of the forties and early fifties involved a man named Mr. Chestnut from Fenton, Michigan. We called him Mr. Apple

Ron Kramer (No. 87), shown here about to tackle a Minnesota ball carrier during his senior season of 1956, was an All-American at Michigan and then went on to play 10 seasons in the NFL for Green Bay and Detroit. *Photo courtesy of UM News and Information Service.*

because he would bring apples to us on Wednesday, which was always a tough practice day.

In 1987, when Bo Schembechler was still coaching, I moved to Fenton and I began to take apples up to the Michigan football team. I haven't missed a week since then. I bring apples to the team, to the athletic director, and to the ticket director. I even take them to the president of the university.

I just wanted to carry on the tradition that Mr. Chestnut started. I remember after a hard practice on Wednesday, you would grab a couple of those apples and they were so good. Just talking about them makes me salivate.

Although Bennie was my coach, Fritz Crisler was very involved with me because he was the athletic director. When I was about to sign with the Green Bay Packers, Crisler took charge.

"Don't say a word," he told me, "I will handle the whole negotiation for you."

He did exactly that, and got me a deal better than anybody.

Bennie was quiet, very unassuming. He gained respect by deeds, not words. He really didn't recruit anyone. He just felt it was a privilege to play at Michigan, and if you didn't want to play at Michigan, you could go somewhere else. He was a great football player, basketball player, and track star. Those were the same sports I participated in at Michigan. There was a connection between us.

Every game we played at Michigan Stadium was the best game there ever was. But football was very different when I played. I played both offense and defense. I kicked off, punted, played end, and even some halfback. On defense, I played linebacker.

My point is that the tradition changes over time. The kids coming up today are playing with equipment that is absolutely phenomenal compared to what we used.

When I wore a face mask for the first time as a senior in 1956, it made football a different game. I could keep my eyes open to watch what was going on. When we didn't wear face-masks, you would close your eyes when someone was going to knock you in the nose. If you didn't, you would have to be Superman. The introduction of the face mask was one of the greatest changes in all of athletics.

But even though the game has changed, there is a connection between all of the players and coaches through the years. Once you are a Wolverine, you are always a Wolverine.

People should know that Bennie Oosterbaan had a great sense of humor, and there is a story I like to tell to show that.

Back then, when you dated a girl, you had to have her back home by 10:30 at night. If she didn't come home by then, she was grounded for a month and you couldn't go out with her anymore.

My roommate was Charlie Brooks. We were both members of the Sigma Chi fraternity. We were both ends. Charlie and I, and other guys on the team, would like to park with our girlfriends at the stadium behind the big high-wire.

One night Charlie was a little hot and heavy with his girl and didn't notice that it was later than 10:30. He was parked in a dark area, and he didn't see that the groundskeeper, Bob Hurst, had come over and locked the gate. Now he is hung up in there with his girlfriend, and he has to climb over the wires and wake up Hurst to get his car out. He was way late, and the girl wasn't allowed to go out again. It was a mess for Charlie.

A few days later, I came home from class and looked in the mailbox. I saw a 7 x 10 postcard with the Michigan Stadium on the front. When I turned it over, it read: "Dear Charlie, it's a wonderful place to play, isn't it? —Bennie Oosterbaan."

After Bennie Oosterbaan died, Kramer took his ashes and spread some at Michigan Ferry Field, some in Oosterbaan's backyard, and some at Michigan Stadium.

JIM MADDOCK

QUARTERBACK

1954–1956

WHEN I WAS PLAYING CATHOLIC LEAGUE FOOTBALL for Fenwick High School in Chicago, I had moments I won't forget. We were playing DePaul Academy. It was fourth and 10, with 10 seconds left in the half. I was the punter. We broke huddle, and before we got to the line, a guy I'd known my whole life named Ed Shannon said to me, "Why don't you run it?"

I thought, "What the heck, 10 seconds left, what could happen?" The ball was centered, and I took one step as if I were going to punt it. Instead I took off around end. Ed was with me, and it was as if we were the only ones on the whole field—as if everyone had already gone to the locker room for halftime. I didn't have to avoid anyone. I just ran around end 50 yards for a touchdown.

Our coach, Tony Lawless, said nothing to me at halftime. So in the third quarter, there was another fourth-down situation. I decided I was going to run around the other end. This time, four guys at the line of scrimmage tackled me.

When I came off the field, coach Lawless said to me: "Maddock, you do that once a year, not twice a game, you fool."

If it had not been for really excellent high school coaching, I probably could not have played for the University of Michigan. Our high school had an excellent reputation. Our coach taught his players the fundamentals. There were people looking out for you all the time. Coach would not encourage you to go someplace where he didn't think you could play. If he didn't believe you could play at a school, he would have something to say to your mom and dad. "If you want him to go there, it's fine," he would say, "but I don't think he will play basketball or football because the caliber of athlete is a little above his aptitude."

Coach Lawless never said anything to you unless he had criticism. And he said it in such a way that you would never forget it. When I decided to go play at Michigan, he didn't say anything to me. That meant I was OK.

Actually, a couple of exemplary people, Ed Madigan and Waldo Lampe, recruited me to go to Michigan. Madigan was an attorney, and Lampe was a general manager at Oldsmobile. When they talked about Michigan, they made you feel that that was the only place you wanted to go. You didn't want to make the big mistake of going somewhere else. These guys were so

Jim Maddock finds some open field to work with during the Army game in 1956. Maddock quarterbacked two consecutive 7–2 teams but failed to make the coveted trip to the Rose Bowl. *Photo courtesy of UM News and Information Service.*

professional. They wore a coat and tie on Saturdays. When we visited Michigan, it was like nowhere else we visited. We had an appointment with the dean of admissions at 9:00 A.M. on a Saturday. The last place we went at Michigan was to the athletic department. At every other school, that was the first place we went. If we went by the admissions office in the car, someone might point it out. The approach was different at Michigan. We were all standing in this 30 x 40–foot office with our mouths hanging open. It was an impressive experience to go to Michigan for the first time.

Three other good friends were going to Michigan, including Ed Shannon. But the reality was Michigan didn't offer me a scholarship at first. We weren't poor, but going away to school was improbable. It looked like I would go to Purdue, but Michigan [coaches] came to Chicago at the last minute and offered me the chance to play there. To me, it was like winning the Most Valuable Player award. It was a big deal.

One of my favorite memories involved Ed Shannon and myself. In 1954 the first game was at Washington, and Ed and I walked out to the field house to see if we made the travel team. We were sophomores. Both of us made it. We just couldn't believe it. If only one of us had made it, it really would have been bittersweet. We just looked at each other and said, "Wow." I can't even describe the feeling.

My wife, Martha, tells me that she never met a group of guys like my football teammates. "They are so genuine," she says, "thoughtful to their wives and so considerate."

Everyone I met associated with Michigan was wonderful. My impression of Michigan coach Bennie Oosterbaan was that he was the kind of man you would want coaching your son. He was wonderful—his heart was in the right place, and his ethics were above and beyond. To Bennie, life was more important. It wasn't what you did on Saturday. It was who you were and who you were working to be. Maybe he was too nice. All three years I played at Michigan, we could have gone to the Rose Bowl. And we had two years, especially, that we were really good. Ron Kramer played with us, and he was the best athlete I've ever seen. What do you want to play? Football, basketball, Ping-Pong? Whatever the sport, he would be the best. Ben lost his only son in the war. Ben really took on Ron as his son. In his mind, I think Ron reminded Ben of himself when he was at Michigan. Like Ron, Ben had played multiple sports. Ron was the most loyal guy to Ben, and vice versa.

For two of my seasons, we should have gone to the Rose Bowl but didn't. We lost to teams that we should not have lost to. They were the kind of losses that probably wouldn't have happened with Bo Schembechler. I think Ben struggled within himself about how to be a little tougher on us. At the end of the day, Bennie was a good man. The love and affection that Ben had for all the players, the coaches, and Michigan was enough to take you through. When it was over, you could say, "I wish we had gone to the Rose Bowl." But football wasn't everything at Michigan. Michigan was everything.

One night, some of my Michigan friends and I were arguing with Notre Dame guys at a party. One friend, Frank Gazzolo, who I had known since kindergarten, made the most awesome statement about Michigan. It stopped us all for about 10 seconds.

"You know," he said, "we can talk about who's the best, but Michigan could terminate its sports program next week—all sports, men's and women's—and nothing would change. Enrollment wouldn't go down. The faculty wouldn't leave. Ann Arbor would still be Ann Arbor. Whether you are in the band or playing football or on the debate team, it isn't you that makes Michigan, it's Michigan that makes you."

There was silence after he said that because he was right. Michigan is an institution second to none. You can talk about the Ivy League, but there are great aspects of Michigan, that go beyond sports. That's what Michigan has meant to me. It was my good fortune—not Michigan's—that I went to school in Ann Arbor. It was a great experience. Michigan sets you up for the rest of your life.

97

Maddock was Michigan's passing leader in 1954 and 1955.

ED SHANNON

HALFBACK

1954–1956

W HEN I WAS A SOPHOMORE IN 1954, I WAS JUST HAPPY to make the traveling squad as a third-string wingback. Tony Branoff was an All–Big
Ten wingback. He was ahead of me, along with Ed Hickey. In the second
game against Army, Branoff was injured and lost for the season. Then Hickey
broke his nose against Iowa.

On Monday or Tuesday of the next week, coach Bennie Oosterbaan told
me, in his own unique style, that I was starting. "Shannon," he said, "you are
all we've got left."

I just thought that Bennie Oosterbaan was a fine, fine man. He was so
immersed in Michigan that it showed in his personality. I went to see him
five or six years after I was out of school, and he brought me down to his
basement. It was a shrine to the University of Michigan. He had all of his
trophies down there. He just loved the University of Michigan. You could
tell by his sincerity how much the school meant to him. When Bennie
coached, he sometimes would get so nervous during a game that the assistant
coaches would have to take over for him.

I mean it when I say he was a lovable guy. He was very proud of Michigan. And that's the way he coached it. It rubbed off on his players. To me,
Bennie Oosterbaan was inspirational.

He had a good sense of humor. The *Chicago Tribune* had a reporter cover-
ing the Michigan–Michigan State game. I had a decent game. But on Sunday,

Ed Shannon, a wingback for the Wolverines for three seasons, arrived in Ann Arbor with teammate Jim Maddock from Chicago's Fenwick High School. *Photo courtesy of UM News and Information Service.*

the headline was "Michigan Defeats Michigan State." The sub-headline was "Baldacci, Kramer, and Shannon Star."

Oosterbaan got the paper and posted the article on the bulletin board. He circled my name and said: "We also have our stars."

Honestly, my performance wasn't that great. But the writer who authored the story was the *Chicago Tribune* golf editor Charlie Bartlett. He was my uncle. Bennie knew the guy was my uncle.

One of my other favorite moments during my Michigan career involved my good friend Jim Maddock. We had known each other since about the fourth grade. We didn't go to grammar school together, but we did go to high school together at Fenwick High School. He was the quarterback, and I was the wingback. Then we went to Michigan together.

At Michigan, I held the ball for the extra-point kicks. Jim would kick. He would get into the huddle and say, "Shannon hold. Maddock kick. Center when ready." The ball was snapped when I opened my fingers. That's how it worked.

In our junior season, we were beating Army by 13 points, and Maddock came into the huddle and said, "Maddock hold. Shannon kick. Center when ready."

The huddle broke and Maddock got on one knee. I said "Jim, c'mon." After all, there were a hundred thousand people at this game. He said, "You can kick it." We were arguing on the field. Eventually, we lined up, and I kicked a spiral that went banana-shape over the crossbar. It was a funny moment. That was the kind of guy Maddock was. Bennie just laughed. My scoring experience at the University of Michigan was 19 points, but that point is the one I will remember the rest of my life.

Fenwick was an all-male Catholic high school, and it turned out lots of college football players. John Lattner was three years ahead of me at Fenwick, and he won the Heisman Trophy playing for Notre Dame. Our coach, Tony Lawless, prepared us so well that we were ahead of other players. We knew a lot about the game of football. But because Fenwick was a Catholic school, most of the priests wanted us to go to a Catholic college. As a matter of fact, the year I graduated from Fenwick, there were 225 guys, and 42 of them went to Notre Dame. But a great guy named Bill Lampe recruited us to go to Michigan. He made us believe Michigan was the place for us.

I wasn't a star at Michigan. But I held my own. We had a very good team and some talented players. Terry Barr was a great football player. He had natural speed. He was a hurdles champion in Michigan. He could travel. He would pull away from defenders. On defense, he would take chances because he was fast. He played safety and made tackles behind the line of scrimmage He just knew where the ball was going.

It was a pleasure to be the teammate of Ron Kramer. You could throw the ball within a 10-yard radius of him and he would get it.

I wear my letterman ring all the time. I'm proud of the accomplishment. I loved Michigan. It was a great experience. My father was self-made. He didn't go to college. My dad wanted me to go to Michigan, and I had a lot of confidence in him. It was important to me that he and I be in agreement on a school. That's how much I respected him.

In my junior year, my older sister Pat died giving birth to twins who both lived. My family was overwhelmed by grief. Four months later, my mother died, probably from a broken heart.

My mother and father used to come up on Friday before my games. But after my mom died, leaving my father by himself, he started to come up on Thursday for my Saturday games and stayed at the Union. Then he started coming on Tuesday before a Saturday game. He enjoyed my college experience as much as I did. It was like he was playing the game, too.

Ed Shannon was 165 pounds, but he even spent time as a fullback and linebacker, as well as a wingback, at Michigan.

GEORGE GENYK

TACKLE

1956–1959

I'LL NEVER FORGET WHEN I WAS NAMED CAPTAIN of the team in 1959. I was actually really surprised by it. I can honestly say it was better than being named All-American. Bennie Oosterbaan came up to me and said: "Congratulations, George. You're the unanimous pick." I was speechless. But there was only one vote that wasn't cast for me. It was my own. It was an honor to be picked, and it was definitely not expected. The honor of being the captain and representing your teammates is unbelievable.

I followed Michigan in the newspapers and on TV as a youngster. I loved their winged helmet. It really attracted me, and I thought they were really cool. I read about the Rose Bowl teams and the dominant tradition Michigan stands for. We were very poor, living on the East Side of Detroit, and I tried to play baseball, but you needed a glove, which for us cost too much. Football was the only sport that supplied the equipment.

With the tutelage of my brother, who played at Pershing High School in Detroit, I was drawn to the sport. Despite my success at Pershing, Michigan was one of the only schools that did not actively recruit me. But they recruited two of my buddies, and my friends told Michigan about me.

Back in Detroit, I had a chance to talk to Bennie Oosterbaan and some other coaches. I took a test to qualify academically at Michigan and passed. I was very fortunate to have the academics to get into Michigan, and I felt it was an absolute gift from heaven.

When I finally got in, they said I was too small for a lineman. I played some freshman ball but had a very interesting experience along the way. At that time, the freshman played separately from the varsity team, and we would scrimmage them occasionally. During this last scrimmage, we faced off against the first-stringers, and we actually beat them by one point.

There was a little twinkle in Oosterbaan's eye that afternoon as he watched the success of his freshman, which would be the future of Michigan football. The following spring brought new challenges. My father passed away right as spring ball was underway. I was only 18 years old. I had obligations at home to fulfill, but I made it back in time for spring ball. At the time, the spring squad was split into six teams. I was on the fourth team and felt I was really on the borderline. In this particular game, it was the white team versus the blue team. I was on the white team. Usually, the blue team would kick the white team's butt.

But this was a defining moment for me. I was on defense and it was the first half of the scrimmage. Jimmy Pace, the All-American running back, was readying to run a sweep. I spun out of a few blocks and was one-on-one with Pace. Usually, he would brush right past you, but not on this day. He tried to make some moves on me, but I just nailed him. At the half of the scrimmage, I was put on the blue team. They felt I could play. As a side note, I believe my father's death served as added motivation. When he was living, he was unable to see any of my games because he was working to provide. But on that day, I think he was there to see my defining moment.

103

After the spring game, I was awarded the John Maulbetsch Award. It recognizes the player who is most likely to succeed at Michigan. I didn't think I deserved it, but it was quite nice of them to think I was worthy of such an honor.

There are a number of games that really stand out. One in particular is of course against Ohio State in 1959. It was my final game at Michigan Stadium. We won the toss and elected to be on defense. In that season, Ohio State was picked to win the Big Ten. The electricity in that stadium was higher than usual, and we were absolutely pumped up. On the kickoff, our defensive end John Halstead went down and put a big hit on the receiver. He knocked him out cold, and he was hemorrhaging from the ears. He dropped the ball following the hit, and we recovered. The player had not even hit the tunnel after being carried off the field, and we were in the end zone with a score. It was the hardest-hitting game of my career. I had friends at the game who

George Genyk played guard for three seasons and captained the 1959 squad. *Photo courtesy of UM News and Information Service.*

couldn't believe how hard-hitting it was. We ended up winning the contest. It was a great feeling to knock off Ohio State.

In 1984 Bo Schembechler approached me. We were at the Bluebonnet Bowl and my sons were alongside me.

"George, how ya doin'?" he boomed. That's Bo, never forgetting a name. It caught me off guard. I introduced him to my sons.

"This is one of the true Michigan greats," he said, talking about me.

"Whoa," I replied. "The last time I played against you, you were an assistant coach with Ohio State."

"I know it," he answered. "We were doing everything we could to block you, and we just couldn't block you." It was very interesting to me that 20 years after the fact, somebody was thinking about you. It was one of the greatest experiences I've had at Michigan.

It was another Ohio State game, this one during my junior year that I distinctly remember. Our quarterback was Bob Ptacek, while Brad Myers was our running back. Dean Clark was Ohio State's All–Big Ten standout running back. It was late in the game when it was decided we had to stop them on fourth and inches. We had a linebacker by the name of Dick Syring. Ohio State opted to run a dive play, and it was Clark who had the ball. The first guy to hit Clark was another one of our linebackers, and he ended up sending Clark out with a bruised thigh. But as the pile cleared, I turned around and saw Dick lying on the ground. He had a dislocated shoulder. He was writhing in pain. I looked at him and asked if he was all right. With pain in his eyes, but fire as well, he asked: "Did he make it?"

"No, you stopped him," I assured him. It was very momentous because we fed off it and drove to their 1-yard line. The game was tight, 20–14 in their favor, and it was first down with about 20 seconds left in the game. But we fumbled the ball, and they recovered. I just remember the deafening sound of the crowd. It was a sellout, and it was just like a vacuum. I remember heading back to Ann Arbor with a real headache.

As a kid, I really loved that Michigan helmet. Putting the winged helmet on was a dream come true. I can remember running out there with the helmet on and just thinking, "Holy Christ." The crowd, the music, it just sweeps you into the moment. I received that thrill every time I ran out there. Another great story was about a fellow who never dressed. But for the final game of his career, he was allowed to dress. I'll never forget his reaction when we sprinted out of the tunnel. He was using every four-letter word in the book.

"Oh my God, it was worth it," he exclaimed. "All those years of work but not playing. It was all just worth it for this moment." Although I can't recall his name, I can never forget his reaction to running out to a packed Michigan stadium. It's an unbelievable experience.

To me, being a Michigan Wolverine is a dream come true. It is the epitome of tradition of a great school, both academically and athletically. The

105

tradition, the football, and the camaraderie is probably the most dominating life experience I've ever had. The tradition, the stadium, the pride of being a part of that is amazing, and the quality and type of people associated with the program are what many schools try to emulate. But they can never really be what Michigan is.

George Genyk was a high school football coach in Michigan for more than 30 years. His son, Jeff, is head football coach at Eastern Michigan University. George now serves as a coaching consultant for Eastern Michigan University.

The SIXTIES

BILL FREEHAN

END

1960

WHEN I LEFT THE UNIVERSITY OF MICHIGAN to sign with the Detroit Tigers in 1961, my deal with my father was that I wouldn't receive any of my bonus money until I had earned my Michigan degree.

The pride and tradition that Michigan stands for is what sticks out in my mind about my experience playing football and baseball for the Wolverines.

I went to high school in St. Petersburg, Florida, and both Florida and Florida State recruited me for football. But I was very familiar with Michigan because I had lived in Detroit in the summers. My grandparents had a home there. When school would get out, I would head north for better baseball competition. I played in some tough, tough leagues in Detroit. Dave DeBusschere, Alex Johnson, Willie Horton, and three or four other guys who went on to play major league ball were playing in those leagues at the time. [Johnson was the brother of Michigan football standout Ron Johnson.]

In Florida you were only playing against white players. In Detroit you were playing against some of the best black and white players in the country.

Don Lund is the reason why I went to the University of Michigan. He was the Michigan baseball coach. He was also a former major league player. He also had played football, basketball, and baseball at Michigan, and Bump Elliott was the football coach. He had also played football and baseball in the late forties.

Bill Freehan played one season at end for the 5–4 Wolverines in 1960, then left school early to sign a contract with the Detroit Tigers, for whom he played 15 seasons in the major leagues. *Photo courtesy of UM News and Information Service.*

When I agreed to commit to Michigan, I was originally on a baseball scholarship. But I walked into Don's office and asked him if he would mind if I also played football. He gave his blessing. By the end of the week, football coaches called me in and told me I was on a football scholarship.

Back then, you weren't allowed to play collegiate athletics as a freshman. Instead you would play freshman ball, and during the varsity games, you'd end up shagging the ball for the varsity

But as a sophomore I played baseball and football. In football, I played both ways and started six or seven games. There were probably only two or three guys playing as sophomores. I actually kicked some field goals. The season went by quickly. We were 5–4.

The following spring I hit .585 in baseball, which was a school record. I don't recall any one play as a football player. However, I remember going 5-for-5 against Western Michigan in baseball. As a sophomore, I was already an All-American catcher, and the big question was whether or not I would come back. Back then I was called a "bonus baby" because, at the time, I was the highest-paid kid, or close to it, ever to sign to play professional baseball.

I will never forget the friendships—in both football and baseball—that blossomed into lifetime friendships. In 1962, a year after I signed my contract with the Tigers, Michigan won the NCAA championship in baseball. I still had buddies on the team. I had won some summer league championships with some of them. They mailed me, letting me know the "onus was off our back." Even though I was in the minors and not physically with them, they still considered me a member of the Michigan family. Those friendships meant a lot to me. They still do to this day.

Although I left school early to play for the Tigers, I did come back to finish my degree. By the time I saw my Tigers' bonus money, it had grown considerably because my father had invested well. The deal I struck with my father was a great motivation to finish my work on a degree. Obviously, my wife and I were happy when I finally earned my degree.

The "M" ring is given to seniors, but the school had a special presentation for me because I came back semester after semester to earn that degree. I'm very proud of that ring, as I am the ring I earned winning the World Series with the Detroit Tigers.

Bill Freehan was an 11-time All-Star catcher for the Detroit Tigers. He won five Gold Gloves and helped the Tigers win the 1968 World Series.

TOM MACK

TACKLE

1964–1965

WHEN I WAS BEING RECRUITED, Michigan had not successfully recruited anyone in the greater Cleveland area in a four- or five-year period. And I was not a particularly good high school football player. My eyesight was extremely poor. I didn't play with glasses, so I had really bad hand-eye coordination. Back then in high school, you played both ways. I was a defensive end and an offensive end. But I couldn't catch the ball because I couldn't see it. I'd have to listen for it. That didn't work very well because the only time I heard it was when it went by me, or when it hit the ground.

I was probably a better swimmer in high school than I was anything else. That's one of the major reasons I got to go to Michigan. As a swimmer, I competed at a state finals level. My swim coach had gone to Michigan, and for the three years that I swam, he glorified and emphasized how wonderful Michigan was. In conjunction with my football coach, the two of them convinced a recruiter in the Cleveland area that, by my junior year in college, I would have matured and become a pretty good athlete. I was behind the curve in terms of my physical maturity. Most important, I could get into Michigan academically, while a lot of other people couldn't.

All of those different factors gave me the opportunity to be recruited by Michigan. I was interested; I qualified academically; and I was a football player who was from the greater Cleveland area. That was as much luck as anything else. . . . Deep down I hoped that someday I could be a good enough athlete to actually play at Michigan.

As a freshman, the best thing that happened to me was that the school bought me contact lenses. It was the era of one-platoon football, when you had to play both ways, and freshman weren't eligible. You spent your fresh-man year trying to stay in school and trying to beat the varsity. They were the only people you ever played besides yourself. You also tried to establish yourself among your peers. There were about 28 kids who had scholarships. At first I was overwhelmed because, with the exception of me, almost every-body seemed to be either all-state or All-America. More than once I sat there and said, "How did I get here?" I just kept going back to how lucky I was that the swim coach and the football coach had argued so hard, that I was somebody that matured late, and Michigan wanted somebody from the Cleveland area.

My sophomore year, I started out as the third- or fourth-team end. Since we played both ways, that meant the first two teams, and occasionally the third team, got to play. I remember the big thing was: Would you get dressed for the game and would you play? You could usually tell because the trainers didn't bother to tape you if they didn't think you were going to play. I was in that category.

Near the end of the year, a couple of people got hurt, and I got all the way to what I considered second team. That's when the most embarrassing inci-dent of my life as a football player occurred.

President Kennedy was shot the day before our last game of the year ver-sus Ohio State. The game was postponed for a week. We played the Saturday after Thanksgiving up in Ann Arbor. I thought my time had come because I was officially on the second team at this point. I remember [coach] Bump Elliott saying, "Second team, get ready to go in." He was on the sideline, looking us in the eye, and he had his hands on our shoulders to push us toward the field, saying, "In, in, in," as he went down the line. He got to me and said, "Sit Down!" I was absolutely crushed. But I figured nobody noticed. Unfortunately, we lost the game. I went home to Ohio at Christ-mas, and my neighbor, who was at the game as an Ohio State fan said, "Gee, I saw you ready to go in and then you sat down. What happened?" I said, "Well, that's life." That was the highlight, or lowlight, of my sophomore year. I did not get a letter.

Guard Tom Mack (center) provides the escort for ball carrier Mel Anthony during a record run of 84 yards in the 1965 Rose Bowl. Mack considers this play a factor in getting his Hall of Fame NFL career off the ground. *Photo courtesy of UM News and Information Service.*

In the spring of 1964 the NCAA changed everything by going to two-platoon football. To me, that was what changed my life at Michigan. By going to two-platoon football, the coaches told me that they wanted to make me an offensive tackle, instead of a two-way defensive and offensive end who couldn't catch. I was thrilled! The biggest doubt I had was that I was 6'3" and weighed 215 pounds.

At the same time, Michigan hired Tony Mason, a high school coach from Niles, Ohio. He was a very big Michigan supporter and had sent between a half dozen and a dozen players to Michigan over a five-year period. Tony became the offensive line coach. Bump was always nice and classy, but a bit distant. He wasn't a buddy; he was more of a father figure that you looked up to. He was clearly the head coach. Getting Tony Mason was the single most significant event that took us from not being winners to being winners.

That spring, coaches made me an offensive tackle. I went from the end of the bench to receiving an award called the Meyer Morton Trophy for the Most Improved Player during spring practice. I guess I really was, because I went from being the butt of all the jokes about the kid who couldn't catch to being very effective as an offensive tackle. It wasn't that I was so big and strong; I had very good speed. In fact speed, more than any individual thing from a physical point of view, was why I was successful playing pro football.

114

We came back that fall and collectively we knew that we could be a good team. Early in the season, we played both Air Force and Navy. The service academies had extremely good teams. Navy was a great team, ranked No. 2 in the country. Roger Staubach had won the Heisman Trophy the year before. We beat them—we beat them pretty badly. Everybody looked at each other and said, "We can really be good!"

When we went down to Columbus to play Ohio State, we hadn't defeated the Buckeyes in four years. But in our minds, there was no question that we were going to win. We shut them out 10–0 and headed to the Rose Bowl. What made it exciting for us was that, of the 22 kids who started, 14 or 15 were from Ohio. It meant a lot more to the kids who had been recruited by OSU. For me, it was going home and proving that I belonged as a football player because Ohio State didn't even call me. They didn't even give me a sniff.

There was a play in the Rose Bowl that gave me the visibility that probably helped me get into pro football. It was a little fullback quick-pitch play to Mel Anthony. He went around the right corner, I threw a block, and either missed or fell down. I got up, took off, and ran down the field with him. Until a few years ago, Mel had the record for the longest run in the Rose Bowl. It was 84 yards. There's a picture of me jogging next to him. He was running full speed, and I was kind of jogging. I guess I had fairly long strides. More than anything else, people wanted to know who the hell the tackle was that was as fast as the fullback! I ended up getting drafted by the Rams as an offensive lineman because I had that great speed!

I can't think of many schools, or many places, that evoke both the pride and continuing sense of accomplishment that you have when you've played at Michigan. You represented the school, and the school accepted you. It was something I didn't grow up planning to do; Michigan was one of those schools where it was almost too high to set as your goal. The interesting attitude was you didn't want to embarrass the school by the way you presented yourself in professional football. You feel the same way about business. As an engineer, I've worked a long time, and I'm proud to say that I'm a graduate of the University of Michigan. I feel very lucky.

Tom Mack played 13 seasons for the Los Angeles Rams and earned All-Pro honors five times. In 1999 he was inducted into the Pro Football Hall of Fame.

RICK VOLK
QUARTERBACK/HALFBACK/ SAFETY
1964–1966

A LOT OF THINGS FELL INTO PLACE FOR ME. In those days, if your university had money, they could offer as many scholarships as they wanted. Bump Elliott was the coach, and during his Michigan playing days, he was also a teammate of my uncle, Bob Chappuis. Bump was his halfback, and I'm sure Uncle Bob said something like, "I have a nephew that looks pretty good, why don't you look at him?" That's how it happened. That's why I got the chance to go to Michigan.

I really hadn't been recruited by Michigan much, I came from a small high school, and I'm sure Uncle Bob mentioned something. We sent film to Michigan, and they invited me up. I met Bump and talked to him, and he said they'd like to have me come up there.

When he told me, I said, "I'm coming!" There wasn't any question. It wasn't like me to tell them I was going to wait—that I had three or four other appointments and I'd let them know. It was just a great feeling. It was an emotional time because I always wanted to go to Michigan, and it happened for me.

Bump made it possible, and Uncle Bob had a lot to do with it. It was just one of those things. Today it might not have worked out for me; you still have to go out there and do it. I had an opportunity.

Rick Volk breaks up a pass against Ohio State in 1964. Volk played in the 1965 Rose Bowl with Michigan and then went on to play 12 seasons in the National Football League. *Photo courtesy of UM News and Information Service.*

Being from Ohio, I had a lot of good-natured ribbing about going to Michigan. For example, my dentist in Wauseon was an Ohio State grad. Whenever I went to see him, I'd be in the chair with a cavity that needed filling and he'd drill deep and say, "That's for the interception that you had against the Buckeyes!" It was just good-natured.

Of course, everybody in my hometown knew that, if I had the chance to go to Michigan, that's where I was going. I'd loved Michigan ever since I was a little kid because of Uncle Bob; he's such a great guy.

My grandma and grandpa would tell me stories about Michigan when Uncle Bob was there and about his teammates that would come to Toledo to stay overnight—all the characters that came down and all the stories about going out to the Rose Bowl by train.

We'd go up into the attic, and there would still be boxes of fan mail that Uncle Bob had not opened up yet. This was probably back in the late fifties. It was usually grandma and me. She'd open up these things, and there would be money in some of the envelopes so he could buy a stamp to send back his autograph. It was just neat, sort of in my blood. It didn't matter what other people said, I was headed to Ann Arbor!

118

Back in the fifties and early sixties, Michigan wasn't really a powerhouse; they were a middle-of-the-road team at that time. Bump was there for 10 years, and he was the one who started to get it turned around. We had that team my sophomore year in 1964 that went to the 1965 Rose Bowl. We were the fourth Rose Bowl team that Michigan had sent out.

To think back from the twenties, even before that, since Michigan started playing football to be the fourth team to go out to Pasadena. Well . . . there were a lot of teams that came through the gate at Michigan and never made it to the Rose Bowl.

We played Oregon State and won 34–7. We won the Big Ten and the Rose Bowl. Oregon State had a good team that year, but we had a great team and came through. It was our group of seniors who were really our leaders, and then we had some juniors and sophomores who filled in and played well and contributed.

Everything seemed to mesh that year. Bob Timberlake was the quarterback; Tom Mack, who played with the Rams and is in the [Pro Football] Hall of Fame was a lineman; Bill Yearby was an offensive tackle; Jim Conley was a defensive end. We had a lot of guys. Frank Nunley and me, and a few other sophomores, such as Jim Detwiler, Carl Ward, and Dave Fisher. We all sort of fit in.

Michigan is about history. You're representing a tradition of great players and coaches. You can go back to Fielding H. Yost, Benny Friedman, Fritz Crisler, and Benny Oosterbaan. You can go right down the list: Gerald Ford, Tom Harmon, Bob Chappuis, the Elliotts, and the Wisterts.

All over the country, people know Michigan. It's just the tradition, that's what Michigan is. It's the fight song, it's the alma mater. I love to sing that, it brings tears to my eyes every time I sing it. That's what I think about Michigan—all the great players and coaches.

You need to have the right people. You need to have the right chemistry. In my sophomore year at Michigan, we had good leaders with our senior group, and we had some younger guys who filled in. It was just good chemistry. You need that wherever you go to be successful—people playing together. It's team, it's not an individual thing. The team is the thing.

I'd rather be lined up with a guy who really wanted to go to Michigan than somebody who wanted to go to Michigan just because they wanted to go to the NFL.

Rick Volk played in three Pro Bowl games and two Super Bowls, and was twice voted All-NFL during a pro career that spanned 12 seasons.

RON JOHNSON
HALFBACK
1965–1968

WHEN MY PARENTS WERE INVITED INTO THE PRESIDENT'S BOX to enjoy my final home game at the University of Michigan, it was a proud moment. My father had a fourth-grade education, while my mother completed the 10th grade. In the midst of folks who boasted doctorates, master's degrees, and bachelor's degrees, my parents were the center of attention. My parents could have been uncomfortable around people with backgrounds in higher education. Instead, everyone was going goo-goo and ga-ga over them. It proved to me again the excellence of the University of Michigan.

My parents were adamant about my pursuit of an education. My opportunities were endless. But Michigan was without a doubt the best option for me. Both the athletics and education were outstanding. As insistent as my parents were about a top education, I can't emphasize how important education was to me. Several schools convinced me that I should have taken physical education as my major. But coach Bump Elliott would not hear of it. I entered into the School of Engineering in 1965.

Obviously, football complemented my zeal for an education at Michigan.

I came from a very proud background. I was surrounded by a number of great influences, including my parents and teachers. At that particular time, black pride was swelling to an unprecedented level. I was blessed to be where I was. In school, I was very studious. My grades were high, and coupled with

Ron Johnson picks up some of his single game–record 347 yards against Wisconsin in 1968. The All-American had five touchdowns in the game and finished with 1,474 career rushing yards at Michigan before embarking on an NFL career. *Photo courtesy of UM News and Information Service.*

football, I was sought out by several universities. Michigan stood out from the rest because of their willingness to quench my thirst for education. I'll never forget Bump's ear-to-ear smile when I inquired about a degree in engineering. He arranged for me to meet the dean, and my decision was sealed. Bump was also very candid about my playing time as a sophomore. While other universities attempted to sell me on playing time as a sophomore, Bump revealed to me that such an option would be slim to none. I appreciated his honesty, and it enhanced my opinion of Michigan further.

My career at Michigan was a great one. I have fond memories and experienced a number of personal milestones in my four years as a Wolverine. As expected, I saw limited action during my sophomore year, but it didn't take very long into my junior year before I started turning heads.

It was only the third game of the 1967 season when Navy came to town. Only two weeks earlier against Duke, I rushed for 85 yards and garnered attention for my first performance of the year. The contest against Navy was an awakening. I broke out for 270 yards and scored two of our three touchdowns. Although we ended up losing the game, my career at Michigan officially took off.

During my senior year, we really kicked some butt. We went 8–2, and although one of our losses came against Ohio State, we really came together during my senior season. We climbed as high as No. 3 in the country before Ohio State knocked us off our lofty perch. Despite the final loss against our bitter rival, my senior season was still a wonderful experience. In fact, the game prior to the Ohio State game proved to be one of the finest in my career.

We may have been looking forward a bit to the Buckeyes game when we faced Wisconsin, and it showed when we headed into the tunnel at the half, trailing the Badgers. As we made our way to the locker rooms, one of Wisconsin's wide receivers started yapping in our direction.

"This is mighty Michigan?" he taunted. "You guys aren't anything."

His comments were all we needed. We marched onto the field after the half and thoroughly dominated the listless Badgers. By the end of the game, I had tallied five touchdowns and galloped for 347 yards on the ground. It was my finest game as a Wolverine and still remains the highest rushing total in a single game at Michigan. In the end, we had Wisconsin's loud-mouthed receiver to thank for our second-half dominance.

My career day happened to be the last I would play at Michigan Stadium. It was also the day my parents sat with the president in his box. It was an unbelievably special day for my parents and me.

Although several of my career marks still rank high at Michigan, I hold firm to the belief that records are made to be broken. At one time or another, I've held several records, but just as many have been broken. It is extremely humbling to be at the top of many records still. And if the opportunity ever presented itself, I'd still have some bragging rights, too. While those records still hold a special place for me, there was a milestone that truly stood out from the rest.

Being named the captain in 1968 was the highest honor bestowed upon me at Michigan. I was the first African American to earn the captaincy, and it was a very special moment for me. From a social standpoint, it was very important. It made me feel proud that my teammates, black or white, truly believed there was no difference between us. It only made my commitment to my team that much stronger. We weren't viewing from a racial standpoint. The captaincy was awarded to the man whom we all felt would best represent and lead that particular team. I was blessed to be that man chosen to lead the 1968 Michigan Wolverines.

There were two other fellows who could have made great captains for our team. To be chosen from a pool of very capable candidates was the highest reward I received in my lifetime. Of all of my athletic accomplishments, it is the one prize I hold closest to my heart.

The greatest work in my life came at the University of Michigan. I thank God every day for the opportunity to be a Wolverine and for His will leading me to Ann Arbor. My parents left the decision up to me as to where I wanted my collegiate path to end. It was by the grace of God that he gave me the sensibility to choose Michigan. I couldn't have made a better choice.

> Ron Johnson ranks ninth in total rushing yards in a season at Michigan with 1,474. Johnson enjoyed seven seasons in the NFL and was a two-time Pro Bowl selection.

TOM GOSS

DEFENSIVE TACKLE

1966–1968

WHEN I CAME TO MICHIGAN, AN INTERESTING PROCESS was taking place. The Southeastern Conference had not yet been integrated. When Tennessee came to me and my family, they actually wanted me to go to a black college, Middle Tennessee State, for one year and then become their first African-American player. My father, who was very influential in my life, thought about that and said absolutely not.

I traveled around to a lot of schools, mostly traditional black colleges, from Tennessee State to Grambling. Michigan was not part of my thought process. However, up in Ann Arbor, there was an assistant coach, Hank Fonde, who was Michigan's backfield coach. He had a brother-in-law, who was a lawyer in Knoxville, who had been sending him all these articles about me.

The next thing I knew, Michigan was knocking at my door, but I was headed someplace else. I was going to one of the traditional black colleges where I had met several young ladies that had my interest. At the end of the day, it was my father who said, "You're not going there. You're going to Michigan." My father sent me to Michigan.

In those days, there were normally three African Americans on scholarship in every football class at Michigan. If you check the records from that time period, I don't know why, but there were always three. Then all at once, the year after I arrived, Michigan brought in all these players—Ron Johnson and a whole crew.

Tom Goss in action during the 1968 season. He recorded 16 tackles in his final game at Michigan, the 1968 loss to eventual national champion Ohio State. *Photo courtesy of UM News and Information Service.*

There was a change taking place, on campus where they recruited more African-American students. When I got to Michigan, there were very few African-American students. So to find someone to date, you would date someone from Eastern Michigan, Michigan State, or try to find someone on campus. The next year, it was a gold mine! In fact, I picked my wife out of that next year's class, and we've been married ever since.

I had a great relationship with Bump Elliott because, as I got into my fifth year, he saw me as the senior citizen on the team. Still to this day, my teammates talk about the red shirt that I used to have. For some reason, I would be "injured" every Monday, Tuesday, and Wednesday. With that red shirt on, you couldn't be hit. But on Thursday, Friday, and Saturday, I was ready to go. Bump accepted it as long as I played well. But my teammates still ask me, "How did you get away with not having to go through those drills on Monday and Tuesday?" They always make a comparison to when Bo came in, and they tell me, "Ain't no way that Bo would have gone for that!" And they are probably right.

My last game in a Michigan uniform is the game I will always remember. It was against Ohio State in Columbus. The score was tied 14–14 at halftime. They were ranked No. 1 in the nation, and we were playing them tough. In the second half, our quarterback Denny Brown was knocked out in the first series. Our backup quarterback, Don Moorhead, came in and separated his shoulder during the second series.

There was still two quarters to play, and both of our quarterbacks were out. Back in 1968, you could only travel with two quarterbacks. So Jim Betts, a quarterback in high school, but a defensive back for us, took over. He had very few reps during the week, so it was three-and-out the rest of the game.

Ohio State just physically dominated us. I remember some of our young guys, Marty Huff and Henry Hill, both of whom would later become All-Americans, standing on the sideline in shock. The Buckeyes were pounding us with Jim Otis and John Brockington. It seemed like we were on the field forever. They wouldn't get more than three or four yards, but we were so physically tired. I had 16 tackles that game, just by being on the field so long. There was no way I should have had 16 tackles that day.

At the end of the game, Woody [Hayes] called a timeout so he could go for two, when they led 48–14. This man called timeout to go for two?! All I was thinking was, "I wish I had one more year to come back." At that moment, the Michigan–Ohio State rivalry went to a whole new level. We left a lot on the field. Nobody likes to be disgusted the way Woody disgusted us that day!

I was a fifth-year senior and graduated in December. When Bo [Schembechler] came in, he offered me a coaching job to be one of his graduate assistants. I thought it was a big deal. I had always wanted to coach because I believed my technique was pretty good and I could share it with the guys. I put on my coaching hat, and the first mistake I made was that I was late coming onto the field. Bo said, "What are you doing coming out here late?" I looked around and thought, "I don't know who this guy is talking to, but I'll let him talk." I went over and stood behind the defense. We ran a play, and I didn't get out of the way in time. I got mixed up in the play. Bo ran over and said, "God damn it, what are you doing?" It was one of his early tirades, and he pointed his finger at me. I thought, "What in the world is this?" I took off my hat, threw it down, and walked off the field. I didn't talk to Bo for two years! He pissed me off that badly.

I was in the Detroit area, and I don't know how it happened, but Bo and I ran into each other and started talking. We made up, and Bo asked me if I would help him recruit. I recruited Harlan Huckleby, Curtis Greer, Tom Seabron, Ron Simpkins, and several others for him from metro Detroit. Our relationship became stronger because we were getting whomever we wanted. That was a fun time. Over the years, I grew to love the man like everyone else because I understood him. But when he came at me . . . that was a different day.

127

One of the things that drew me back to Michigan was so many people reaching out to me without my asking, simply because I was a Michigan Wolverine. Having someone offer to help, you don't know how huge that is in a young man's life. When a successful individual would take the time to sit down and talk to me about various career paths, it was overwhelming.

Going into my junior year, I had someone say, "Tom, I know you want to be a coach, but you might want to consider business as an alternative." For a black guy, you didn't hear of many black guys having business opportunities. Being from Tennessee, I was either going to teach, coach, or be a preacher. That conversation was the catalyst that moved me toward what eventually became my gift back to the university. I have done that with a lot of athletes over the years, counsel them about their other opportunities beyond playing ball.

When I was Michigan's athletic director, we invited the 1947 national championship team, the "Mad Magicians," out to the 1998 Rose Bowl. We matched offensive lineman up with offensive lineman, and those older guys talked about what it meant to be a Wolverine to young guys like Jon Jansen. That was one of the more special events I've witnessed and one of the best suggestions I ever received. We gave them national championship rings because they didn't have rings. Fifty years later, a Wolverine was still a Wolverine.

Tom Goss served as Michigan's athletic director from 1997 to 2000. As a player, he earned All–Big Ten honors in 1968.

CECIL PRYOR

LINEBACKER/DEFENSIVE END

1968–1969

IT WAS QUITE AN ADJUSTMENT TO GO FROM COACH BUMP ELLIOTT to Bo Schembechler. They were two different characters, two different personalities, two entirely different people. They handled players differently; but young people are resilient and we made the adjustment.

Bo often admits that when he came in he was tougher on us, his first team, than any of his other teams because he had to set his standards. He had to develop his program, a certain attitude that he wanted his players to have. As you get older, you understand it. I didn't agree with it back then. We used to have our little arguments all the time. But we're good friends today.

We had philosophical differences. He was the new guy! We had been there! We had gone through all sorts of hell, and then he comes along and subjects us to even more hell. Some of us thought that that wasn't quite fair. Usually, I wound up being the spokesman for that kind of thing. Bo didn't respond very well, because it was his way or the highway. But we opened his eyes, and his mind, and got him thinking. We used to yank his chain, too.

During that time it was long hair, thick sideburns, big Afros, and beards. Bo had this issue about facial hair; he didn't want anybody to have facial hair. A couple of guys got together and wanted to talk to Bo. We said, "Hey, Bo, you've got to understand. It's a cultural issue. Black guys have to have hair on their face. We need to have long sideburns, long muttonchop sideburns. That's just part of our culture." Bo went for that; he came into our team

Defensive end Cecil Pryor (No. 55) sizes up a Wisconsin receiver during a game in 1969. His Wolverines went to the Rose Bowl that season, but coach Bo Schembechler suffered a heart attack the night before the game and was recovering in the hospital when Michigan faced USC on New Year's Day.

meeting and said, "All right, no white guys can have mustaches or sideburns. Black guys—you can have mustaches and sideburns." We all just busted out laughing. He bought into it hook, line, and sinker.

The game that I will always remember is the 1969 Ohio State game. We were primed for that game. We remembered that score, 50–14, from the time that last gun went off [in 1968]. After that game, seniors-to-be Jim Mandich, Tom Curtis, and I pulled together all the guys that were coming back onto one bus. We made a commitment right then—whatever it takes to right this wrong, we're going to do it next year. If anybody didn't want to buy into it, they could go sit on the other bus with the seniors. We had a mission to accomplish, and we weren't going to stop until we accomplished it. We began that mission the day after that 1968 game. Bo didn't have anything to do with that. He didn't know about it. It was a pact that was made among all the returning teammates.

Despite what you may have heard, I didn't knock out Rex Kern before the 1969 game. There was a fight in the tunnel because they tried to precede us down the tunnel before the game. Mandich was always first, and I was always last to head down the tunnel. I hadn't come out of the locker room yet, and I heard a commotion going on. By the time I got out the door, the battle was full-blown. Half the guys were already down the tunnel and heading out onto the field. The other half was battling with Ohio State players.

Officials, cops, and coaches—all of the adults—broke it up. It was just a shoving match. You get two teams attempting to go down the tunnel at the same time, and it's Ohio State and Michigan, the year after Ohio State went for two to win 50–14, and you'll end up with what we had. It was a mêlée. But, again, I didn't knock out Rex Kern. I've even heard stories in which I tore the door off the visitor's locker room and sought out Rex Kern to beat him up. In the middle of their locker room! There was a fight in the tunnel, and I was involved in that. As far as the rest of the Rex Kern story—that's an urban legend. That's probably as old as the story that is true about nuclear physics.

Education was my major, not nuclear physics. The nuclear physics thing came about before the 1970 Rose Bowl. Back then, we taped our pregame shots, those things that you used to see on ABC, at Crisler Arena. We were wearing suit coats, and they had 22 of us up there; the 11 starters on offense and the 11 starters on defense. We were introducing ourselves in front of a camera, and everybody was going up and saying, "Hi, I'm Dan Dierdorf. I'm from Canton, Ohio, and I major in education. I'm Jim Betts. I'm from Cleveland, Ohio, and I major in Kinesiology." This went on and on. It was very boring and I thought, "I've got to liven this thing up."

So I was standing back watching and thinking, "What could I do to lighten the party up?" I didn't know what I was going to do until the camera came on. As soon as the camera clicked on, it hit me. I said, "Hello, my name is Cecil Pryor. I'm from Corpus Christi, Texas, starting right defensive end, and I major in nuclear physics." I looked straight at the camera and said it as honestly and sincerely as I could. All these guys were standing around, and they started rolling. The camera guys, they didn't have a clue as to what was going on, so we didn't reshoot it. It was two or three weeks before the game, and they left it like that.

When it was shown, it was like the shot heard around the world. I was getting phone calls from NASA. They sent me a couple of tickets to come down and interview for a job. I started getting all these letters and phone calls from

131

people all around the world whom I had never heard of. I thought about that guy, the Great Imposter, and how he was working his act and wondered if maybe I could get away with it. Then I thought, "No, I'd better not. I don't want to end up in jail." I cashed the tickets NASA sent me, kept the money, and never went to Houston, or Washington, or Cape Canaveral.

Not having Bo there at the Rose Bowl was quite a shock. Obviously, no one was prepared for it. We really didn't know about his heart attack until the next day. We realized he wasn't in our meetings, but no one told us anything, I think, until we were on our way to the stadium.

I went up to see Bo a couple of days after the game. I stayed out there because I was headed to the Hula Bowl. Bo was still in the hospital in the ICU. He told this story in his book about me coming to see him. He kept passing out and waking up. First he sees his mom, passes out again, wakes up and sees his wife, Millie. Then he passed out, woke up, and I was standing there! He thought I had come to pull the plug on him because we used to fight all the time. I had just come to see him. He always wondered how I got in to visit him, and that's another story.

No one was allowed to see Bo except Millie and his mom. I went to the hospital after everybody left for the day, and they wouldn't let me in. So I went down to the doctor's lounge and got a set of white scrubs and a white lab coat. I grabbed a clipboard, put a stethoscope around my neck, and said, "Dr. Pryor here to see Bo Schembechler." I didn't have a name tag on, but they just ushered me right on in. I hung out with him, we chatted for about a half hour, and then I left.

Being a Wolverine means I'm part of a great tradition that no one can take away. My kids know about it, my grandkids will know about it, and their grandkids will know about it. That's all it has to be.

Cecil Pryor recorded 15 tackles, including 5 solos, against USC in the 1969 Rose Bowl. He finished his career with 106 tackles, including 9 tackles for loss.

JIM BETTS
HALFBACK/SAFETY
1968–1970

About 175 colleges were trying to recruit me during my senior season at Benedictine High School in Cleveland, but I didn't know that at first.

Legendary Augie Bossu, who had played at Notre Dame, was my coach. He prevented colleges from contacting us during the season. He didn't want distractions. Following our final senior game, a buddy of mine, Larry Zelena, and I each received a box that contained hundreds of letters from recruiters. After we had sifted through most of the letters, coach sat down and asked us about our priorities heading into college ball. What traditions were important to us? Could we play as sophomores? We ran through lists of questions and then whittled our choices down to where we wanted to go.

I had visited six schools in the Big Ten and was pretty sure it was where I wanted to be. What stood apart from the rest was Michigan. Bump Elliot, who was the coach at the time, and Don James, his assistant, had covered the Ohio area extensively. Bump came in, sat down, and talked to my mother for about two hours in our house. Following their departure, my mother looked at me and said, "You're going to Michigan."

Even though my mother had her mind made up, coach James was instrumental in sealing the decision for me. I wanted to play quarterback, as I had in high school. Most colleges were interested in moving me to defensive back. Don assured me I would be brought in as a quarterback and would actually play at quarterback. I was sold.

Being a Michigan Wolverine is something that is very special. Obviously, everyone doesn't have the great fortune of being part of the Michigan tradition. You are associated with an athletic organization that isn't just renowned in the nation; it's world-renowned.

Look no further than the local store. Michigan has some of the highest-selling merchandise in the nation. The winged helmet is instantly recognizable and has been duplicated by lower division schools. It's a program coveted by a lot of folks.

A funny story about my recruiting is that Bo Schembechler actually tried to get me to play for him—but he was coaching at Miami of Ohio at the time. I obviously turned him down and went to Michigan instead. When he took the job at Michigan, he let us in on a little secret.

"For all you guys who snubbed me at Miami to come here, now you have to deal with me at Michigan," Bo said.

He really gave it to [Dan] Dierdorf, who had come to Michigan instead of playing for Bo at Miami.

It was definitely different when Bo came in. Bump let his coaches run practice more. Bo was very hands-on.

It was a tighter, more difficult practice regiment. The structure of practice was extremely organized, and we always moved at a very quick pace from hash mark to hash mark. And I'll never forget how much we ran. Our conditioning was second to none. Bo's hard-nosed, but fair style definitely set us up for the magical season we had.

We always joked around that our motivation increased because Bo pissed us off at practice. We were so sick and tired of beating up each other that we jumped at the chance to pound other teams on Saturday.

Obviously, the big moment of my junior year and Bo's first year was beating Ohio State. It was when Bo sold his vision to everyone and taught us all to believe. If you read the papers that year about the Buckeyes, they were billed as the team to beat in the nation. They were all but handed the national championship. In fact, some papers wrote about Ohio State possibly beating professional teams. But when the Buckeyes rolled into Ann Arbor that year, they ended up limping out.

We knew heading into the game that we were going to beat them. Our run started against Minnesota, where we had a comeback win. We rolled off a bunch of wins, which led us to the game against Ohio State.

Now, there was already tension before the game even started. On the Friday before the game, we would do walk-through drills in sweats. The Buckeyes

Jim Betts picks off a pass against Texas A&M during his senior season of 1970. Betts came to Ann Arbor as a quarterback, played some as running back, and went over to the defensive side his senior year.

were on the field first, doing their drills. Before they left, they lined up on the tunnel on both sides. As we made our way to the field, some guy made a nasty comment, and all hell broke loose. Woody and Bo were trying to separate guys as we were all fighting like cats and dogs. When it was finally settled, someone from our squad yelled that we'd beat 'em tomorrow. And we did.

The Rose Bowl was a letdown because we found out about Bo's heart attack prior to the game. Our focus was taken away, obviously, and we didn't play like we could have. We were more concerned with our coach, who was laid up in a bed. And I don't think anyone could have really blamed us for that.

During my tenure at Michigan, I played a variety of positions. Although initially I was brought in to play quarterback, I was featured at running back, wide receiver, and then finally defense. It was a humorous story as to how it happened, too. Dick Hunter, who was one of the defensive coaches, approached me at the start of practice during my senior year and asked if I wanted to play defense. I jumped at it, knowing that I probably would not have been a starter if I were on the offensive side of the ball.

I waltzed into Bo's office and let him know of my personal decision. "You don't come in here and tell me what you're going to do," he said matter-of-factly. "I'll tell *you* what you're going to do."

I wasn't satisfied with his answer. I let him know I didn't want to sit on the bench for my final season at Michigan, behind a guy whom I felt was better than. Of course, Bo had a few choice words for my thoughts and then grandly replied: "You'll play both positions." I settled for that decision and ended up playing both defense and offense. I loved defense because I could really hit someone. In the offense we ran, it was usually the quarterback taking the hits. Now I was the one unleashing the hits. And I loved it.

To this day, when I return to Michigan to watch a game, I get goose bumps watching the guys hit. In fact, a big hit is the only time I really jump up. When I can see the guy coming, readying for the hit, I'll yell, "Pow!" as soon as he unleashes it. I don't think my wife likes it when I do that, though.

My four years as a Wolverine were some of the finest in my life. It truly is something to be a part of the tradition and legacy that is Michigan football.

The Wolverines were 25–6 in Jim Betts' three varsity seasons.

MARTY HUFF
LINEBACKER
1968–1970

WHEN I GOT RECRUITED, I ACTUALLY PICKED INDIANA. I don't know why, maybe because I was young. But my mother had cancer pretty badly, and I liked Michigan because it was closer to home. I had visited quite a few colleges: Michigan, Michigan State, Notre Dame, and a few others. Twice I went down to Ohio State. I hate to say it, but I thought Ohio State was a great college. I really liked Woody Hayes. Woody came up to my house on a third recruiting visit and brought my mother some flowers because she was dying. He didn't say, "Hi" or "Good-bye," just jumped back in his car and drove back to Columbus. He was a pretty cool guy.

The only bad thing is, two weeks after I started at Michigan, in September, my mother died. It was coming, my mother's death, we all knew it. She hung on longer then we expected. She was just a warrior, a very tough lady. I'm not sorry that I picked Michigan; it ended up being a good choice.

At the time, freshmen could not be on the varsity. I was basically on the "meat squad." I was a grunt. We were all grunts for the varsity. We had to stick together. It was very important to go through that year because it made our freshmen class extremely close.

Bump Elliot was the coach, and he was on a pedestal. He was a very kind, laid-back individual and an extremely good coach. He had the hearts of the players in his hands. Bump didn't have such a great season in 1967–1968. We weren't that good. We were half-and-half, and we got slaughtered by Ohio State, which won the national championship.

When Bo came in, we were all curious. Bo was more of an extrovert. He was just kind of like, "Hey, here I am. I am going to make it happen, so you better pay attention." He was good. From the beginning, it took right off. He knew how, through diplomacy, to get the respect from his players. He was extremely good at that and very tough. Bo could be tough and diplomatic at the same time.

Physically, I worked hard to try and increase my muscle and increase my speed. Really, it's all mental. Jim Young was my linebacker coach and he was extremely intelligent. He would make us meditate a lot of times. He wanted us to imagine doing something great. It really helped. It kept us aware at all times. It kept us, more or less, in control when we were out on the field. Instead of going completely bananas and berserk, we were under control.

When he first started it, I was like, "What the hell? He's a weirdo. Who is this?" But when we started to realize what he was doing and took it more seriously, it was a better situation for everybody. It was kind of cool.

It helps when you can take yourself out of the element and eliminate all your negatives; you're going to get a lot of positives. A lot of negatives come back, but you'll still have a lot of positives on your side when they do. It's important for everybody to think about what they are doing because everybody gets in a rut and starts getting upset and stressed. To all of a sudden say, "Wait a minute, I'm going to stop for a minute," and then when you come back, surprisingly, you find it's not as bad as it was.

Jim Young was very positive about everything. He just said, "This is the way it is." He approached everything with a positive, no negatives. He was a great defensive coordinator and linebacker coach. He made a big impression on me.

In my sophomore year we played Ohio State, and they beat us so badly, I don't even want to tell you what the score was. The next year, my junior year, we really wanted revenge, and we had a very good team. We didn't say anything because back then guys didn't put their mouths on paper. We whipped their butts, basically. We were a 17-point underdog and beat them 24–12.

It all started in 1969. When we beat Ohio State, they were supposed to be the "world team." It solidified everything that we expected from each other. I was a very lucky person to be involved in something like that.

138

Linebacker Marty Huff makes one of his three interceptions during the Purdue game in 1970. His son Ben carried the Michigan tradition and played for the Wolverines' national championship team in 1997.

The legacy of Bo Schembechler started right there. Michigan Football was resurrected, and we were headed for the Rose Bowl.

When Bo suffered his heart attack on the eve of the Rose Bowl and Jim Young took over the team, we basically said, "Oh, shit, what do we do now?" We were just numb sitting in the Rose Bowl. We didn't have time to sit there and reflect. We didn't have time to do anything but go out there and play a game. And we played a pretty good game. Southern Cal beat us 10–3 on a pass to Bob Chandler. We played good defense. They were a good team, but we should have done better. But it was still wonderful to be there.

Superficially, we wanted to win that one for Bo, but I don't think our hearts had time enough to realize what happened when we played the game. If we'd had three days to think about it, we could have regrouped and let it build up a little bit, but it happened overnight. It was, "Oh, he had a heart attack . . . breakfast is ready, you'll be suiting up in four hours." We were like, "OK?"

I got lucky a few times getting into the end zone—the dummy threw it to me. I remember the first game my sophomore year, we played Duke. The quarterback threw it right to me, and I went 40-some yards for the touchdown. I was in shock when I got there because my whole team passed me going to the end zone. I think I was in the right spot at the right time. Mike Phipps did me an honor; he threw me three interceptions in one game. I might have been a pen pal to him, I don't know. I don't know why he did that.

It felt good to be an All-American, but I'm not into all that stuff. My children love it more than I do. It felt good to be appreciated, but it did not compare to the fact that I got to wear that uniform.

My son, Ben, played at Michigan on the 1997 national championship team. They might have invited him up because he was my son, but the thing is they realized how good a football player he was. He did all the work. He's an amazing kid. He did everything he was told and he became a great football player.

Ben and his teammates lived at my house. I fed them all year long, damn near every weekend. None of them had any money, and I was just 45 minutes down the road. They'd say, "Mr. Huff, can we have some chicken or ribs?" It was ridiculous, I almost had to take out a bank loan to buy all the food. It was kind of funny and enjoyable; talking football with my kid and all his friends.

When I was going to Michigan, my dad, Ralph Huff, was down in Toledo, and I used to bring my buddies down there—Jimmy Betts and Dick McCoy. We'd come down there and eat because we didn't have any money. My dad would barbecue half of Toledo for us, he was amazing. I did the same thing for Ben. I was proud to be at Michigan but more proud that my son went there.

In his three seasons at Michigan, Marty Huff had nine interceptions, 266 career tackles, scored a touchdown on a blocked punt, and called defensive signals.

JIM BRANDSTATTER

TACKLE

1969–1971

AS A 10-YEAR-OLD KID, I WAS WATCHING MY BROTHER, Art, play football at Michigan State. He was a great athlete. Art probably was the most highly sought-after athlete out of the Lansing area until Magic Johnson—that's how good he was. In his junior and senior years, he was not treated well by the Michigan State staff. I'd see him come home after games with a look of disappointment on his face. I'd hear my mom and dad talking to him, trying to pat him on the back to buoy his spirits. I was 10, my brother was my hero, playing for the hometown major-college football team, and I got the sense that this shouldn't be happening. The more I learned, and the more I observed, I realized Art was not getting the proper treatment from Michigan State. I thought, "You know what? If my goal is to be a collegiate football player, MSU is not the best place to go based on the treatment of my brother."

Michigan recruited me, as well as a bunch of other schools. Bump Elliott was a class act. When he visited my home, Bump was very respectful to my parents and my dad's background at Michigan State. Bump talked more to my dad about their days as Michigan and Michigan State players, than he did trying to recruit me. He basically got to visit an old foe that turned into a friend. As he left, Bump said, "Well, Mr. Brandstatter, we think your son's a fine football player. He'd be a great asset to the University of Michigan. We sure would like to see him come there. I hope you guys talk about it; if Jim doesn't mind taking my offer seriously."

I went down to Ann Arbor, stayed with some guys, watched some spring football, and said, "You know what? I like the atmosphere of this place. I like Bump. I think this is the place I want to be." Hindsight being 20/20, I can tell you without hesitation that this was the best decision of my life.

Bo [Schembechler] and I didn't hit it off right away. Dan Dierdorf and I didn't like him very much. When Bo came in, I was a sophomore and Dan was a junior. Bo was extremely demanding. That first spring football was a very physically and mentally difficult period because Bo wanted to find out whom he could trust. If you couldn't handle his spring football, then you weren't cut out to be his kind of football player. The sign "Those Who Stay Will Be Champions" was tested that first spring. A lot of guys quit. Those who stayed, though, went on the next year, 1969, to become champions by beating Ohio State.

I used to write letters home. One of them I wrote: "This guy is unfair and he shouldn't treat me like that, but I'll be darned if he's going to get me to quit." It goes back to that whole issue of what kind of guy you are. I was just as stubborn and bull-headed as Bo was. I wasn't going to let him beat me. No matter how hard it gets, no matter how tough it may be, I'm going to hang in there. That may be an old trick; Bo's a brilliant guy at handling people. Perhaps that's the type of guys he wanted with him. I would bet money that, if you talked to players from that period, many of them were thinking, "I don't know how much more I can take, but I'll be damned if I'm going to let him get to me." Those are the guys Bo went to war with and won championships with. Bo's smarter than all of us.

142

In the late sixties and early seventies, a football player was a part of the establishment at the University of Michigan. It was a time when women were burning their bras; men were burning their draft cards; Vietnam and the protests against the war were everywhere; and African Americans were growing big afros as a sign of their cultural heritage.

Members of the football team weren't viewed in the highest regard from some other parts of the campus. Bo made it clear to us that the outside influence of social unrest had no impact upon what we were doing as football players. We were all fairly adequate at this game or we wouldn't be there. And what was wrong with getting as good as you possibly could in a physically and mentally demanding game? None of us felt that there was anything

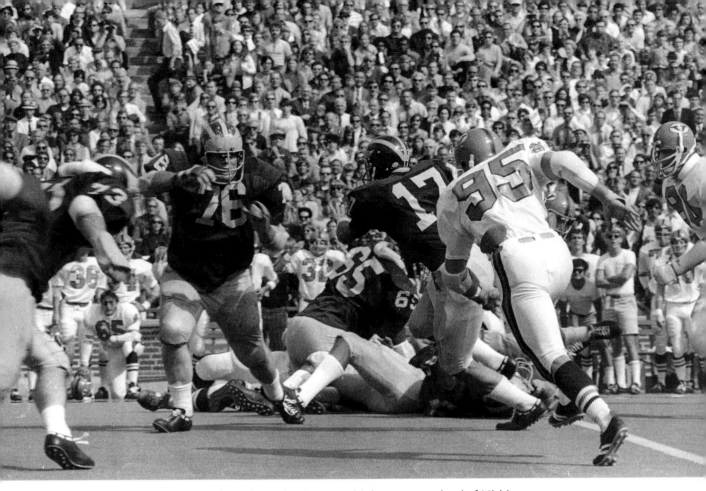

Jim Brandstatter chose the Wolverines over his hometown school of Michigan State and came away with 28 victories in three seasons on the offensive line.

wrong with it. Players embraced what we were doing as something that was good and positive for ourselves and the university. It was the old bunker mentality; the people on the outside don't mean a damn thing. What's most important is the family. That was the football team.

There wasn't any color barrier or social barrier on our team. You were out there in the same foxhole, fighting the same enemy, going through the same issues. You see each other at your absolute worst, and you see each other at your absolute best. You try at all times to be supportive of your teammates. If you support them, the better the team gets, which means the better you get. That's the way team sports should be.

Everyone in the world cringed at the thought of playing Ohio State in 1969. They were the best thing since sliced bread. But we knew we could beat them. We were in our locker room and we wanted them. Bring on the Buckeyes! As sophomores, my class felt responsible to do our best for guys like Mandich, Dierdorf, Caldarazzo, Craw, and Moorhead. We felt we had to play our best for our leaders—Cecil Pryor, Tom Curtis, Brian Healy, and Marty Huff. We had to do our best because those were the guys who went down there in 1968 and were humiliated. We were going to do everything we could to come out the victor.

It was a great sense of pride to win that game against Ohio State. It made me feel that I was a small part of history. Many consider the 1969 victory over Ohio State to be as a watershed mark in the great tradition of Michigan football. I'm extremely proud that my name happens to be associated with that game, and most important, with that 1969 Michigan team.

I fully realized that I made the right decision coming to Michigan when we were playing Michigan State, at Spartan Stadium, my senior year of 1971. I was playing offensive tackle, and I played maybe my best game. Bo likes to kid me that I played despite him. But then he gives me a left-handed compliment, telling people I started on a team that went 11–0; I couldn't have been that bad.

Playing well in East Lansing, against Michigan State, where I had grown up, was so gratifying. My mom, dad, and brother were sitting in the stands. My brother, Art, was actually broadcasting the game for Michigan State. This was my way of giving Art some credit, giving him some respect—that I would come back, in the archenemy's uniform, and perform so well.

After the State game, every one of my teammates, without exception, came over especially to pat me on the back. Telling me how glad they were that this happened. It made me feel that they cared about me. It was great we won, but the team knew how important it was for me. That told me these were the guys that I wanted to hang with.

Jim Brandstatter became the host for the weekly television program *Michigan Replay* in 1980. He continues to host it today while also providing color commentary for every Wolverines football game.

DANA COIN

LINEBACKER/KICKER

1969–1971

I WAS PART OF THE LAST CLASS EVER RECRUITED BY BUMP ELLIOTT, and the transition from Bump Elliott to Bo Schembechler was hellacious. You're recruited by this father figure in Bump, who's a gentleman and just a great guy. He represented the University of Michigan as well as any person ever has. Bump went into administration after the 1968 season, and Michigan hired this guy whose last name you couldn't even pronounce. I remember when they first hired Bo, all the sportscasters in the area were butchering his name pretty badly.

Bo came in and immediately established his program. He told us, "We know how to win. We're from Miami of Ohio. We come from a winning school that has produced many top college coaches who know what they're doing, so you guys need to have confidence." Then the papers started running articles about the "cradle of coaches" and all the great coaches that came from there.

We started a conditioning program that was like boot camp. There were a lot of guys who didn't believe in what he was pitching. We went through winter conditioning, we went through spring football. In the first spring he was there, all the kids went home after the spring term was over—except us. We stayed another week and one-half and played football because Bo hadn't gotten his 20 days of spring practice in yet.

Dana Coin boots a field goal against Texas A&M in 1970. Coin also played linebacker for three seasons.

When we came back in August, there was a joke—that there was this traffic jam down at State and I-94 because everyone was leaving the team. I bet we lost about 35 players from the time he came in and started winter conditioning through the first couple of sessions. There were seniors, juniors, and some sophomores that left; these were all guys that Bump recruited.

It was in double sessions the second week that Jim Young came up with the saying, "Those Who Stay Will Be Champions." He posted that around the locker room to say that if you do what we ask you to do, and do what you believe in, it will pay off. We had lost so many guys. "Those Who Stay Will Be Champions" came out of a fear that they would lose all their good players or run them into the ground.

You respected Bump as much as you respected anyone in college football, but Bo's whole approach was to come in and establish himself, his discipline, his system. This is the way it was going to be. He wasn't going to let anyone steer him in another direction, regardless of who recruited the kids or what Bump's philosophy was.

Personality-wise, they were completely different. Both were guys whom you loved, but you loved them in different ways. Bo and Bump were the type of guys you would go to war with anytime and anywhere. But their delivery and their whole style of how they developed young men into real men was a little different.

147

My first encounter with Bo was one I'll never forget. We had a team meeting, and he shook everyone's hand. We had a pretty good freshmen class, which Bump recruited, and George Mans had a lot to do with recruiting all the Detroit-area guys who were on that team. Bo had obviously watched film of our freshmen games, and he looked at me and said, "Coin, I hear you're a kicker, huh? I can tell you right now, there ain't going to be any goddamn specialists on my team."

So he set the tone right there. You were going to be a player, or you weren't going to play. Of course, I also had played linebacker and ended up eventually starting in a three-linebacker set in my senior year. That's my first recollection of Bo.

I think 1969 was special because of everything we went through to get there, and then we proved on the field that we could win and win with Bo's system. We took it on the nose pretty well from Missouri early in the season, and we lost to Michigan State that year, too. We took a pretty good team into the Ohio State game and we were 17- to 22-point underdogs, depending on what line you were looking at.

I remember barely touching the field because we were so jacked up for that Ohio State game. It was all channeled energy; we had a mission the whole week before that game, and we really believed we could win. Bo was the chief lauder that whole week and convinced us that was true. He knew Woody, he had coached for Woody, and he told us, "They've got a great program, but let me tell you men—they don't dress any differently than we do, they don't have any better players on their team than we do."

We were looking at all these All-Americans they had, but we had beaten some pretty good teams that year. We were on a big roll going into that game from an offensive standpoint. But if you look at that game, it was really won by defense.

Bo will tell you that that was the most important game of his career because it solidified all the things that he had been teaching. It was all the things he taught us about "Doing It My Way" and "Those Who Stay Will Be Champions." And, sure as shootin', the guys who went through the rigors and his Marine-like training came out on the front end of that saying, "I'll follow this guy anywhere now."

The key thing for that year was the fact that we did win, and the seniors on that team—the Jim Mandiches, the Dan Dierdorfs—bought into the program and turned out to be great senior leaders. The following years were a little bit easier, even though Bo didn't change his methodology.

I'll never forget going from my freshman year to my sophomore year. Jim Young had already pegged me as second-team linebacker behind Marty Huff. I met with Jim Young and Bo just before the start of spring ball, and Bo looked across the table and said, "You know, I think you're a pretty good football player, Coin. But I'm not going to invest my time and my coach's time in somebody who's not going to be academically eligible, so you're going to play on the scout team this spring. If you get some shots in there, we'll try and put you in where we can. But we can't waste our time."

You talk about a wake-up call! I think I had a 1.8 GPA. So I went to school all summer, aced both the spring and summer term, and got Bo's message load and clear. I think I graduated with a 3.0 GPA in education.

Bo really believed that you were there for the reason of getting an education. Football was a part of getting a degree from the University of Michigan. That was the expectation Bo had. He would keep on guys, know when they missed classes. He'd counsel them, get them any help they needed.

We didn't have a tutoring program back then; we had a study hall at the Michigan Union Monday through Thursday. That's the thing about being a Wolverine, you can't really say you are, even though you've thrown the uniform on and gone out and competed, unless you've walked out of there after four or five years with a degree. There's still that little piece of sheepskin you have to qualify for to be a real, true Wolverine.

On November 13, 1971, Michigan defeated Purdue 20–17 on Dana Coin's 25-yard field goal with 26 seconds left in West Layfayette, Indiana.

BILLY TAYLOR
TAILBACK
1969–1971

DURING MY SENIOR YEAR AT BARBERTON [Ohio] High School, I had 57 college scholarship offers. It was still a toss-up about where I was going to go when Ohio State coach Woody Hayes came to my house to meet my mother. My mom was pretty impressed with Woody, but she had also heard good reports about Michigan coach Bump Elliott.

Personally, I wanted to get farther away from home than the 120 miles from Barberton to Columbus. I had just returned from a recruiting visit to Michigan, and I was wearing a Michigan sweatshirt when Woody came to my school to get me. My French teacher was speechless. Here was Woody, bigger than life in our classroom. Everyone in the room was gasping for air. She brought him back to my cubicle where I was sitting with my headphones on listening to French tapes. When Woody spotted my shirt, he said: "We've got to get you a real shirt."

Woody got excited when he talked about football. He was really into the stories he was telling my mother and me about a recent Buckeyes' practice

"Billy," he said, "you should have been at that practice yesterday. Jack Tatum came up and knocked the hell out of the ball carrier."

My mom's house was a strict Christian home, and when Woody used profanity, I caught a glance from mom. She was peeping over the top of her glasses. She shook her head. At that moment, I knew I wasn't going to Ohio

State. When I say strict, I mean I wasn't even allowed to watch pro football on Sunday in our home because my mom and aunt thought the game was "too worldly." I had to go find another place to watch Jim Brown and the Cleveland Browns

My mom and I still went out with Woody to the Brown Derby for dinner. He was a very personable guy. But my mom just loved Bump Elliott. My mom also looked into the academics, and that sealed the deal. Ohio State is a good school, but it's not Michigan. I just liked the Michigan campus, the atmosphere, and the people. And Bump was running the I formation, which was also appealing.

At that time, Bo Schembechler was recruiting me for Miami of Ohio. He had also gone to Barberton High School. Our moms knew each other. I went to Miami on a visit, along with Thom Darden, who would also end up playing at Michigan. We didn't much like Bo because he got us up at 6:00 in the morning and had us doing timed sprints. He also had us playing basketball to check out our quickness. When you are being recruited, you wanted to have fun and party. But Bo had us lifting weights and running distances. Coaches would squeeze your arm, and say: "You are a little soft there. You need to tighten up."

We didn't want to play for Bo Schembechler. So you can imagine what I thought when I picked up the *Akron Beacon Journal* over Christmas break and saw that Schembechler was going to be coach at Michigan. And he brought his coaching staff with him.

When Bo saw me for the first time back at Michigan, he said: "Hot damn it, Taylor, you thought you got away from me, didn't you?" Not only didn't I get away from him, he became a very important person in my life.

When I came to Michigan in 1968, I was a part of the largest collection of black athletes ever to come to Michigan on scholarship in the same year. A close bond formed among us. [Thom] Darden, Reggie McKenzie, Butch Carpenter, Glenn Doughty, Mike Taylor, Mike Oldham, and myself—we were all roommates. We had a house on campus, and we were called the Den of the Mellow Men. Remember, this was the time of the Black Action Movement and Vietnam protests. Bo wanted us to stay out of politics. But we all decided to stick together, and live together. And we vowed we were going to be part of a championship team together.

That latter objective fit well with what Bo was planning during the 1969 season. He told us all season that our big game would be the last game against

Billy Taylor (No. 42) was one of the Wolverines' most celebrated running backs of all time, but his Michigan experience was the most meaningful to him when he fell on hard times after his football career and had to pick himself back up.

Ohio State, and we were going to beat the Buckeyes. We played one game at a time that season, but always in the back of our minds we prepared for Woody Hayes and Ohio State. Bo and I were both from Barberton, and we both took that game very personally. Guys from the Den of the Mellow Men were all starters as sophomores, and we were playing with a great group of seniors like Dan Dierdorf, Garvie Craw, Jim Mandich, Don Moorhead, and Cecil Pryor.

Ohio State was ranked No. 1 coming into the game in Ann Arbor. None of the newspapers, even in Detroit or Ann Arbor, believed we had any chance to beat Ohio State. In one newspaper, I read: "Michigan has two chances of winning this game, slim and none." To this day, I've never seen a Michigan team that came together like we did in that game. Sometimes in a game, the offense doesn't show up until the second quarter or the defense doesn't show up at all. It's difficult to have everyone playing well at the same time. But in this game, we were all there from the beginning.

We were all ready for Bo to talk to us, like he always did before a game, especially a big game like this. We expected a long oration. But it didn't happen. He turned the bill of his cap to the back and said: "Our own newspapers are saying our chances of winning this game are slim and none." He glared around the room slowly. "I'll tell you what, we are going to go out there and kick their ass." He slammed the chalkboard with his fist and knocked it over. Everyone had tears in their eyes.

You had to be a real man to get out of the Michigan locker room that day. Players were pushing to get out of the door. When we took the field, no one felt their feet touch the ground. In those days, I think there was a metal floor in the stadium, and the noise level was incredible. You couldn't hear yourself talk when you got onto the field. Even when Ohio State scored first, we knew we were going to win. It was 24–12 at halftime, and that's how it stayed. I have a tape of that game, and up and down the line on offense and defense, Michigan players were at the top of their game. What a great team game we played.

Individually, my biggest run came on my last offensive play at Michigan Stadium in 1971. It was against Ohio State. We trailed the entire game, and we got the ball deep in our own territory with several minutes left. Just before the offense took the field, Bo called us together and said, "This could be our last possession, and we want first down after first down, and we aren't stopping until we get the touchdown."

That's exactly what we did. On a third and long, Bo called on me. I was a senior, and Bo had always preached that seniors had to step up and make the big play. I remember the play like it was yesterday. When we broke huddle, someone said: "Everyone on their blocks, everyone on their blocks." I told myself that I was going to score. When the ball was pitched, it was almost like slow motion. I could see our line cracking. Bo Rather made a crackback block, and I saw a guy flipping. Fritz Seyferth was leading me around the corner. There were about four people in front of me. There was one defender

153

with a true shot at me, but Fritz took him out. Another Buckeye guy came out of nowhere, but I outran him. I went into the end zone untouched for the winning score. That gave us an undefeated regular season and a Rose Bowl bid.

I have a bobblehead of the late Bob Ufer doing play-by-play of that run: "Billy Taylor is down to the 20, down to 15, down to 10, 5, 4, 3, 2, 1. Touchdown, Billy Taylor, Touchdown! Billy Taylor scores a touchdown from 21 yards out. The crowd is going berserk."

Michigan was probably the most important experience of my life. I'm proud as a peacock that I went there. The lessons I learned as a Michigan Wolverine prepared me for life. Bo, Bump, and my teammates taught me never to give up, even when the odds were against you. If you are knocked down, get back up. That was Michigan's teaching. Those lessons would become more valuable later in life.

At the lowest point of my life, I was ready to give up. I had never been in trouble, but I have a tendency to do things in a big way. When I got into trouble, man, did I get in trouble. I was severely depressed and drinking. I had lost my mother, and then a young lady that I was dating was stabbed to death. My uncle shot and killed my aunt and then killed himself. This all happened within a nine-month period. From that point, there was drinking and a downhill spiral. The bottom fell out when I was charged with aiding in an armed robbery. An acquaintance robbed a bank in Barberton, I was sitting in a car waiting for this person. With all the tragedy that I experienced, this person was able to pressure and trick me into being associated with him. But I was there. I made the bad decision. I had to pay the consequence. I spent two and one-half years in prison.

During that down period, I was ready to give up on life and myself. Then I realized that's not my nature. It was the teachings of Michigan that helped me understand that. Bo had drilled in us the idea that we should have the self-confidence to overcome any obstacle. Here I had fallen so low that I had to pick myself up. I recalled all that we had gone through at Michigan with my roommates and teammates. I thought about that 1969 game. I realized that I had made a mistake and I needed to overcome that.

When I was in prison in Milan, Michigan, I became the first inmate to begin and complete a graduate degree while in a federal institution according to the records at the time. I did it with all As and one B.

To understand what kind of man Bo Schembechler is, know that he helped in the selection of my attorney and with the fundraising for the cost of the attorney. He helped work it out so I could get my master's degree in prison. When I reported for prison in Oxford, Wisconsin, Bo Schembechler flew out there with me to lend his support.

Billy Taylor earned his doctorate in educational leadership at the University of Nevada–Las Vegas and now works at the 35,000-student Community College of Southern Nevada.

The
SEVENTIES

GORDON BELL
Tailback
1973–1975

I ACTUALLY SIGNED A NATIONAL LETTER OF INTENT TO GO TO NOTRE DAME. The only reason I did that was because I'm Catholic and one of my best friends from high school football, Joe Allen, wanted to go to Notre Dame. We had always said we were going to go to school together. I'm from Troy, Ohio, and in January or February of my senior year we had eight inches of snow on the ground when Joe took a recruiting trip to Florida. He flew into Florida, where it was 85 degrees with Gator girls and everything, and the next thing I knew, Joe was going to Florida. I was like, "Oh, God, what am I going to do now?"

Luckily, I called up Bo and explained to him what had happened, and he said, "We're out of scholarships. Let me call you back tomorrow." He ended up calling me back saying, "Get up here you little son of a bitch." That was my introduction to Bo—"you son of a bitch." So I went to Michigan.

All along I had an affinity for Michigan. Even when I was a senior in high school, before colleges started coming around, I had a Michigan jersey that I wore in practice. Most of the people in my school were going to either Miami of Ohio or Ohio State. My colors in high school were scarlet and gray. I just wanted to go some place different. I didn't want to go to a place that would just be a continuation of my high school. I also wanted to go far enough away—but not too far away—that my parents could come to see me play.

Gordon Bell's three Michigan teams lost a total of three games during his career.

In 1971 I took a recruiting trip to Ann Arbor. It was my first time there, and it was the weekend of the Michigan–Ohio State game. Woody Hayes tore up the yard markers on Thom Darden's interception. I recall feeling very comfortable being in Michigan Stadium.

What really got me going was that we had three types of weather driving up there that day: snow, sleet, and rain. Right before the game started workers had to squeegee the field because there was snow on it. Just when Michigan was coming out of the tunnel the sun came out. It hit the satin front of their two-toned pants. There was gold all over the field. It was perfect for me. It was a sign that Michigan is where I would end up.

I had a good relationship with Bo. At that time, Bo was like Woody, "three yards and a cloud of dust." The tailback would run up there—there was no East to West—everything was North and South. I wasn't a North and South runner. I wasn't a conventional I-Back.

It frustrated Bo sometimes because I'd get in there and I might see a hole. If the hole was blocked, I would slide to another hole, or I'd dart to the outside and do something else. One day I remember him telling me, "You're the only person I'll let do something like that." It was because I could get to the outside. I had an instinct to find a spot and make something happen when there was nothing.

Bo was stubborn, but what could he do? I was the kind of running back that averaged five or six yards a carry. That helped. If I wasn't going anywhere, or if I was getting stopped behind the line of scrimmage every time, he wouldn't have let me improvise. I proved that I could do it, so I kept on doing it.

During the last game in 1973, the 10-10 tie against Ohio State, I was standing on the sidelines with everyone else when Mike Lantry lined up for the game-winning field goal. We all had roses in our mouths; we just knew we were going to the Rose Bowl. But he missed that kick. It stunned us a little bit. But we figured we played well enough in the second half to come back from a 10-0 deficit to tie it up and we had a chance to win.

We thought we were the better team and believed the athletic directors would vote us into the Rose Bowl. Unfortunately, Dennis Franklin was hurt; he had bruised ribs and a sore ankle. They voted against us because they didn't know if Michigan would be the best team to represent the Big Ten if Dennis wasn't healthy. That was our only opportunity to go to the Rose Bowl. We thought we should have gone if it was fair, but they voted against us.

When Bo came in and told us that we weren't going to the Rose Bowl, he was upset and crying. We were pissed, too. Other teams around the country, 4–5 teams from other conferences, were going to bowl games. We didn't lose a game that year, we had that tie, and we weren't going anywhere. Up until my senior year, we hadn't gone to any bowl games, and we had only lost two games. It was mind-boggling to us why everybody else was going to bowl games with worse records, and we were sitting at home. That led to the Big Ten changing the rules. In my senior year, three or four Big Ten teams were allowed to go to bowl games. That vote was very pivotal in changing the rules.

It was great being in the same backfield with Rob Lytle because opponents couldn't key on me. They had Rob to contend with, too. You'd take one out and the other one would take his place. You really couldn't get a rest facing us. Usually at Michigan, you have one featured running back, and that was the tailback. He was the guy who gained most of the yards. But during my senior year and his junior year, we were the only running back duo in the nation to have more than 1,000 yards each. We got along great; we were roommates on the road for two years.

Dennis Franklin was quarterback my sophomore and junior year, and Rick Leach became the quarterback my senior year. Rick was good as a true freshman quarterback. He was mature for his age, and he ran the offense well. One good thing about him was that if they keyed on me, he would run it up in there.

Rick Leach proved himself in practice. That's where the proving ground is; if you can't make it in practice, you're not going to make it. Our defense that year was ranked third in the country against the run. When we had scrimmages, you weren't playing against Podunk kids. You were running against Michigan's defense, and you had to do well.

Michigan was a lot of hard work, dedication, and emotion. There's pride in being affiliated with a group of guys that paid the price with you. There's pride in knowing that Michigan is one of the top academic schools in the country. There's pride in knowing that your school is well known across the nation. When people ask you where you went to school and you say, "The University of Michigan." They kind of perk up a little bit and say, "Oh, you went there?" I love everything about Michigan. The state is great, the outdoors. It's great to know that when people see that block "M," it stands for something.

As a senior, Gordon Bell was voted Michigan's Most Valuable Player by his teammates. In 1995 the award was changed to the Bo Schembechler Award.

ROB LYTLE
TAILBACK/FULLBACK
1973–1976

T HE FUNNIEST BO [SCHEMBECHLER] STORY I HAVE INVOLVES a guy by the
name of Greg DenBoer. He was a tight end and would sometimes stut-
ter, especially when he was nervous. Back at that time, we would wear the
wide-mesh jerseys during summer practices. For whatever reason, Bo was
angry about something Greg had done and had his finger in Greg's shoulder
pad. Greg's trying to explain himself, but for whatever reason, Bo barks: "Go
get back in the huddle." Bo's whistle was on an elastic string around his neck,
and somehow it stuck in Greg's jersey. I don't know exactly how it happened.
But when they turned, the elastic snapped back and smacked Bo right in the
back of his head. The next thing you see is Greg running with Bo screaming after him.

"Get your ass out of here, I don't ever want to see you here again!" Here's
Greg, 6'6", and Bo, not even 5'11", chasing after him. It was so funny. Once
we had Bo settled down, we explained that the whistle had gotten stuck in
the jersey. But I'll never forget Greg DenBoer running for his life.

But it was because of Bo that I chose Michigan. I had the opportunity to
play anywhere I wanted. I was recruited by many of the big-name colleges.
I narrowed it to Michigan, Ohio State, Notre Dame, and Alabama. But in
the end, it came down to Michigan and Ohio State. After meeting with Bo,
there was something about him. We just clicked. He'd told me how every
school was telling me I was the best thing since sliced bread. He said that he

162

would have liked to tell me I would rewrite the record books at Michigan. "But to be quite honest with you," Bo said. "If you sign with us you'll be the second team tailback and whatever you do from there is a bonus to you." He was the only one who laid it on the line for me. He had integrity and was straightforward. I liked that.

Both Bo and Woody [Hayes] were intense. Both ran similar programs and boasted great integrity. When I went to Michigan, I already believed Bo was a legend, even though he'd only been there for four years. What he had done in one season wrote him into the record books after knocking off rival Ohio State. I felt both universities were interested in you—the human being—and not as much with what you liked about football. Notre Dame's Ara Parseghian and Alabama's Bear Bryant also had similar approaches. My meeting with Woody encompassed only about 15 minutes of talking football. Instead, since both Woody and I were history buffs, it felt more like a professor teaching a student as we discussed history. After I signed with Michigan, Woody refused to speak to me. Although he was one of my biggest fans, he never said another word to me. He would send things to me through friends at Ohio State. But he would never directly deal with me.

163

The rivalry between Michigan and Ohio State is simply known as "the Game." Even those outside the rivalry know it as "the Game." The camaraderie between the players, however, is something to be seen. For example, a couple years ago the Diabetes Society ran a benefit for [former Buckeye] Jack Tatum. He had lost a leg as a result of his diabetes and almost lost another. Jack was in real bad shape. But [former Buckeye and offensive lineman] John Hicks brought him back to Columbus, and a bunch of us from Michigan came to show our support. We still busted each other's chops about our respective teams, but the camaraderie between the hugs showed the mutual respect between the teams on and off the field.

We really struggled against Ohio State my freshman year and fought to an ugly 10–10 tie. It was so bad that Woody even said to Bo before the teams left the field: "Hey, kick their ass out in California for us, too." He didn't think they'd be going to Southern California. But that was a year we were denied by the Big Ten. Instead, you had a 10-win team not playing in a bowl game. We lost out on the Rose Bowl because of a single vote I attribute to politics. It was absolutely criminal.

It was devastating. I can remember Bo coming in and telling us the bad news during that 1973 season. We'd never seen him break down like he did

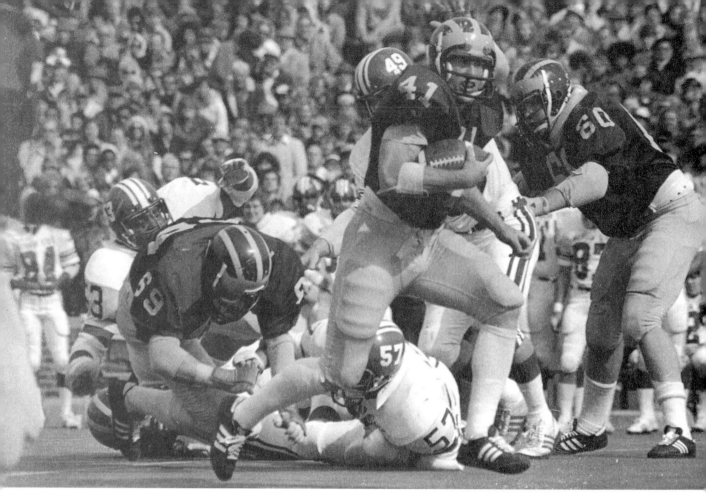

Rob Lytle breaks free for a big gain against Michigan State during the 1976 season. Lytle amassed more than 3,000 yards of offense at Michigan before going on to have a successful seven-year NFL career with the Denver Broncos.

that day. This guy was physically down and it looked like he'd suffered a heart attack. I can't imagine the toll it took on him to explain to kids between 18 and 21 that they were going home after Thanksgiving and not playing again.

He had to explain that, despite their undefeated record, they weren't good enough to play in a bowl game. It seemed every other school was playing in a bowl game except the undefeated Wolverines. We had a second chance my sophomore year, and were denied again because of Mike Lantry's "supposed" missed kick. In the past, the rule barred repeating champions to participate in multiple Rose Bowls. Eventually, that rule was changed. However, the Big Ten would not allow any additional teams within the conference to play in any other bowl games besides the Rose Bowl. That was until money started to talk. The Big Ten realized other schools were receiving money for their appearances and soon the rules changed again. But can you imagine a 10-win team not going to a bowl game three years in a row? It's unthinkable.

We had great respect for the guys before us. Had it not been for Dennis Franklin, Dave Brown, and the countless other guys who were seniors, juniors, and sophomores when I was a freshman, we never would have been in the position we were. Those guys paid the price. They went 30–2–1 in a three-year time frame but never went to a bowl game. If it weren't for them, the Big Ten would have their crazy rules to this day. Without their sacrifice, we probably would not have played Oklahoma in the Orange Bowl in 1975.

My sophomore year was a rebuilding year but featured something I'll never forget. The single play that stands out more than any other happened against Ohio State. We were losing 12–10 despite the fact that we had totally dominated the game. We finally had a nice drive going and pushed to the Ohio State 7-yard line with time expiring. The year before, when we tied them 10–10, our kicker Mike Lantry just missed a 50-yard field goal. He had another shot later in that game, but he ended up shanking it. I felt so damned bad for the guy. But a year later, we were on the 7-yard line and Lantry came out to kick again. As he kicked, I was the wingman blocking the wing, and I had a great view of the kick. I still say the kick was good. He kicked it straight, and it went high through the uprights. But these were the days prior to back judges and extended uprights. That ball was good. I've seen films of it and if there were refs there today, they would agree with me that it was indeed good. But Woody carried a big stick. And those referees weren't going to rule in our favor. They ruled it no-good. I felt so damned bad for Lantry. He went to Vietnam and fought for his country, and then he comes back and was shit on like that. It was too damned bad.

There were a lot of freshman and sophomores playing during my junior year. Despite our youth, we still had a great season and ended up going to the Orange Bowl.

The Orange Bowl against Oklahoma was a smack-down, hard-hitting game. They had a phenomenal team and were crowned the national champions following the game. Bo and the coaching staff had taken a team that was so green and molded them into real competitors. Oklahoma scored on two big plays, but we stymied them for the rest of the game. We ended up losing 14–6, but it was a fun game to play in.

But the best game I ever played was the 22–0 shutout against Ohio State in my senior year. It was pretty gratifying, especially doing it in Columbus at the Horseshoe. It was really nice to be able to walk out and hardly see a soul in that Horseshoe when we left. I think it was the most satisfying time in my career. I remember watching the clock run down in that game, and Bo was taking people out of the game. I'm walking off the field and looking around at the silent stadium. It was the greatest feeling I ever had on a football field. The frustration of not winning for three years and having it culminate on that field in Columbus was an unmatched feeling.

We laid an egg in the Rose Bowl during that same season. New Year's Day fell on a Saturday that year, and it should have felt like a regular-season game. We were supposed to have a tune-up scrimmage the week before the game. But things just fell apart. They canceled the scrimmage, in fact. Because we had such great practices in Ann Arbor prior to leaving for California, I think we peaked too early. I have no idea what happened. It's a game that still haunts me as a contest we should have won. Earlier in the season, we'd lost to Purdue. But we didn't deserve to win that game. We'd made too many costly mistakes. But that 1977 Rose Bowl game will always haunt me as a game we should have won.

166

Being a Wolverine shows how Michigan players are all about team. I can remember seeing other schools that paraded their All-Americans and Heisman Trophy winners around. At Michigan, it was always about the team. It was very much like the Marine Corps: Semper Fi. The guys took care of each other and still do to this day. That says a lot about the program and it's what I take away from the Michigan program. It was the greatest four years of my life and nothing has come close to it.

Rob Lytle's 3,307 career yards is ranked sixth all-time at Michigan. His 26 touchdowns are tied for ninth all-time at Michigan.

LES MILES
GUARD
1974–1975

WHEN I WAS BEING RECRUITED, WOODY HAYES SPOKE at my high school banquet. I had great respect for Woody—he was a wonderful man. But I was just attracted to the Schembechler-style of guy. Now that I'm aware of the way recruiting works, Michigan was interested in me because Ohio State was interested in me. And Ohio State was interested in me because Michigan was interested in me. I may have been a product of being on an undefeated high school team and a guy from Ohio with whom Michigan wanted to beat Ohio State.

Ohio State came down to visit me a couple of times, and I just don't know how sincere their interest was. The factor that steered me toward Michigan was that they offered the best education. I was really attracted to the educational element of it all. And there was this coach with a long name at Michigan who had just beaten Ohio State in 1969. It appeared that that might continue for some time. I was recruited throughout the Big Ten, but when I went to Michigan, the challenge of "the best" called me. The young Bo Schembechler seemed to represent that in an extraordinary way.

Bo was fiery and emotional in those early seasons. I was fortunate enough to play for him and then come back and coach for him. I never felt like the fire dimmed much for Bo. I always felt that he was most "on," and the most talented, in front of his team. I felt that he had a passion for his team, his

Les Miles (No. 63) prepares to throw a block on a Navy defender in 1974. Miles played two seasons under Bo Schembechler and then followed his mentor into coaching.

players, and the situations they were in. He reacted, mostly, with a thought-out response that was driven by passion.

I fought for the little bit of playing time that I got when I came to Michigan. I had a lot to learn. In high school our offense did very little of what Michigan did. I was small and needed to do a lot physically to get on the field. I was definitely a product of the program. It was a very revealing ride. Michigan asks you to grow up and to contribute.

Michigan became me and I became Michigan. I never gave any thought to whether or not I had made the right decision in going to Michigan. I was so loyal to what I was going through with those Schembechler-coached teams—the difficulty in the classroom, the cold weather, the stadium, and playing Ohio State for the championship—that I never second-guessed my decision to go there. The experiences that I had at Michigan were only the very best.

After I graduated, I was in business and doing very well. I had the opportunity to make a good living if I continued in business. My dad and I really talked it out, trying to figure out what I really wanted to do. I always felt that the hardest objective I ever accomplished was getting my degree from Michigan and playing championship football. If there was something that I could live a life doing, it was helping young guys who needed an experience like I had had at Michigan. I could teach them to pursue excellence; I could go back and help somebody do that. I felt that coaching would be a calling worth spending a life on.

I was very fortunate to be around a coach who had those values of education, hard work, and doing the right thing. I went back and talked to Bo about joining his staff. He told me, "No. You've lost your mind. You're not going to make any money. You're going to work long hours." Bo really told me, very honestly, what I was in for. He also said that there was no guarantee that I could become a college coach. He told me that there were a lot of good coaches in high school and that was something I should consider. I said, "Coach, I know what I want to do. I will be the hardest-working grad assistant that you ever had." I sold him, but he made me go through a time frame of about a year before he said, "OK. You can show up." I showed up and spent three years at Michigan as a graduate assistant and a year at Colorado. Bo pointed me in the right direction.

169

Coaching was not work for me. It's something I enjoyed doing. Even though I worked long hours, I was never tired. As a coach, your job is to do whatever needs to be done to prepare the players to play their best and put the team in the best position to win.

It was a sad day for me when Bo left. I had come back to work with Bo and coach. I knew that Michigan would not be the same. Not that it wouldn't be better or have the opportunity to be greater, but I knew it would be without Bo. There was some adjustment to be made, but Gary Moeller did a wonderful job. He united his staff and pointed out things that the team needed to do. He went at it very strategically. I was grateful that he kept me on his staff.

A couple of incidents stand out while I was coaching the offensive line at Michigan. We were playing Notre Dame. I was on the sideline with Bo. Steve Everitt was my center. We had broken a draw right up the middle for a touchdown. Steve Everitt went down. I was standing on the sideline and someone came over and said he thought Everitt had busted his jaw. I was very concerned. I went out on the field and saw that Steve had broken his jaw in two places, one high underneath the ear and one just below the chin. His jaw, the freewheeling bone, had separated from his teeth; so he was talking without the ability to make words. He couldn't operate his tongue with his teeth to communicate. Steve was trying to say, "Don't worry, I'll be fine. Just take me to the sideline and I'll be fine." I remember there was plenty of blood.

Everitt was taken to the emergency room and had his mouth wired shut. That memory was a pretty distinctive one. I don't recall ever looking into the face of a guy with an injury like that. The doctors plated his jaw in two places and gave him a new face mask. He started and played three weeks later against Illinois.

Dean Dingman played his last game for Michigan in the 1991 Gator Bowl against Ole Miss. We only scored 35 points, even though we put up 715 yards. I don't think they ever stopped us. Desmond Howard was the big playmaker; we were throwing screens to him and throwing the ball down the field. Our offensive line ended up getting the Gator Bowl MVP trophy; every starting offensive lineman got it. It was the first time that I had ever been around an offensive line that was rewarded like that.

Dingman was always really possessed to play at a very high level. He did not want to come out of that game. I was trying to substitute and I asked him, "Dean, what do you want to do?" And he kept saying, "I want to play, and I want these guys to play with me. I want them to play hard." Dean turned to his crew and said, "We're going back in for one more series, and I expect you to play your ass off." That is exactly what they did. I'll never forget, knowing that that would be his last game. Dean was a great player, a great competitor. He didn't have all the natural ability in the world, but he had a ferocious heart. I'll always remember that day, when Dingman said, "Frankly, damn it, this is my last series. I want to play it with my teammates, my best players, and best guys."

There is a special breed of people that play at Michigan. They are goal-oriented, they want the very best. They want a great education, to play on a championship team, and to do things right. I was fortunate to be around them.

In every professional endeavor that I have ever had in football, my fundamental background at Michigan has helped me tenfold. I'll never be able to repay the memories or abilities that I was allowed to gain while at Michigan. I'll never be able to repay the good fortune that I've had in my life, personally or professionally. I was so fortunate to be able to go to Michigan and be coached by Bo Schembechler.

Les Miles was a member of the Michigan coaching staff from 1980 to 1981 and from 1987 to 1994. He is currently the head football coach at Louisiana State University.

CALVIN O'NEAL

LINEBACKER

1974–1976

BELIEVE IT OR NOT, MY FIRST CHOICE WAS MICHIGAN STATE. I was going to be a Spartan. However, in the process of recruiting, first it was Michigan State, then it turned to Michigan. Michigan State had a transition ready to take place between Duffy Daugherty and Denny Stoltz. I felt I would probably get lost in the wash there. I would have gone to Michigan State, but for whatever reason coaches didn't come back to give me a formal commitment for months. During the whole recruiting process, Gary Moeller, who was recruiting me for Michigan, was in Saginaw every week. He went to my basketball games and track meets. He followed me through the process. "Mo" would communicate with me on a regular basis.

One day I was in our gym at Saginaw High and the telephone rang in the coach's office. By chance I just happened to be outside the office. I answered the phone, it was Moeller. He was calling my high school coach, Oarie Lemanski, to see if I'd made a decision. I told him I was going to Michigan right on the spot. He got Bo on the phone, Bo congratulated me, and the rest is history.

I got home that night and had a limo in my driveway. It was the guy from Michigan State who was recruiting me. He came up to take me and my mother out to dinner. We went to a local restaurant, and he tried to persuade me to go to Michigan State. *Bleep, bleep, bleep, bleep, bleep*—there's a lot of

Linebacker Calvin O'Neal played on three Big Ten championship teams from 1974 to 1976, and captained the squad in 1976 with Rob Lytle.

bleeps in there because that's how the conversation sounded. After dinner, I went home and the phone rang. It was Denny Stoltz calling me to see if I was going to go to Michigan State. I gave him no commitment. To make a long story short, I went to Michigan. It was the best decision I ever made in my life. I felt that Michigan really wanted me from day one, and they showed it.

Bo was in his fourth year when I was a freshman in 1972. I got him very early in the game. He was pretty fiery. Let's just say you didn't want to rub him the wrong way. Not only were the players afraid of him, but I think that all the assistant coaches were too. If he said something, you got it done.

Throughout my whole career at Michigan, I only had one encounter with Bo. I still say to this day, I was set up. I was playing on the freshmen football team and we were going to play at Notre Dame. The bus left at a certain time, and freshmen coach Denny Brown accused me of being late for it. A lot of guys were standing around the door of the bus, but we weren't on the bus yet. When I got on, he said, "You're late!" I didn't know how to respond.

I said, "I don't think I'm late. I was outside the door talking, and when the bus driver said it was time to go, I got on the bus." He told Bo, and Bo confronted me. I said, "Bo, I didn't do anything." He jumped in my face and got on me pretty bad. That was the only incident I ever had with Bo in my five years at Michigan. Denny Brown had set me up.

Once I committed to being part of the team, I never had any other issues with Bo at all. Whether you were a regular player or a demonstration player, if you were committed to football, going to class, and working hard every day, you were one of Bo's guys. I looked forward to working hard and doing the work we had to do to win football games. Bo's way was my way. I enjoyed it. There weren't many days when I didn't have fun working out, going to school, and playing games.

What I really liked about Michigan was at the beginning of the season, we would sit down as a team and set our goals. We would come up with our individual goals, offensive and defensive goals, and a total team goal. When we sat down to do that, we knew we were getting ready to take this championship home. Bo was at the front of the room with the yardstick, banging it on the wall, saying, "This game we should win, this game we should win, and this game is a red-letter game, this game we . . ."

When Bo went through the entire script, it was classic. We were putting together the battle plans for the year. That probably didn't mean a lot to other people, but it really meant a lot to me. When he did that, that was my signal that Michigan was ready to go fight, and here's what we're going to do. I was fortunate to be on three Big Ten championship teams. We had some really good seasons, but Bo's battle plan was the one situation that made me realize that it was a big deal to be a Michigan Wolverine.

Being a captain is something you earn at Michigan. I was extremely proud that my teammates elected me captain. I still am today. It's a big deal. We had a football reunion at which pictures were taken of all the All-Americans, coaches, and captains at Michigan. It was tremendous to be in a picture with all those other great Michigan captains. We were the leaders of our teams.

I was captain in 1976 with Rob Lytle. It was a great combination. When something went wrong, the guys came to us. If there was an issue coming down from the coaches, they came to us to deal with it. We solved any kind of problem we had on the team, regardless of what it was. The most satisfying aspect of being a captain was that I had to earn it. It wasn't given to me.

In 1976 I can honestly say I had no issues with anybody on that team. I felt good about everybody. That's how close we were as a unit. It didn't matter whom you were or what position you played, we were one unit. We played as a team, and we won the Big Ten title. Michigan instills tradition, which means being able to play together.

There's a sign at Michigan that says: "Those Who Stay Will Be Champions." That's a profound statement. When you're a high school player coming in, you see that sign, and you ask yourself, "What does it take to be a champion? If I just stand here and do nothing, am I going to be a champion?" It's a pretty simple answer. No.

You need to do whatever it takes for the team to continue the championship tradition of Michigan. I worked as hard as I could in every facet of the game to improve myself. I was always one of the best-conditioned athletes on the team. I lifted weights a lot, probably more than most people did; I still have the Michigan bench press record of 550 pounds, five times. Nobody has broken that record, and it's been 30 years.

The reason I worked that hard was to make sure I did everything I could do to help Michigan win, keep the tradition going. I wanted to win every individual battle I fought against an offensive lineman. I wanted to play inside the context of the team that was preached so much at Michigan. You want to work hard, work smart, and work together as a team. You never want to let down any of your teammates.

Calvin O'Neal was twice named All–Big Ten and was a consensus All-American. On November 6, 1976, he had 24 tackles at Purdue, which is Michigan's single-game record.

MIKE KENN

TACKLE

1975–1977

SEEING WOODY HAYES STEAMING ON THE SIDELINES after the Wolverines gave him an ass-kicking is a great sight. That memory is one that stands out from my playing days at Michigan.

It was 1976, and I remember it more fondly than any other game from my career. We were visiting the Buckeyes in Columbus, and it was Archie Griffin's final game at Ohio Stadium. By far, it was the hardest-hitting football game I ever played. After a scoreless first half, Bo delivered a stirring halftime speech. Fired up, we shoved the ball down their throat on an 80-yard touchdown drive. Our defense forced Ohio State to a three-and-out, and then we scored again. We were up 13–0, but to really rub it in Woody's face, Bo went for two points. We converted, increasing our lead to 15–0. Soon it was 22–0. We played cat-and-mouse until marching down to the Ohio State 15 with the clock winding down.

In the midst of the drive, Bo called a timeout. We shuffled to the sideline, and Bo informed me that I was done for the day.

As stunned as I was to leave the game, I walked off the field feeling absolutely splendid. All season long we had schemed to beat Ohio State. Everything we did was in preparation for our victory against Ohio State. Being removed from the game helped me revel in the moment.

Remember, there were at least eighty thousand fans in the horseshoe in Columbus. At that very moment, there was dead silence. I couldn't hear a

Mike Kenn looks to make a tackle against Minnesota in 1976. Despite a long, successful career in the NFL, Kenn says he cherishes his Michigan years more than anything else.

sound coming from fans in that stadium. There were no boos. The usual jeers directed our way were nowhere to be found. It was hilarious.

As I made my way to the 50-yard line, inching closer to the field to watch the last seconds of the game, I spotted Woody on the other side, arms crossed and a huge scowl on his face. There was not a player or a coach within 10 yards of him. It's not an embellishment. He was angry. I laughed my tail off, and I knew it was the greatest victory I would ever savor.

How I found myself at the University of Michigan is an interesting story. Growing up, I had an absolute fascination with Michigan. It was the only school I wanted to attend. I was a celebrated high school athlete in the Chicago area, but the problem was I was 6'6" and weighed only 192 pounds, playing defensive and offensive tackle. Initially, I was contacted by a number of different schools, but because I was so skinny, many shied away. I was contacted by Michigan at one point and made a visit to Ann Arbor. I also went to Arizona and Illinois. But when letters of intent came out, I had no offers. That prompted me to visit the University of Cincinnati because my family could not afford to send me to a large out-of-state university. Cincinnati coaches wanted to sign me. I was hesitant, even though I thought it might be the only scholarship offer I would receive. I really had no interest in the school and told my parents that collegiate football looked out of the question.

Meanwhile, I pestered Michigan coaches to death. They continued to say they had interest in me, but it seemed like they would never offer me a chance to come there. Where the story gets funny is when a University of Arizona recruiter contacted me. Six months after letters of intent were signed, Arizona coaches decided they wanted me to come there to play football. I was ecstatic. I had a great visit to Tucson, and it was a hundred times better than Cincinnati. After returning home, I gave my verbal commitment to Arizona. The coach asked me if I considered that binding.

"Absolutely," I said.

Arizona's next course of action was to have a coach fly to Chicago and have me sign the letter of intent. Only then would my commitment to Arizona be final. I told my parents the news, and they were elated. But as fate would have it, I was not destined to be an Arizona Wildcat.

A few hours later, Bo Schembechler called and let me in on his plans for me.

"Mike," he boomed, "we'd love for you to be a Michigan Wolverine."

"Well, Bo," I laughed, "that's great, but I have a problem."

He countered with one burning question.

"Do you want to be a Michigan Wolverine or not?"

There was no way I could turn it down. So after hanging up with Bo, I looked at my parents and laughed again. When the next day rolled around, the recruiter from Arizona called from the airport, asking for directions. I decided to break the news about Michigan to him over the phone. I apologized and explained that I always wanted to attend Michigan, and that's where I intended to go.

He cursed me up and down. When I hung up the phone, my parents asked me what had happened. I turned around and said, "Wow."

Not more than five minutes later, the phone rang. It was the head coach of Arizona, who just happened to be the former defensive coordinator at Michigan. He cussed me out left and right about going back on my word. I felt bad, but as an 18-year-old, I didn't understand the complexities of the situation. Long after the fact, I understood that it was just business and I was looking out for my best interests. My career at Michigan speaks for itself.

When I finally arrived at Michigan, I had bulked up by 30 pounds. All the coaches were seated around the table in a meeting. Bo looked up and greeted me.

"Kenn, how're you doin'? Welcome to Michigan." It was funny. Bo never called me anything but Kenn until I graduated from Michigan. I told him how happy I was to be there and he proceeded to ask me what position I wanted to play. I let him know that I'd be willing to play any position on the field.

He looked around the room and said, "Who wants him?" Coach Hanlon said he'd take me, and that was the brilliant start of my offensive tackle career.

During training camp, my brilliant offensive career was slightly derailed. I dislocated my left elbow and was shelved a while. There were rumblings of my scholarship being a waste. I worked my tail off to rehabilitate and ended up seeing some playing time near the end of the season.

We were beating the hell out of Northwestern during my freshman season, and Bo sent all the freshmen out for a series. It was a huge thrill. Even recovering from injury, it was an awesome experience to be playing college football in front of one hundred thousand fans.

Returning for my sophomore season, I bulked up again, adding 45 pounds to my once-meager frame. My new appearance impressed Bo.

"Damn it, Kenn, is that you?" he barked.

"Sure it is, Coach," I laughed.

"Damn, Kenn, you look great," he said. "What the hell did you do?" I explained I'd lifted weights all summer and pushed myself pretty hard.

"Welcome back," he said, slapping me on the back. "It's good to see you."

My workouts had paid off. I found out later they were planning to red-shirt me following my disappointing injury. Following training camp, I found myself to be bigger and stronger, and the coaching staff noted this, too. Following an injury to one of our starters, I was slotted in full-time. But the injury bug struck again. Someone fell on my leg, and it ended up broken. That would end my season, and I missed out on the Ohio State game and the Orange Bowl.

For my two final seasons, I was lucky enough to participate in two Rose Bowls. Although we lost both contests, they were still surreal experiences. Following the loss to Washington in the 1978 Rose Bowl, Bo called me into his office.

"Now you know, Kenn, you still have a fifth year of eligibility."

I stared blankly at him. "No, Coach, I don't," I corrected him.

"You only played for three seasons," he protested. "You sat out your fresh-man year, so you have a fifth year of eligibility." I reminded him of the Northwestern game when he allowed the freshman in for a series.

"Well I'll be a son of a bitch," he said.

I enjoyed a long career with the Atlanta Falcons, but I look more fondly upon my years at Michigan. I forged many friendships and received an out-standing education from one of the top institutions in the country. I always believed Bo helped mold us from boys to fine men. My career is living proof of that.

Mike Kenn spent 17 seasons in the NFL as an offensive lineman. He was selected to five consecutive Pro Bowls and was named All-Pro three times.

RUSSELL DAVIS

FULLBACK

1975–1978

W HEN I WAS RECRUITED, IRREGULARITIES AND ILLEGALITIES were rampant in college football recruiting. I was offered inducements by many different schools. They ranged from schools saying they would get my girlfriend into school on a cheerleading scholarship to offering homes and cars for my parents. I'm not lying. It was mind-boggling.

Tom Reed was the assistant who recruited me for Michigan. When he came to visit, my father, Russell Davis Jr., told him; "My son can't be bought."

"Good," Reed answered. "That means we have a chance."

Prior to going to Ann Arbor for my official visit, Tennessee made the biggest mistake a school can make in recruiting. Tennessee brought in the top running backs around the country on the same weekend. We sat around and compared notes. How many yards do you have? Tennessee was a top candidate for me because it had a great track program. That's why Harlan Huckleby was visiting there, as well.

When I visited the University of Michigan, Huckleby was also there. So was Rick Leach. The three of us hit it off. It was no secret then that all three of us were going to Michigan. The reason I came to Michigan was the camaraderie I felt. There were other prevailing reasons, too—the football prowess of the school and the uniform. As shallow as that sounds, I loved the Michigan uniform. Penn State didn't stand a chance with me because of their uniform. My parents loved Joe Paterno, but I could not get past that uniform.

Russell Davis explodes for an 85-yard touchdown run against Stanford in 1976. Fullback Davis, tailback Harlan Huckleby, and quarterback Rick Leach formed the offensive nucleus of the teams that went to three straight Rose Bowls in the midseventies.

Before I committed, Bo [Schembechler] came to my house. We were in the living room talking when the phone rang. It was Woody Hayes making a recruiting call. Bo said, "Give me the phone. Give me the phone." At the time, I didn't understand the relationship. He began to rip Woody. It was as if he were saying, "I'm here and you're not. Ha, ha, ha." When it was done, my family was looking around at each other thinking, "What just happened here?"

I didn't start playing football until my junior year of high school. I was a track man. My father was a career military man and retired to Woodbridge, Virginia. We moved there in early summer. This was pre-Nintendo. I was playing football and running races in the streets with my newfound friends. The guys kept telling me to come out for football. I started watching practice. The coach, Red Stickney, asked me if I wanted to come out for the team, and I said did. When I said I wanted to play running back because I was fast, Coach chuckled. I was 6'1", 195 pounds, and that was big back then. I'm sure he thought I was going to end up on the line. But he made a good coaching decision and gave me a chance. Once they gave me the ball for the first time, I ran like I had no sense at all.

After only one season in high school football, I had run for more than 2,000 yards. As a junior, I had also cleared 6'9" in the high jump. With my statistics and athletic ability, I had 250 colleges after me.

My father was an only child, and he was a first sergeant in the army. He did two tours of duty in Vietnam. He was not anybody to mess with. I wasn't concerned about Bo Schembechler being a tough coach. Bo didn't get into me a whole lot. Growing up, I always did what I was asked to do. I would ring a doorbell and run. Then I would feel bad about whose doorbell I had rung. I never strayed too far from what was expected of me.

Although I was considered the top tailback in the country, Bo didn't hesitate to move me to fullback. Initially, I don't think I was comfortable with the idea. But you have to depend upon the wisdom of those leading you. I wasn't that rational at the time. There had been schools that I turned down because they wanted me to play fullback. Michigan had made no promises.

All Bo said was: "Russell, we would like you to play fullback. This could be an opportunity to play a lot sooner in your career."

183

At the time, I didn't fully understand what that meant. I didn't understand the prowess of Harlan Huckleby. He was a 9.4 sprinter in the 100-yard dash. Coming in from another state, I didn't appreciate his ability. Accepting that move was another good decision by me. As it turned out, Harlan was one of the finer young men I've met in my life. We ended up being roommates. And he was a tremendous football talent. I had to learn a whole new side of the game. In other words, I had to learn to block.

On my first day of full-contact practice, Don Dufek was playing cornerback. My assignment was to be the lead blocker on a wide sweep. I was supposed to kick out the cornerback or turn him inside. I took off fast. But here came this slight guy to take me on. He was much smaller than I was, but he went through me to make the tackle on Huckleby. I laid on the ground hurting, and I remember having this conscious thought: Is this really what I want to do the rest of my life?

But in those situations, if you are a true competitor, you pick yourself up. You start to think, "You may have gotten me this time, but not the next time." I did get up, and eventually I became a decent blocker.

Before my senior season, I remember thinking about who would make the best captain. My two names were Rick Leach and Harlan Huckleby. To be honest, I don't remember how I cast my ballot. But I thought either one would be an exceptional captain. It didn't occur to me that I would end up being selected as the captain. It was one of the most overwhelming events of my life. I didn't have a clue, one inkling that my name would be called out. I mean that sincerely. After all these years, I can't say how humbled and proud I am to see my name on that roll. In my four years at Michigan, we lost only one regular season game per year. It was a team effort to accomplish that feat. But the team that accomplished that decided to elect me as captain. It is a medal of honor that I wear proudly

But I have to be honest and say that my first emotion when I was elected captain was fear. I had never really paid attention to that role until I was in that position. It was overwhelming.

The university honored the 1978 team at a Michigan game a couple of years ago. Leach, Huckleby, and I were among those who showed up. During a long timeout on the field, Leach said, "Let's run a play in the end zone." I was 46, overweight, and had a hard time bending over. We were going to do the old option play. We lined up in the familiar I formation. Leach called the cadence, "On one." I couldn't get in the three-point stance, but we said, "On one." We took off. I was expecting Leach to give me the ball. And just like he did when we played, he pulled the ball from me, faked the pitch to Huckleby, and ran into the end zone.

We all laughed. That was what we always used to get on Leach about. We always used to joke that he should have given me the ball or pitched it to Harlan. To us, he never made the right decision. But we always won with Rick Leach.

Russell Davis gained 2,550 yards rushing during his Michigan career. His best day was a 167-yard outing against Purdue in 1977. He played four seasons for the Pittsburgh Steelers.

HARLAN HUCKLEBY

TAILBACK

1975–1978

WATCHING DENNIS FRANKLIN PLAY AGAINST OHIO STATE when I was around 14 or 15 years old is my first memory of Michigan football. Dennis Franklin was a black quarterback, and I hadn't seen too many black quarterbacks playing at the time. Dennis played his butt off and had a hell of a game, but Michigan ended up losing. I was really upset about it because Michigan got down inside the 5- or 10-yard line twice, but Bo [Schembechler] refused to kick a field goal. I just really fell in love with Michigan watching that game.

My first experience of recruiting was when Bo came to recruit some guys ahead of me when I was a junior in high school. I was sitting up in the eighth-floor lunchroom at Cass Tech, and a guy came up to tell me that Bo Schembechler wanted to meet me. I remember thinking that the guy was kidding. Then another guy came up and told me that our coach wanted me to get downstairs because Bo Schembechler wanted to meet me. I was think-ing, "If two guys have been sent up, maybe he's there." I went down and boom, I met Bo. I was really surprised by it because I had shown some talent in track, but was just starting to show promise in football.

During the recruiting period, when I was a senior, I was home from school with a cold. I was still undecided about my college choice. Joe Bugel, who ended up coaching the Washington Redskins, was recruiting me for Ohio

State. He called Cass Tech, but I wasn't there. Bugel then called the house, and I told him I was sick. That evening, Michigan was having a dinner for all the local recruits, which I couldn't attend, but my parents did. Bugel and Woody [Hayes] ended up coming to my house at about 6:00 P.M. and stayed until 8:00 P.M. They came around the time my parents left and ended up leaving before my parents came home. It was kind of a strange visit from Woody Hayes.

It's different to have Woody Hayes at your house trying to sell you on going to Ohio State. Woody recruited the old-fashioned way, going house to house shaking hands. You could see how he could get players to commit from the inner city. If my parents would have been there, they would've been taking pictures with him for sure. I talked more with Bugel, I didn't really relate to coach Hayes. I do know that his players all loved him—before he started going off the deep end.

Woody knew everything about Lewis Cass. He was a total history buff. I think he was a history teacher. He had a passion for it, but here I was sitting in my house listening to Woody go on and on about the guy my high school is named after. I'll be honest, as a teenager, Lewis Cass wasn't on my mind. I was thinking, "Lewis Cass . . . yeah, right."

In the end, it came down to Michigan and Ohio State because I have relatives in Columbus and I had an interesting recruiting trip there. I stayed in Neal Colzie's room in an apartment he shared with Archie Griffin and another guy. I remember asking Archie, "Where am I going to sleep?" He said I could sleep in Neal's room. I asked, "Where is he? Is he gone? What if he comes back?" Archie said, "Nah, he's not coming back. He's still out." It seems that Colzie stayed out on the coast after the Rose Bowl and said the hell with school. But really, I was going to Michigan the whole time. I started to become a real fan while watching them play on TV.

The best part of recruiting was meeting Russell Davis. We met on a recruiting trip to Tennessee. Somehow Russell and I gravitated toward each other and started talking. I was feeling pretty good about the season I had had as a senior, picking up 1,000 yards, a bunch of touchdowns, and going to the city championship.

I was asking Russ what his stats were. Russ told me he had more than 2,000 yards rushing and, in his championship game, had had 300 yards and six touchdowns. The numbers he threw out were just amazing, so I changed the conversation. The funny part about it is that you'd never know any of that stuff unless you asked him directly about it.

Harlan Huckleby tries to get around a Michigan State defender during the 1976 game. Huckleby and Russell Davis ran roughshod over Big Ten defenses en route to three straight league titles.

Big Russ was also at Michigan the same weekend I was. We were at this frat party. He had this huge overcoat on, and he's a big guy. He was from the South, and I guess it was cold as hell to him. I remember joking with him about it. We decided right then that, if we both signed with Michigan, we would be roommates.

Rick Leach was also on my recruiting trip. In high school, I heard so much about him. He was outstanding and played everything. It took special skill to hit a baseball like he could, play point guard in basketball, and ultimately play quarterback at Michigan as a true freshman! If you know Rick, you'd think he was a brother if you didn't see him, the way he acts and talks. Rick, Russ, and I became good friends right away, we all jelled.

I would get into some trouble with Bo. I had a car up at school, and I accumulated a number of parking tickets. I was a bit neglectful about prompt payment of these tickets. My car ended up getting impounded. We had to get it out. Bo said he didn't want to see me driving. He said, "You've got to take that car and park it."

One Sunday after a game, which both Russell and I played well in, we were going to go to breakfast before we went to watch film. I jumped into the driver's seat of my car, and Russell said, "Hey man, Coach told you not to drive it." I said, "Oh, man, screw that." We were going to a restaurant on the corner of Packard and State. Because I wasn't really thinking, I drove by the football building. Just when we were cruising by, Millie [Bo's wife] was dropping Bo off. He saw us and initially smiled and waved, as if saying, "Hey guys." I was about to crap my pants. We smiled and waved back. As I drove by, I was looking in my rearview mirror at him. Bo turned and dropped his head with this look on his face like, *That son of a bitch.*

188

We drove on, ate breakfast, and then went to our meeting. Bo would always give a little talk before we broke down into offense and defense. After he addressed the team, Bo came to me and said, "Mr. Huckleby . . ." He gave me a quick talking to. As he was talking to me, it was like he was trying to touch my back by poking his finger through my chest. I knew he probably really wanted to do something to me, but he couldn't. Instead he explained to me, vigorously, what I had done wrong.

The greatest moment in my Michigan career was a game we played at Purdue my junior year. My buddy Russell had a killer game where he flat out ran some guys over. Purdue always played us tough, especially in West Lafayette. It was a clear and somewhat chilly autumn afternoon. We couldn't get anything going until we started using Russell between those tackles. Boilermakers were jumping on, but they couldn't take Big Russ down.

We ran the option, Leach went through his reads, and handed it off to Russ while we carried on our fakes. As I ran to the sideline, I had a perfect end-zone view of the entire play. On this particular run, Russell made me swell up with pride thinking, "Yeah, that's my man. That's how you do it. That's how you win a game." He became our captain when we were seniors, and the reason why was Russ always came up big in games.

What it means to be a Wolverine is being a part of the great history of Michigan. It's about the memories, friendships, and the accomplishments of the team. Being in the huddle, looking at the faces of those guys you played with, and trying to get the job done. There's always that excitement and freshness to Michigan football. Every year it's renewed for a big fan like me.

Harlan Huckleby rushed for more than 100 yards 9 times during his Michigan career. He finished his career with 2,624 yards and 25 touchdowns.

RICK LEACH

QUARTERBACK

1975–1978

I THINK I WAS THE FIRST ATHLETE IN THE STATE OF MICHIGAN to be all-state in three sports: football, basketball, and baseball. I just loved athletics and loved to compete. I loved the competition, and I wanted to win titles. That's what I was all about. It was always about the team.

When I was being recruited, my biggest drawback in going to the University of Michigan was that people were saying, "You're a throwing quarterback. There are other programs where you can throw and do the things that you've done. If you go to Michigan, you're going to be pigeon-holed into something that really doesn't match up with what you do."

That may have been true, but my dad told me, "You've had success in athletics, you're an athlete. Is it more important for you to go somewhere where maybe you throw 30 times a game and win half your games, or do you use your athletic ability to compete for Big Ten championships based on what they've done and who they've got there now? What's important to you?" That was a big factor.

Even before I signed my tender, my football scholarship, I was in a very unique situation. I had a lot of notoriety playing baseball, and the Major League Baseball draft comes up in the late spring/early summer. I had a lot of pro scouts talking to me, and more and more of them started showing up at my games. One in particular with the Philadelphia Phillies wanted to sit down with me and my dad and make an unofficial offer.

Rick Leach runs the option against Notre Dame in 1978, one of the finest moments of his brilliant, All-American career. Widely regarded as one of Michigan's best quarterbacks to ever take a snap, Leach went on to play 10 seasons of professional baseball.

It was a stroke to my ego. I was a 17- or 18-year-old kid, and they wanted to offer me money, so I was willing to listen. Well, I had no idea, but they were offering a six-figure contract, which in today's society would be a multimillion-dollar deal. I had never been exposed to something like that, and to be quite frank, my first reaction was, "Where's the pen? Let's get this done!"

I'm sure my dad saw my reaction, knew what was going on, and said to the scout, "Can you give us some time? I want to talk to my son."

My dad went to Michigan and had a Michigan background. He played on a national championship baseball team, and he just talked about what the school meant, what Michigan was all about—the alumni body being the largest in America and what opportunities would be before me if I continued and did the things I thought I could do at Michigan.

He brought reality back into focus and he again asked me, "What's really important to you? Because if this money, which is certainly a lot of money, is that important—if you go and do accomplish the things at Michigan that you think you can, there's going to be all that money and more after that. In football or baseball, whichever, if you can stay healthy, I really believe that. You can't put a price on going to a school like Michigan and having four years being around kids your own age, growing up and maturing, having that college experience—socially, academically, and athletically."

It made me think, "What else could be out there that I was looking for?"

So when you talk about the Michigan experience, I got exposed. But really more than anything, I just had the kind of relationship and love for my dad that, if he would go through all these things, thank God, I had at least composure enough to listen and believe in what he told me.

Other than my own father, I have more respect and admiration for Bo Schembechler than any man I've ever been around for a multitude of reasons. He was a surrogate father away from home, and especially in my situation as a freshman quarterback, he was even more significant. From the time that he announced I was the starter, Bo took me under his wing as much as possible.

Looking back, I never thought there was a lot of pressure being the quarterback at Michigan, being the point guy for a program like that, being exposed to everything—college life, the campus, playing in that stadium on national TV and the pressure that comes with it. I never felt it because of Bo.

My freshman year, Bo told me, "Hey, there's one guy you've got to keep happy and that's me. I'll do everything I can to help you, nurture you, but understand when you're the Michigan quarterback, there are certain responsibilities and things that come with that. But as long as you keep me happy, don't worry. There's going to be multitudes of things you don't even know are coming your way yet, but I'll be there to go through this with you." That's all I needed.

When I think about the games, the four Ohio State games stand out because of the schools, the tradition, and the coaches—Bo and Woody. I never really had any interaction with Woody Hayes. I had the hatred; but really, it's respect. I watched those previous games before I was a player, and I watched him tear down the sideline marker. I knew that he never said "Michigan"; it was always "the school up north." I heard the story about making a coach push an out-of-gas car over the Ohio line because he wasn't going to spend a nickel in Michigan. I ate that up whole-heartedly.

In fact, I was real brave when I was a senior and we went down there. At one point in the game, we called an option play-action pass. Our primary guy wasn't open, and I started to scramble just a hair. Then I saw, out of the corner of my eye, Roosevelt Smith slip into the backfield. I floated a pass out, and he went in for a touchdown.

We were all hugging and screaming in the end zone, and I heard, "Look, look, look!" We looked over at Woody just punching himself in the face. Two-fisted—*boom, boom*. It happened on that side of the field, so I kind of ran half-circle—I was real brave as a senior, knowing I didn't have to play them again—and I yelled, "Hey, Woody, maybe you know now, we're Michigan! We're not 'that team up north!' We're Michigan!" And then I sprinted off the field.

But really, it was just about respect, because almost everything they did was parallel to what we did. Every game, at that point in time, had everything—the Big Ten title, national ramifications, the whole nine yards. It was life or death back then.

Early in that game, I had scrambled and got tackled along the sidelines. A guy fell on me and kind of wishboned my legs apart and tweaked my hamstring. It kept getting worse and worse. It was one of those things where Bo kept asking me every time I came off, "Are you all right? Can you keep going?" Of course, I was sitting there, saying, "Hell yes, I can!" I didn't care. It was my last game, my senior year, and I was not coming out.

The bottom line was that, after the game, it was hard walking off the field. It was my last game. We had just won the third game in a row against Ohio State. Some trainers had talked to me and the coach, and people were coming in the locker room, and I saw my dad. I don't know how he got in, because normally the room is closed. Through the course of my career, in both football and baseball, my parents never missed a game—home or on the road. My dad was a coach and did a lot of things in bringing me up. I was sitting at my locker and was out of energy. I was hurting with my leg, but I was just so jubilant as to what happened and winning the game.

My dad didn't say a word. He sat down, hugged me, and we both just started crying. I remember that moment with him as one of the special things that we've done. He was so proud as a dad, which I understand now with my kids going through things. I was so proud just knowing I was able to do these things that made him really proud.

It was the culmination of the end. We knew we had a bowl game, but basically that was the end of my career. Knowing how he felt about Michigan, Bo, and everything, I look back because we didn't have to say anything. It was right there. We talk about it to this day. In the culmination of these things that happened to me, that's one of the special moments I'll have till I go.

Rick Leach is one of the few athletes in modern times to become an All-American in both football and baseball.

GEORGE LILJA

CENTER

1977–1980

WHEN I WENT ON MY RECRUITING TRIPS MY SENIOR YEAR, we were allowed four visits to colleges. My third visit was to Michigan and the fourth was to Miami of Florida. It was wintertime on my trip to Michigan. I remember being on the campus, with all of its tradition, and walking into the stadium, which was filled with snow. Michigan Stadium was so huge when I walked in on the 90th row and looked down at the snow-covered field.

Chip Pederson showed me around during my recruiting trip. It was really cold and dreary. I don't remember the campus being all that attractive. What drove me to Ann Arbor was when I walked into the weight room; there were all these pictures of championships and great players hanging on the walls. I could just feel the aura of all the years and tradition that Michigan holds. I felt that if there was any way I could add or be a part of that tradition, I wanted to go to Michigan.

The last meeting I had on my recruiting trip was with Bo Schembechler in his office. I sat down with him and said, right off the bat, "Bo, I want to come here." It was two weeks before you could sign a letter of intent, so he came around his desk, put out his hand, and I shook it. He said, "Now you told me you're coming here, and if you change your mind, the wrath of Schembechler will haunt you the rest of your life." I said, "Yes, I definitely want to be a part of the Wolverine tradition."

George Lilja (No. 59) gets ready to snap the ball to quarterback John Wangler during the 1979 Ohio State game. Lilja was an All-American at center and a team captain during his senior season in 1980.

It was cold, and a foot of snow was on the ground when I came back home to Chicago. My next trip was supposed to be to Miami. Even though I wanted to go because of the weather, I had to tell the Miami coach that I was canceling the trip since I had already given Bo my word.

As a freshman, I didn't want to be late for anything. We used to have this training table in South Quad where they had all this food for us. On the last day of training camp, the upperclassmen got to go back to their apartments and the freshmen to the dorms across campus—rather than our training camp dorm where they had bed-check. We still had to show up for breakfast and practice the next day.

The next morning, I went to the training table in South Quad. I walked in, and there were five chefs standing by themselves with all this hot food laid out, but nobody was in the room. I got my plate and was thinking, "Man, I must have missed practice. What is going to happen to me? What is Bo going to do?" I went through and got my food, went to the dining area, and ate my breakfast. The workers kept coming out making sure I got enough to eat and that everything was fine. I finished up, left, and went to practice.

That night at the meeting, Bo came in and was upset about something. You could tell whenever his glasses got to the front of his nose that something was bothering him. He took command of the room really quickly, looked at all of us, and said, "I want to know who went to breakfast this morning." I raised my hand. I was the only guy. He said, "Lilja, stand up." So I stood up, and he said, "Were you the only one at breakfast this morning?"

I thought he was going to yell at me, but he started pounding the blackboard and said, "If I'm going to pay $1,000, I want my players there! And nobody shows up except one?! I'm going to have you guys running up and down. This is the last time this is going to happen." Bo looked at me and said, "Sit down, George." I sat down, and he went to turn to write on the blackboard. He half turned around, smiled at me, and said, "Well, George, did you get enough to eat?" Everybody in the room started laughing, which broke the tension. I'll never forget that smile, that grin.

Bo knew how to motivate his team, and he knew how to motivate each individual player. When I was a captain as a fifth-year senior, we took a bus to Michigan State to play the Spartans. Michigan's tradition is that, on Friday night, we travel up to Michigan State by bus because we're just going to

East Lansing. At the end of the evening, after you had a meal and they showed a movie, you went back to your room.

After getting to your room, your position coach would come in and check the game plan with you. You usually roomed with someone at your same position, so the backup center, Jeff Felten, was my roommate. Coach Schudel came in and went over the game plan, telling us what to expect from the Spartans and what to do in the red zone. The last person to check in is Bo.

This particular time, Bo came in a little different, a little peppy—and when he was happy, he called me "Georgie." He came in, and I had my feet hanging off the edge of the bed. He grabbed my toe and said, "Hey, Georgie, I think we have a little game down at the stadium tomorrow, do you think we should show up?" I looked over at Jeff, kind of smiled, then looked back at Bo, and said, "Yeah, I think we better, Bo." He said, "OK, that sounds good. Have a good night." He turned the light off and left. I looked at Jeff and said, "Wow, that was kind of a light moment."

Three weeks later, we were down at Columbus about to play Ohio State. Same scenario, we were in our rooms, and our position coach came in and went over the game plan. I should have been alerted to the fact that this was Ohio State week and we turned it up a notch, but I thought that I was going to play along the way that I did at Michigan State. Bo came in, and I said, smiling at him, "Hey, Bo, we got a little game at the stadium tomorrow, do you think we should show up?" He grabbed me by my T-shirt and said, "Not only are you going to show up, you're going to play the game of your life!"

My roommate pulled the covers over his head. Bo ran out of the room and slammed the door. I looked over at Jeff, and he had just started to breathe again. I told Bo later that I had never gone out and played harder in my life than I did in that Ohio State game.

Bo knew how to motivate you at the right time and what to say because he had been around football for so long. He knew what it would take to win.

There was a kid named Art Balourdos, who came up to a Michigan football camp that I spoke at for 10 minutes. He played the center position, was from Chicago, and ended up going to Michigan. He requested my number. It amazed me how from just 10 minutes of speaking, you could connect with people like that.

Awards are nice, but over time they kind of wither and you forget. It's the friendships that last forever, the impact you have on people. I was at the right place at the right time and had great coaches and teammates who played alongside me. I worked extremely hard in the weight room to prepare myself to compete at Michigan, which allowed me to be chosen All–Big Ten and All-America. I just feel fortunate.

I can picture myself going into my freshman year as a boy and leaving my senior year as a man because of the impact that Bo Schembechler, my coaches, and my fellow teammates had on me. To go through adversity and overcome it is the lesson you learn, specifically, at Michigan. You use those lessons the rest of your life, and that makes you successful. You can't really teach that in a classroom, but the life experiences that you get as a Wolverine, you'll take with you the rest of your life.

George Lilja was co-captain of Bo Schembechler's first victorious Rose Bowl team. Michigan defeated Washington 23–6 in the 1981 Rose Bowl.

MIKE TRGOVAC
MIDDLE GUARD
1977–1980

It's kind of weird because I grew up in Ohio as a big Ohio State fan. When I was little, my dad and I used to work in the yard on Saturday afternoon, and we would be listening to the Ohio State game on the radio. I can remember we would always sit and wait for Archie Griffin to get his 100 yards. He went through that span of I-don't-know-how-many games in a row that he had 100 yards.

As a matter of fact, when I was a freshman or sophomore in high school, I always went down to Columbus for the state wrestling tournament. My younger brother and I got on the field—when they had Astroturf. We actually cut a piece of the turf off. I had to stuff it under my brother's shirt and snuck it home. We were scared that my dad was going to catch us. We were young guys, and if he caught us, he would have done what fathers did at that time.

It was the middle of my senior year, and I was one of the Ohio kids who actually was heavily recruited by Ohio State. I was just kind of halfway thinking about Michigan at that time, but I went to a game there and I really loved it. It was the Michigan-Minnesota game, and my mom and dad drove me up to Ann Arbor.

That's when I met Bo Schembechler for the first time, and I just fell in love with him. I thought he was exactly what I was looking for in a coach. He was fair, tough, and personable all at the same time. You could see that he was a

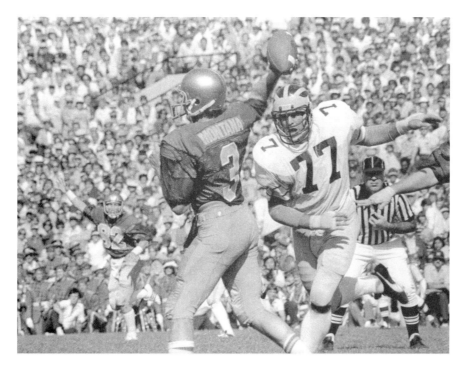

Mike Trgovac of Ohio chose the Wolverines over the Buckeyes as a recruit and then helped Michigan win three of four games against Ohio State.

guy with whom you could have fun, but he was also no-nonsense. That's what I needed because I was a little bit of a free spirit, and I needed someone to keep his thumb on me. I knew at that point, right there, that I was going to Michigan.

I went to the Michigan–Ohio State game in Columbus that year, and I think Michigan won 22–0. It would've been Rick Leach's sophomore year. Actually, I was a guest of Ohio State and left my seat. I left my mom and dad, walked over to the Michigan sideline, sat there, and watched their players. It was obvious Michigan was kicking their butt that day, but it was just a weird feeling as I sat there and watched them. I remember looking at Rick Leach and all those guys, thinking, "These guys are pretty cool."

Woody Hayes came to my house, pulled me downstairs in my bedroom, and gave me the old speech about, "Hey, you're an Ohio kid. Do you know what it's going to mean after you're done playing to work in the state of Ohio? You're going to get a lot of business contacts." Because he pulled me down in my bedroom, by myself, and I was a senior in high school, I was terrified. So it was really hard for me to tell him no, but I didn't say anything then.

Woody brought his wife to my house, and my mom and Woody's wife went to a garage sale together during that recruiting trip. My mom actually loved Woody and his wife. I believe her name was Anne Hayes; my mother fell in love with Mrs. Hayes. There were a couple of days before the signing date, and I knew where I wanted to go, but I was scared to death to say it. I wanted to be an Ohio kid going to Michigan.

My mom said, "Wherever you decide to go to college, I'm going to knit you a nice afghan." The next day when I got home from school, there was a bunch of scarlet and gray yarn on our kitchen table. My dad got mad at my mom and said, "Don't try to influence the kid like that, get that damn stuff out of there." I told my mom, "You may not want to buy that scarlet and gray yarn yet." She said, "What do you mean?"

I knew I wasn't going to Ohio State; I just didn't want to tell anybody. Finally, my dad took me downstairs, and I told him, "Look, I want to go to Michigan." We called up Ohio State and told them. The coach from Ohio State kept trying to come to the house, and my dad wouldn't let him in. He said, "Look, this kid made his decision and he's going to Michigan." I thought, "Thank God that's over with." I knew for a month where I wanted to go to school, I was just really afraid to say it.

I was a wrestler in high school, and I made it to the state finals, which were in Columbus. I was in the big-school category, and the guy I was wrestling signed with Ohio State. The guy's name was Luther Henson, it was a big match: Luke Henson vs. Mike Trgovac. Trgovac signed with Michigan and Henson signed with Ohio State, and Woody Hayes was there.

There were a lot of people rooting against me, obviously because of my being from Ohio and going to Michigan. I ended up beating him for the heavyweight state championship. That was huge because it was built up as the Ohio State vs. Michigan match in St. John's Arena.

In the summertime in June, you play in the Ohio All-Star game. It's the North vs. the South, and I was playing for the North. Well, I ended up being the defensive MVP of the game and the offensive MVP was Brian Dickey . . . B. J. Dickey. Woody Hayes was at the game and was pissed off, livid, out of his mind, because these two Ohio kids going to Michigan were the MVPs. There were a lot of people in Ohio pissed off about that. "Even if they played well, why you would give it to them? They're going to Michigan!"

We had lost my junior year to Ohio State on a blocked punt, and Earle Bruce went 11–0. That was the only time in my career that Ohio State beat me. The next year we went down to Ohio State, and Ben Needham, Andy Cannavino, and myself were from Ohio. We were also three of the seniors on that team, along with Mel Owens. I just remember Andy—he was so emotional before the game and really going crazy.

It was about the third or fourth play in the game, and they ran a sweep play over to the Ohio State sideline. Andy made the tackle, and Earle Bruce was standing right there. Andy grabbed Earle Bruce and started yelling at him, "We own this line! We own this line!" I was standing next to Andy and remember thinking, "This dude is freaked out." He just grabbed Earle Bruce and started yelling at him; he was yelling at all of us, treating us like we were all his stepchildren.

I thought to myself, "I don't know how this guy is going to be able to call plays or call checks." He ended up doing it the whole game, but he was just out of his mind. He was just so fired up and wanted to win that game so badly, having lost to them the previous year. We ended up winning it 9–3. As a defensive player, you like winning games 9–3.

There are so many times when I have decisions to make, I find myself thinking about how Bo would handle this or do that. Bo pops into my mind a lot because I'm in the profession he was in, and I remember how he handled certain situations. I don't always do the exact same thing, but without him even knowing it, he's been a guide in my career.

It's a proud feeling to play for Michigan, a school that has such great tradition—not only from an educational standpoint, but in its football program—of doing it the right way.

Mike Trgovac is currently the defensive coordinator for the Carolina Panthers. He has been a coach in the NFL for 10 seasons. Prior to his work in the professional ranks, Mike served as a defensive coach for several teams. He spent two seasons as a coach with Michigan before moving on to Ball State in 1986.

STAN EDWARDS

FULLBACK

1977, 1979–1981

WHEN I CAME TO FALL PRACTICE AS A FRESHMAN AT MICHIGAN, what amazed me was how the coaches paid so much attention to detail. They didn't let go of any aspect of the game. They would get on you about your foot alignment, the number of inches your feet needed to be apart. At the time, I thought it was nitpicking.

We were probably the most well-prepared college football team in the country. Coaches always added new wrinkles each week, special plays put in for certain teams. Our coaching staff would look at these teams in film sessions and say, "Aha, here is something that we can exploit." And it would work 90 percent of the time.

Every time we took the football field we knew we were going to win. Now, we never went undefeated—there would be a fumble here or a play there that would cost us. But we never went into a game wondering if we were going to win. We always had the mindset that we were going to win.

I came close to not going to Michigan. When I went to the University of Miami [Florida], O. J. Anderson was my host out there. I visited Ohio State, and it was absolutely the worst visit I had. I was there at the same time the Ohio Player of the Year was there, and Woody Hayes spent all of 10 minutes with me. To make it worse, it was probably 10 degrees in Columbus. Coaches wanted you to have a good feel for what it was like at Ohio State, so you stayed in the dorm. You didn't stay in a hotel. In my dorm, there was something wrong with the heat. It was freezing. I went on Friday and was supposed to come home on Sunday. I went home on Saturday.

UCLA and Texas were two intriguing possibilities. When I visited Texas, Earl Campbell was heading toward his senior year, and people were saying he was going to be a Heisman candidate. We ended up playing in the backfield together with the Houston Oilers.

But I thought I could beat out the guy who was with Earl and play right away. The same was true at UCLA. I thought I could play earlier there than at Michigan because Michigan already had Harlan Huckleby, Russell Davis, Roosevelt Smith, Lawrence Reid, and Kevin King. They had a lot of backs. I was thinking I wouldn't play right away at Michigan.

But during the in-home visits, Bo Schembechler called my mom and told her what he wanted for dinner if she wouldn't mind fixing it for him. Back then, he was a legend. Everyone on the block knew he was coming to my house. Everyone was peeking out of the house when his car pulled up. It was a big deal.

Bo came in my house, loosened his tie, unbuttoned his top button, rolled up his sleeves, and took his biscuits and worked them around the gravy in the plate. He licked his fingers at our table. There was no pretentiousness. He made himself at home. It was him and [assistant coach] Bill McCartney.

He looked at my mom and said, "Shirley, your son Stanley will get the best education that the college can offer. He will play in front of the largest crowd at any college every weekend, and he will play on TV more than anyone else."

That's all my mom needed to hear. "You are not going anyplace but Michigan," she told me.

As it turned out, I did play as a freshman at Michigan. I will never forget my first collegiate carry. We were on the road in Champaign, Illinois, and we were blowing them out. Bo called me to the line and told me I was going to get my first carry. I told him I was ready.

I had been moved to fullback in camp, and Bo called a quick-hitting trap play for the fullback. The play was perfectly blocked. There was no one between the goal line and me. I should have scored on a 40-yard run. Instead, I tripped at the line of scrimmage and fell. I don't know if it was the turf or the paint on the field. But I tripped. And certainly no one forgot that in the meeting room the next day.

The first time I came down the tunnel, I couldn't believe I was there. I was in shock. I was in the back of the line. When you get to the end of the

Stan Edwards sprints for a touchdown against Kansas in 1979. Edwards went on to play in the NFL, as did his son Braylon, a Michigan All-American wide receiver who was drafted in the first round of the 2005 draft by the Cleveland Browns.

tunnel and it stops, you are like a herd of cattle. Everyone is bouncing and jumping because the adrenaline is high. You hear someone say, "Let's go!" Then you hear the band firing up "Hail to the Victors." The very first time I ran out there, I only went 20 yards and stopped. I started running slowly, looking around, and saying, "Oh, my God. Oh, my God." I spent the entire first quarter looking around. I couldn't believe the atmosphere.

I was so proud that I was able wear that winged helmet and run out of the tunnel and touch that banner. As the parent of [All-American Michigan player] Braylon [Edwards], my focus is on my son. But as a family, it means an awful lot to us to have a second-generation Michigan player, especially given how well he has played.

Actually, he didn't have a lot of options coming out of high school. I almost had to convince Michigan that he was going to be a pretty good player, even though he didn't have the high school statistics. Michigan had 20 or 21 scholarships, and he was given the 19th one. Michigan State was the only other Big Ten school that offered him a scholarship. He had schools like Akron, Eastern Michigan, and Vanderbilt interested in him. Braylon was starting to say, "These other schools are showing a lot interest, and Michigan isn't calling."

But I wanted him to go to Michigan. When I was choosing a school, I wanted a top-notch, upper-tier program. I knew when I was done with my football program, I wanted a school with a good following. Schools with a long tradition of winning and academic excellence have a strong alumni presence. Guys may have played well in college and had a good pro career, but some don't participate with their university because that university isn't attractive to them. I liked the prestige of Michigan. You are proud to have gone to the school. I wanted the same for Braylon.

There weren't a lot of differences in the football program that I knew compared to the Michigan program Braylon knew. A lot of today's Michigan coaches either played for, or coached under, Bo Schembechler. The tradition and philosophy are the same. He and I laugh about how we had similar experiences. Most issues that are talked about, most of the slogans on the wall in the locker room or meeting rooms are the same. That's very comforting to know. We could share in the same traditions.

There are similarities between Bo and coach Lloyd Carr. Lloyd is a very straight shooter. He wants to run a program that is high in integrity. He wants to make sure all of his players get the best out of their ability. You earn the right to play at Michigan. And Lloyd wants to make sure you come with the intention of graduating. I thank Lloyd for keeping the tradition going.

Bo was a master of coaching, motivation, and preparation. No one was better. Everyone warned me that Bo wouldn't be the same guy who recruited me. I remember one time he said, "Who recruited you? We should have never given you a scholarship. You are the worst player we ever recruited." And you believed Bo because you knew he had coached great players in the past. He had an immense amount of credibility in your mind. You spent your time trying to prove yourself to him.

Lloyd was hard on Braylon, just as Bo was hard on me. And he should have been. Every player needs to understand that life is about being at your best in tough situations. I was a model athlete, and Bo would tell you that. But he was hard on me. Huckleby would run a play and make a mistake, and Bo would say, "Now Harlan, next time you should do it this way."

I would run the play the same way, and I would get yelled at. "Get him out of here. I don't want to see him," Bo would say.

That was part of the initiation process. I came in and worked hard, and Bo still called me everything but a child of God. He did that to everyone. He was just making sure I pushed myself.

Maybe I needed that because I ended up starting as an 18-year-old in the 1978 Rose Bowl against Washington [rushing for 74 yards and catching a 32-yard touchdown]. The game is shown on ESPN Classic now and then. When I watch that game, I find it interesting how the game has evolved. That's the one difference between the game I played and the game Braylon is playing. When Braylon and I watch that replay, the linemen look skinny, and I look frail. Braylon says I look "little."

"Yeah, but I was quick," I say.

Stan Edwards had six 100-yard rushing days at Michigan, including a career-best 164 yards against Purdue in 1980. He played six seasons in the NFL, five with the Houston Oilers.

BUTCH WOOLFOLK

TAILBACK

1978–1981

THE MAIN EVENT I REMEMBER ABOUT MY CAREER at Michigan was helping Bo clinch his first Rose Bowl victory against Washington on January 1, 1981. It was great to watch him enjoy it, and it was like a giant weight had been lifted from his shoulders. I recall when they came to get us from Pasadena and took us to NBC studios in Burbank. It was 4:00 in the morning, and the television folks wanted Bo and me because I was the Rose Bowl MVP.

Even though it was the crack of dawn, Bo was wide awake. In fact, he told me later that he hadn't slept a wink. Instead, he came out with a big cigar in his mouth and a huge grin on his face. Even while we were in the limousine, Bo wouldn't sleep. He had that big cigar sticking out of his mouth. I slept in the back. But every now and then I would wake up to peek on Bo. He just kept puffing on that cigar. He really tried to play it down, but we all knew how thrilled he was to finally win the Rose Bowl.

I was happy to share those moments with Bo. There was a great deal of pressure for that one game. Michigan had come close in years past only to fall short. No one could have ever imagined the pressure we felt. Granted, we were only there for four years and felt just a shred of the disappointment Bo felt. We adopted the pressure and the frustration. We combined all of the years of frustration that Michigan had built up, coming so close to winning

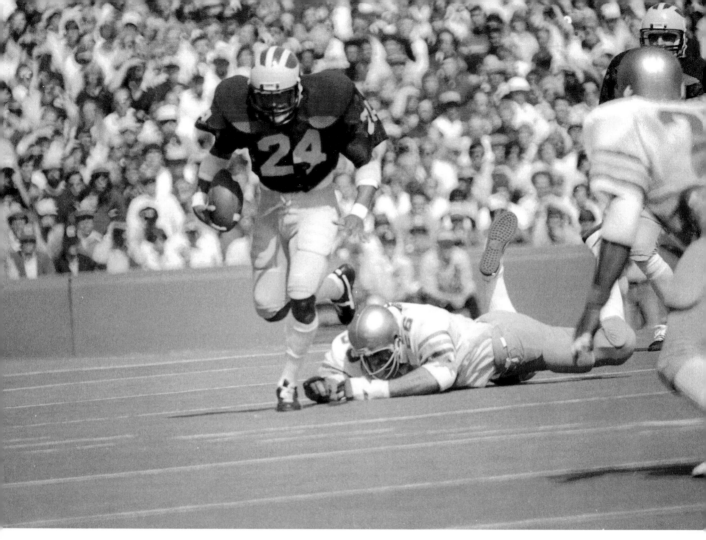

Butch Woolfolk slips past a tackler against Notre Dame in 1981. Woolfolk presently stands as the fourth all-time leading rusher after an All-American career at Michigan. He was drafted by the NFL's New York Giants.

the Rose Bowl. We remembered it before the game. We didn't forget it in the tunnel coming out. And we focused on it in the huddle, too. For that final game, we knew what we there to do. Our sole determination was to win that game for Bo. Washington never had a chance.

To say that I was destined to be a great running back at Michigan would have been a strange thing to say when I was in high school. I was determined to go to USC. I lived in New Jersey and was unaware of the mystique and traditions that surrounded the University of Michigan. But after my visit to Ann Arbor on a recruiting trip, I was sold on Wolverine football.

I knew Michigan was right before I even got back onto the plane. I was impressed by the first-class facilities and the intentions the coaching staff had on championship football. They didn't talk about anything but winning championships. In addition, Bo was going to allow me to play both football and track at Michigan. In high school, I had not only been an All-American running back, but also an All-American sprinter. I had won the national championship in both the 100- and 200-yard dash. Running track was very important to me, and the opportunity to do both football and track was a huge draw. Overall, my trip to Michigan was first-class all the way, from mentality to facilities, and I knew it was a program I had to be a part of.

When I finally became a member of the team, my career was a special one. In the past, Michigan had been known as a traditional "three yards and a cloud of dust" school. When my career came to a close at Michigan, I was the third leading rusher of all-time in the Big Ten. Now, after all the great running backs that have come through the Big Ten, and Michigan as well, I'm fourth all-time at Michigan. It was no surprise that Michigan had a dominant running game—it was expected. At that time, there were few big-time receivers in Michigan's history, and from an offensive standpoint, there weren't any receivers for the opposing defense to focus on. But it all changed when Anthony Carter came in.

There aren't a lot of teams that can boast All-American running backs and All-American receivers on the same team. There usually weren't enough balls to go around to support such teams. But we were special, and Bo made it happen. We had a very potent offense, and we were difficult to defend against. It was a great way to confuse the opposing defenses, having All-Americans all over the field. We had three or four All-American lineman as well, adding to our strength up front. It was phenomenal to play with such great talent, and we were constantly throwing off even the best of defenses.

To be involved in Michigan football was incredible. If Michigan teaches anything, it is that it takes a team to win. The mystique, tradition, and everything associated with Michigan Wolverine football all revolves around the concept of a team. It isn't about individual accomplishments. It is learning to appreciate the value of a team, seeing teammates lay it all out on the line for the betterment of the team. I saw those guys, the heart and soul of the team, who may not have appeared on stat sheets, laid out on the trainer's table. They may not have been All-Americans or household names, but their role was not small. They were buddies, roommates, and the core of those teams.

Michigan is nothing short of excellence. Even in my professional playing days, the tradition and prestige that Michigan embodies was understood by guys who didn't go there. They may not have liked us, but they had great respect for what Michigan stood for, and they could see how special it was to guys like me who had played there. Simply put, being a Wolverine is the cream of the crop.

Butch Woolfolk rushed for more than 100 yards 16 times at Michigan. He played seven NFL seasons with the New York Giants, Houston Oilers, and Detroit Lions from 1982 to 1988.

JOHN WANGLER

QUARTERBACK

1979–1980

PEOPLE THOUGHT I WAS CRAZY. At the time I was being recruited, Michigan was more of an option team, and my strength was throwing the football and scrambling. Both Michigan and Michigan State were recruiting me pretty hard. Bill McCartney had coached at Divine Child, which was my big rival in high school. He knew me from playing against him as a sophomore and junior. When he went to Michigan as a defensive coach, he started recruiting me. He was as good a recruiter as I've ever been around. I liked Mac a lot, and I liked Bo.

Rick Leach started as a true freshman. I was a year behind him, and everyone said, "You'll never play." But McCartney said, "Hey, if you're good enough, we'll find a spot for you and give you a chance to compete against the best." That appealed to the competitive part of me, to try and see if I could make it at Michigan. Even though my strengths didn't necessarily fit the kind of option football they were running, Mac always said Bo would adapt to the type of quarterback he had.

It really came down to Michigan and Virginia because Michigan State went on probation that year. One of my teammates from Royal Oak Shrine went to Virginia. I had a nice visit there and would have had the opportunity to play early. I also played basketball and was thinking about playing both sports in college. Virginia said I could do that. In the end, it was about being

John Wangler drops back to pass against Illinois in 1980. Under Wangler, Michigan's offense shifted some from the option to a power-football, drop-back passing scheme, where he could best utilize his talented corps of receivers.

a part of Michigan's tradition, playing for Bo, the Michigan degree, and being close to home. Michigan was tough competition for any other school to beat.

In the early seventies, option football was in vogue. Oklahoma, Texas, and Nebraska were all running it. I was a drop-back, scrambling type—more of a West Coast type of quarterback. By the late seventies, Ralph Clayton, Doug Marsh, and Anthony Carter were our receivers in my senior year. All three played in the NFL. When Anthony was a freshman, no one knew how great he would eventually be, but they knew he was special. Ralph was also a great receiver, and Doug was a great tight end. We had the type of receivers who you had to get the ball to. It took a while—Bo fought the transition because we were built to be an option team. Eventually, Bo realized that we could win playing power football and drop-back passing.

I made "L.T.," Lawrence Taylor, famous. The 1979 Gator Bowl was a tough game. It was, statistically, the best start I had in a game. We were playing great. Then we ran a bootleg, and I didn't give Kurt Becker, our guard, time to get out and block L.T. I tried to beat him to the corner, which I found out was the wrong decision. I tried to cut up on him. He tackled me and twisted my knee. I was done.

My injury received a lot of publicity. People were wondering if I would ever walk again. It was bad, but I rehabilitated, and it healed well. I had an injury where I should have sat out for two years. I was injured in January and I probably shouldn't have played that year. I should have come back the following year by getting a medical redshirt for a sixth year. But they weren't really giving those out back then. So I was going to play because it was my fifth year. I had already used a redshirt in my junior year.

By August, Bo figured I might be available. In our second game of the 1980 season, we were getting beat 14–0 by Notre Dame in the first quarter. Bo called me over and said he was going to put me in. I was all taped up, and Bo asked me if I was sure I wanted to go in. I said I was. I was cleared to play, but for Bo it was almost as if he were talking to his son. He called all the linemen together and told them if anybody touched me he would kill them. I came in, and we came back, but we ended up losing on a Harry Oliver field goal into the wind.

Winning the Rose Bowl my fifth year was the best moment of my career. After the game, I was in the end zone with Mel Owens. We were both fifth-year seniors and roommates. The sun was setting. There's not a

215

more picturesque scene than the Rose Bowl when the sun is setting behind the mountains. Mel and I didn't leave the field. We were crying because we had both been through a lot. As Michigan seniors, we had gone out there three times and lost. Mel and I had suffered similar injuries, we were red-shirted our junior years. We both had to fight our way to get to play. It was the culmination of five years of blood, sweat, and tears. It pulled everything together—no one could have drawn a better ending then beating Washington. The crowd was cheering. Bob Ufer was leading the cheers. It was great.

There were some other great moments. Anthony's touchdown catch against Indiana got some big play, and it was memorable. But as far as an outpouring of emotion, it was that feeling of finally winning the Rose Bowl—and being the first team to win it for Bo. After taking all the abuse in the seventies for not being able to win the Rose Bowl, winning it was very special. The monkey was finally off our back.

Fans remember the touchdowns and wins. To me it's more about the people whom I was able to be exposed to and played with, the lessons and values that Bo and his staff taught and drilled into us every day. Those are the things that are really important today. That's how you want to live your life. As an 18- or 19-year-old, you may want to buck a lot of those things.

Bo always had our best interests at heart. It didn't matter if you were Anthony Carter or the 120th guy on the team, Bo would always have time for you. He'd always make you feel special. He always cared about you—how you were doing in school, your family. You couldn't get a better situation. Lloyd Carr has carried that on, as well. I've always said the greatest compliment I could give a coach would be that I would want my son to play for him. I wish my son could have played for Bo. I hope Lloyd Carr stays long enough for my kids to play for him.

Ron Kramer, Terry Barr, and Bob Chappuis were guys who went through the same things you did on the same field. You can't buy tradition. Winning is a big part of tradition. But the block "M," putting on the winged helmet, and the fact that the uniforms have never changed—it's the maize pants and navy jersey—they're all constants of Michigan football. There's a lot of great programs that have dipped over the last 20 years. Michigan hasn't. We may have been 7–4 or 8–3, but we haven't dropped below .500. In this era, that's difficult to do. That's a testament to the foundation that's been built. Every guy who goes to Michigan feels the responsibility to carry on that tradition of excellence.

I'd like to thank Bo from the bottom of my heart for giving me a scholarship and the opportunity to play for Michigan, for allowing me to be a part of—a small part of—the tradition that is Michigan football.

Before his injury in the second quarter of the 1979 Gator Bowl, John Wangler had completed 6 of 9 passes for 203 yards and one touchdown pass.

ALI HAJI-SHEIKH

KICKER

1979–1982

M Y DAD WAS GETTING TWO MASTER'S DEGREES FROM U OF M when I was born in Ann Arbor at St. Joseph's Hospital. We moved to Minnesota when I was a year old where my dad got a Ph.D. from the University of Minnesota. When I was about five or six years old, we moved to Texas. I obviously don't have any early memories of being in Ann Arbor.

I grew up in Texas playing football, and football is king in Texas. This was back in the day when ABC only showed one or two college football games. I saw Michigan two or three times a year. My dad was a graduate and a big Michigan guy. Every time Michigan was on TV, we'd turn them on.

All of my buddies eventually went to Texas A&M. I remember in the late seventies, Michigan played A&M and just beat the snot out of that team. I was the only guy rooting for Michigan that week. I went to school that Monday walking a little taller, telling guys down south, that's how you play football up north.

I had a flair for kicking at a young age. I started kicking field goals in the fifth grade. The recreation league was full tackle, and if you scored a touchdown, everyone usually went for the two-point conversion. My team asked the league, "What are the goal posts for?" They said, "Well, they're mainly there just for decoration to make it look like a football field." We said, "What if someone can kick one through there?" They said, "Then we'll give two

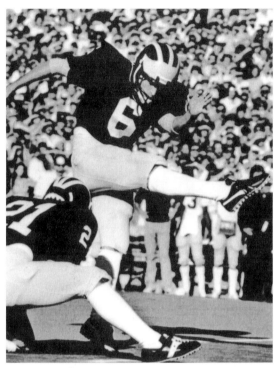

Ali Haji-Sheikh walked on as most at his position did at the time, and he finished his Michigan career regarded as one of the school's best all-time place-kickers.

points for that, one for a run, and one for a pass." From then on we just started kicking field goals and got eight points for every touchdown.

I wasn't very highly recruited at all. I was recruited by small schools locally. But I always knew I was going to walk on at Michigan. We went up the summer before my senior year to my grandparents' house in Munising. On the way back down, we stopped in Ann Arbor. I kicked for Jerry Hanlon and did pretty well. I think I kind of surprised him, being a skinny little kid, weighing about 150 pounds soaking wet.

Back then, Bo never gave kickers a scholarship. They had to walk on and then you had to earn a scholarship. I knew full well going in that it was a one-term shot. My dad was going to pay for one semester. Either I made it and got a scholarship, or I was going back somewhere in Texas to go to school.

I probably put a little too much pressure on myself early in my freshman year, which I guess is understandable being a freshman. I had some opportunities all year. I kicked off all season and put the ball outside of the end zone on every kick-off.

When we were playing Notre Dame, I was surprised because I was only supposed to kick off, but all of a sudden, I heard my name. I had to go out and attempt a 50-yard field goal. I was in no way prepared for that, but I hit it pretty well, just a little bit wide. I was pleased that I got good contact with the ball, considering I didn't think I was going to get in the game in that fashion at all. I tried more kicks, but for the rest of the non-conference schedule, I just didn't do well. I didn't get the job done as a young freshman.

The coaches must have seen enough. They called me in January and said they had an available scholarship. Every semester it was pretty much, "We'll see if it's available." That pressure never left. I wasn't a guy who came in on scholarship, so every year I had to wonder if there was one available. After a fairly good sophomore year, that pressure was pretty much removed. But it was an ongoing deal, which is fine because it's a pressure business.

Bo was very interactive, especially during practice. I loved Bo. He is just a fabulous guy. The older you get, the more you appreciate him. He was a one-of-a-kind guy. He was right in there every special teams practice. He was in there with his yardstick whacking guys. In one practice my freshman year, we were doing these kicking drills, and Bo said, "Next person who misses a kick, I'm breaking this yardstick over his head." Of course, I was the first guy to miss a kick. The next thing I knew, I felt this thump on my helmet and I saw half of the yardstick go flipping off into space.

220

My demeanor is pretty calm. I never really showed any emotion one way or the other. During my senior year, we were practicing, and Bo stopped to watch us kick. I had made five in a row, then missed the sixth one and got back into line. Bo walks over to me and says, "You know, just once when you miss, I'd like to hear you say 'son of a bitch'." I said, "Well, I'll try." This was after four years. You either make a kick or you miss it. You always have to get ready for the next kick.

If you get too emotional about kicking, you start losing your fundamentals. You can't get too pumped up. You don't see golfers get too emotional. Yeah, they'll show it here and there, but for the most part they'll try to suppress it or else their game will start to go south.

Everybody called me Sheikh. If Bo was really mad at me he'd say, "Ali Haji-Sheikh, what are you doing?" If he used your full name, you knew you were in trouble.

It was great being a member of Bo's first Rose Bowl–winning team. Everybody wanted that for him. It was 1981, and he had gone 12 years without winning a Rose Bowl. When that game was over, it was just an incredible feeling—everyone was on cloud nine. You just couldn't believe it—the way we did it, the way the season started with so much adversity. But we pulled it together. In the last six weeks of the season, you couldn't tell us we weren't the best team in the country at that point.

Bo was ecstatic. I saw him about three years ago in the airport, and I chatted with him for about half an hour. Bo told me, "You know what? That 1980 team might have been my best team." That pretty much sums up how he felt about it.

There's a big bond that Michigan has over you. Since 1969 there have been different faces, but the coaching staff has been pretty much the same. It's the same type of coaches, the same demeanors, the same goals, and the same objectives. When I was at Michigan, Lloyd was the defensive backs coach. You're always part of the family, you're always welcome.

If I went back to Michigan, there would still be Jerry Hanlon. One of these days, they'll probably sit him up in a chair. He'll pass away and they won't bury him, they'll put him in a chair because he's been around forever. It's just great seeing Jerry and all of those guys.

When I was in the NFL, being a Wolverine was more important to me than being an NFL football player because you always had that connection with the other guys. I can talk to guys who played at Michigan 10 years before I did, and there's that camaraderie of knowing that we have done the same things. It's like one big family. I get kind of emotional talking about it because it's everything to me, being a Wolverine.

Ali Haji-Sheikh, played five seasons in the NFL, for the New York Giants, Atlanta Falcons, and Washington Redskins. He made All-Pro in 1983 and played in the Pro Bowl.

The
EIGHTIES

JIM HERRMANN

LINEBACKER

1980–1982

I CAME UP TO ANN ARBOR IN THE SUMMERTIME for freshmen orientation. When orientation was over, freshmen football players would usually work out a couple of days with the team. Then you went back home. I said, "Yeah, I'll work out, I've been running." That particular day we were running distance. George Lilja, who was my captain my freshman year, was on the track running. I was running with him. I was thinking, "Oh, I'll kill this guy! He's 280-some-odd pounds and I'm 210. I'll kill him in this thing."

At the end of the workout I said to myself, "Wow!" I realized then that this was a man. George had been through battles. His ability to push himself beyond was incredible. I knew that I was in for something. Here was a guy who was 50, 60, 70 pounds heavier than I was and he ran me into the ground. Michigan was going to be different.

Back then, when freshmen reported, Michigan had freshman football. Just the freshmen were here. So I was practicing with my peers, I was doing well, and I was thinking, "This is OK. I'll fit in here."

Four days later, the varsity reported. We had practiced in the morning, and I remember going to lunch with the varsity. I walked into the lunch room, and Mel Owens walked past me. Mel played the same position as me. I said to myself, "My God, this guy is unbelievable! I'll never play here." Mel was such an Adonis in terms of his body. His physique and muscle structure were incredible.

Jim Herrmann (No. 94) chases after a loose ball during the 1982 Purdue game. Herrmann played three seasons at linebacker before joining Bo Schembechler's coaching staff as a graduate assistant. He is still coaching at Michigan, currently under head coach Lloyd Carr.

Then Curtis Greer walked past me, followed by Mike Trgovac, Ron Simpkins, and Andy Cannavino. I was thinking, "These guys are going to kill me." At Michigan, we matured quickly because we had to—if we wanted to go out and compete. But we got through it as a freshmen class.

One thing that Michigan does that's unique is the freshmen have their own locker room. It helps bridge that first year, which is somewhat of a shock. I always look at the freshmen who come in, watch them go through that same process, and try to let them know, "Look, these guys were freshmen once, too. They looked just like you. They came in just like you. And someday you will be like them. You'll be a man at Michigan."

Everybody talks about Bo's wrath. How tough of a coach he was. Bo cared about the welfare of his players. After my fourth year, I decided that it was over. I wasn't going to play anymore. I walked into his office and I told him that I made a decision, the right decision. I wanted to go into coaching. He looked at me and said, "Great, start next week." I started as a graduate assistant, or G.A.

There were quite a few guys who were coming back for their fifth year from my class. Bo pulled me into his office and told me, "This bridge that you just walked over, there's no going back. You're no longer a player; you've got to conduct yourself as a coach." That has stuck with me throughout my career. He's been a great influence, not only in terms of how to coach and how to be tough on your players, but also that you must care about your players and what's best for them. That's the biggest thing I took from Bo: you must be tough, you must push, you must get them to do their best; but when you care for them and they know you care for them, they'll play their hearts out for you. To me, that's the essence of Michigan football.

Now that I've been through it, I wish as a player that I would have been more serious about the game of football. My playing career would've probably been better for me. I didn't take full advantage of playing at Michigan. When I began coaching, I started realizing what Michigan was all about.

Sometimes when you're in it, you don't really understand the whole scope of what it means to be a Michigan football player. As I look back on it, it's a bittersweet memory. My experience as a player has allowed me an insight that I'm able to pass along to today's Michigan players. Take advantage of being where you are, the situation that you're in, and getting everything you can out of it. As a coach, I try to let them know how special this place is and to take advantage of it.

The camaraderie of being on a team is why we've been successful. Michigan is a team. There are a lot of football teams out there, but they don't play as football teams. They don't play as a unit, as one. There is no "I" in this program. It's about Us. That's why we've been able to maintain where we are and who we are. From Schembechler, to Moeller, to Carr; when guys come in here they realize it right from day one, "I'm part of a team, I'm part of something other than just me." It's that sense that makes us what we are here at Michigan.

Coach Schembechler, coach Moeller, and coach Carr have been an instrumental part of my life. The relationship that I've had with those three men has been special. Their passion for coaching and their love for Michigan are what I'll take with me. I've had opportunities to go other places, but I can't envision myself wearing any other colors than maize and blue.

Why is Michigan different? It's the tradition of Michigan and all that it means to the guys who have played here before, and the guys who are going to play here afterward. I hope that never dies. I hope that college football will still look at Michigan 50 years from now the same way. That's what we want our program to be like. To me, that's what's special about this place.

In 1997 Jim Herrmann was named the winner of the Broyles Award as the national assistant coach of the year.

STEVE SMITH
QUARTERBACK
1980–1983

WHEN ASSISTANT COACH BILL MCCARTNEY CAME TO TALK to me about going to Michigan, I told him I was not very interested in going there because we had thrown the ball so much in high school. I was leaning toward Tennessee or UCLA.

Bo Schembechler then came to my [Grand Blanc] high school on his first visit. He called me out of class. He crawled across a table, poked me in the chest, and said, "You're a Michigan man, and there is no way you are leaving this state."

I didn't decide right then, but it made it difficult to go anywhere but Michigan. Bo claimed I was one of the few people he personally recruited. What really sold me on Michigan was the honesty and integrity of the program. That may sound corny, but it was true. The only promise that was made to me was that I would be given an opportunity to play. I appreciated that. When you come out of high school, you don't worry about competing against other recruits. My only concern was that Michigan had a freshman named Rich Hewlett who had started in the Ohio State game.

But I started three years at quarterback. Probably the game that many remember came in my sophomore year. We were getting beat 21–7 in the first quarter by Illinois. They had Tony Eason. We rattled off 63 points from that point on. We beat them 70–21. It made for a nice memory.

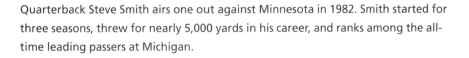

Quarterback Steve Smith airs one out against Minnesota in 1982. Smith started for three seasons, threw for nearly 5,000 yards in his career, and ranks among the all-time leading passers at Michigan.

I played two seasons with Anthony Carter. His junior–senior years were my sophomore–junior years. My memories of him were that he had phenomenal hands, and he was a phenomenal athlete. He was the most amazing receiver—it didn't matter where you threw the ball or how fast he was running. He could either run faster or slower without breaking stride. That's a unique quality. He could always catch the ball out in front of him with his hands. If you underthrew a ball, he would actually slow down without looking like he was putting on the brakes.

He was a really quiet guy. He never said "boo." I watched him get very loud in a USFL game once, and I remember thinking, "I don't remember him ever saying a word in the huddle when we were in college."

When people find out that I played at Michigan, they all ask the same two questions: What was it like to play in front of all of those people at Michigan Stadium? And what was it like to play for Bo?

Bo was fair. I don't think he treated his starters differently than he treated his backup players or his third-string players. If he did, I never saw it. And with Bo, there were only two subjects to talk about. The first one was school and the second was football, and that was the order he put them in.

The tell-all about Bo is this story: I was in Canada for three years [playing in the Canadian Football League], in San Diego for a year, back here for a year, then moved down to Florida for five years. And when I came back here, I didn't go back to the Michigan program. So it had been a number of years since I had seen Bo. He came into my house and met my mom three times. And when I saw him 12, 13, or 14 years later, the first thing he said was, "How's Jimmy doing?"

That's my mom's name. I asked him how he had remembered my mom's name, and he looked at me like I was from Mars. "I remember Jimmy," he said. "How could I forget her?"

Everyone has good Bo stories. One time we were in a Tuesday or Wednesday meeting before a Notre Dame game, and a player came in wearing a Notre Dame shirt. I'm pretty sure it was Cedric Coles. We were in the first big meeting room, and the seniors were in the front with the juniors behind them. When Bo saw the shirt, he went ballistic and threw him out of the meeting room. Everyone was petrified. No one knew what to say. A lot of guys in the back didn't even know what was going on. But soon everyone started to giggle, and finally Bo turned around and said: "What are you guys laughing about?"

Finally, someone asked Bo whether he had actually read the shirt.

Coles had taken a black permanent marker and he had written "Kill" over the top of the "Notre Dame." The shirt read "Kill Notre Dame," but Bo hadn't seen the word "Kill."

Bo made someone go get him, and he started to snicker about it. When Coles came back, Bo just said, "You can't wear those shirts in my room."

The only time Bo ever got into a panic was third down. I remember once we were playing Purdue at home. It was third-and-four or third-and-six— anyway, it was a passing down. I came off the field to talk to Bo, and he kept calling different series for passing. He couldn't decide which series of passing he wanted to call. He hated timeouts, and I said "Bo, give me a play or we are going to run out of time here."

In his own way, Bo then just said, "Piss on it, run a 32." That was a full-back dive. I said, "Bo it's third-and-six." He said, "just run a fullback dive," and pushed me back on the field. Bo wouldn't waste a timeout to save his life.

Bo could be very tough. You would think that, after being a quarterback for a while, if you made a mistake, the coach would just simply say, "Don't do that." Not Bo.

We had a scrimmage once in spring ball. We started the drive at the 20, and we were down to the 35-yard line. He calls a post pattern. The guy wasn't really open, but I threw the ball, anyway. And the defender picked it off. Bo absolutely humiliated me going down the field. Poking me in the chest: "How could you make that pass? What were you thinking?"

231

He wouldn't leave it alone until I got mad.

We started the drive all over again, and we get down almost to the same spot, and he called the same play. I threw it over the defender's head this time for a touchdown.

He turned to me and said, "See? Nice job. Now you did it right."

We had a pretty docile team. Most of the characters on the team got kicked off. Mostly I hung out with the linemen. Guard Jerry Diorio was a good friend. One year in spring football, I was banged up. I had hurt my leg or ankle. Diorio came over one night and said, "It's dime beer night at Dooley's. Let's go." I said, "I can't walk all the way down there."

He said, "I'll carry you."

"No," I said. "You can't carry me all the way to Dooley's from South Quad."

The next thing I knew, he put me on his back and carried me all the way to Dooley's so we could drink dime beers.

My wife didn't know I played at Michigan for the first year we were dating. I met her in Florida. It's a funny story how she found out. I owned a little retail place in Florida, and I was sitting in a chair when I saw a guy who kept walking past the picture window.

Finally, he came in and said, "Are you Steve Smith?"

"Yes," I said, "Why?"

"Did you play football at Michigan?" he asked.

When I said I yes, he told me that he lived in Ann Arbor. He had met me back when I played. In fact, I had dinner at his house.

Then my wife turned around, looked at me, and said, "You played college football?"

"Yep."

"At Michigan?" she said. "You didn't play for Florida or Florida State?"

We laugh about that now. She probably didn't understand the significance of Michigan football until we moved back to Michigan. Maybe I didn't, either.

When you are playing, it's something you do. You don't really appreciate it. But now I'm extremely proud. I really don't have words to describe what I got out of being a Michigan quarterback. It taught me lessons that have nothing to do with football. I went 15 years without ever being late for an appointment. I would be 20 minutes early because that's what I was I taught at Michigan.

Now when I go to Michigan Stadium, I say, "Damn, I actually played here—that's really cool."

Steve Smith passed for 4,860 yards in his career, which ranks sixth on Michigan's all-time list. He once threw four touchdown passes in a game against Purdue.

DAVID HALL
QUARTERBACK
1982–1983

RICK LEACH WAS THERE ON THE WEEKEND of my recruiting visit. He was a year or two out of Michigan, and he said some nice things to me about basketball. I had been in the papers a lot for basketball because my high school, Livonia Stevenson, was having a good season. Rick wasn't trying to put on a hard sell on anybody. He was there talking up Michigan to the whole group and he was very gung-ho. Obviously, as a quarterback, I looked up to somebody who had started 48 games at Michigan. He did so well as a player, it was a big thrill to see him.

My recruiting visit was excellent. It was the Michigan–Ohio State basketball game, a very exciting game, and I met a lot of the players who would become my teammates. I was very impressed with most of the guys and really liked it. I had a lot of opportunities to visit schools, but in the end I just wanted to go to Michigan. It was the perfect combination: a great football program, great academics, and a really great track program. I intended all along to play football and run track. Having grown up in the state, I knew about Michigan. I watched them a lot on TV and also went to their football camp in the summers.

On signing day, Bo came to my house to sign me. I understand he signed Steve Smith and me that day. The assistant coaches signed the other guys. That was exciting, having him come to my house. He didn't say much other

233

than Gary Moeller was coming from Illinois to be the offensive coordinator and quarterbacks coach. Bo also said that he was focusing on getting two quarterbacks, and he was signing me and Steve Smith. I remember his calling a future friend, Vince Bean, from my house to try to convince him to come to Michigan. Vince was still on the fence on where to go.

College was very, very different. Everything is faster, and everyone is faster and stronger. It's extremely challenging to come in and compete at that level. It takes many freshmen a couple of years to rise up to that level. Some freshmen are super-talented and do it immediately, but many of the players worked their way up and got stronger, faster, and smarter on the field. I experienced that challenge, as well.

David Hall, who played backup quarterback to Steve Smith, scores a touchdown against Washington State in 1983. Hall also ran track and broke the school's decathlon record.

Steve Smith was our starter, and I was his backup. They did not give back-ups a lot of playing time. In practice however, the number-two guy fully pre-pares as if he were going to play. It's hard—there's nothing like game time because it's so fast compared to practice. It gets you up to speed. During our preparation for the 1983 Rose Bowl, I recall thinking that, even though Steve Smith hardly ever got hurt, and as tough as he was, that I was somehow going to play. That's part of tricking yourself to prepare and stay on edge.

When Steve got hit, I was surprised that he went down. After seeing the hit, I wasn't surprised because it was an incredible hit. Steve was running an option play and he was moving 100 miles-per-hour toward the safety. UCLA had the perfect defense called. Don Rogers leveled Steve, and he separated his shoulder. Schembechler grabbed me, gave me the plays, and sent me in, no fanfare.

In his mind, I'm sure he was thinking, "Wow! I wish Hall had more play-ing time under his belt." But he was like, "Hey, you know the offense. Here's your plays, go in and do it." Mentally, I was ready to go in.

The fact that Bo didn't pull me aside or say anything special only gave me more confidence. At Michigan, they have confidence in their first- and second-team players to do the job. Bo's approach settled me down a little bit after being rushed into the game in the second quarter.

At halftime, there's so many technical adjustments going on, there's not too much talking other than Bo's saying a few words at the end. I did huddle with Jerry Hanlon and Bo about what offensive plays would work best for us, considering that we were down 10–0. UCLA was not blitzing, and we wished they would, because that meant single coverage on Anthony Carter. But they learned from the Bluebonnet Bowl game the year before not to do that. They also caught on that I wasn't near the running threat that Steve Smith was. My strength was throwing, and in preparing for the Rose Bowl, I practiced throwing and being aggressive in the pocket.

We came out in the third quarter, got a good drive going, and pulled to within 10–7. That was as close as we got—it ended up 24–14.

Coach Hanlon, the quarterbacks coach, said some nice things to me about how I played in the Rose Bowl. Bo did as well. They were very disappointed that we ended up losing. That was the overriding emotion.

Guys on the team were also complimentary about my play. I'll never for-get the kind words from Larry Ricks and his father. Larry was such a great tailback, and he ran so hard in that game. It was good to hear from a senior tailback, a guy who's a class ahead of you, whom you respect a lot, say such kind things after the heat of the battle and a loss. I appreciated it. It's just so disappointing to lose a game that you build up and want to win so badly.

If I had played more during the regular season, would that have made a difference in the outcome of that game? It's hard to say, UCLA was ranked fifth. We were ranked 19th. We fully expected to win the game. That's one thing about going to Michigan that I liked: we expected to beat a fifth-ranked team. And if we didn't, we were terribly disappointed. We're not at all thinking, "Oh, they were ranked ahead of us." At Michigan, you believe that you'll win every game you play.

I did have a fifth year of eligibility in football that I ended up not using because of some knee injuries. Instead, I finished my last year running track for coach Harvey and coach Warhurst. Track ended up being the sport that gave me the most satisfaction. I mean, I love football and I loved playing football for Michigan. I wanted to play more, of course, having started just one game and playing in a large part of a Rose Bowl. I lettered in track before I got my letter in football. In my last year, I broke the Michigan record in the decathlon, which was probably my single highlight, that and playing in the Rose Bowl . . . but had we won the Rose Bowl, it would've won out over the decathlon.

David Hall earned seven letters at Michigan in three different sports: four in track, two in football, and one in basketball.

ERIK CAMPBELL

DEFENSIVE BACK/ WIDE RECEIVER

1984–1987

I ALMOST DIDN'T COME TO MICHIGAN. I had the chicken pox when Bo [Schembechler] came to visit me in Indiana. Bo went to my high school, and I wasn't there. My parents called me and said, "Bo wants to see you." I said, "I'm sick, I don't want to see anybody." I didn't care who it was. The next thing I knew, the doorbell was ringing and Bo was getting me out of bed, making me sit in the house and talk to him. That's Bo. That's what he did.

My dad, John Campbell, was a legendary track coach. He's in the Indiana Hall of Fame and also in the National Track Hall of Fame. I had to run track. That's why I was heavily recruited. I was an All-American in track. I had the best track coach ever in the history of athletics, but football was my first love. I wanted to play for the best football coach. That's why I came to Michigan, to play for Bo.

One day during practice my freshman year, I was catching punts and Bo said, "I'm going to call you Soup." I said, "Soup? Where'd that come from?" He didn't say anything, but one player heard it. He jokingly started calling me "Soup." It stuck. That nickname will be with me for the rest of my life. It's funny that Bo gave me that name, because growing up I wasn't called that, nobody thought of it.

Bo also called me "Clarence." He claims it was from his old Ohio days, when he played baseball. He knew a pitcher named Clarence Campbell, and that's why he called me that. Bo gives nicknames to everybody. He gave me two! Even if you didn't like the nickname, you don't say no to Bo because . . . he is Bo.

I was highly recruited as a wide receiver. Even though I was a tailback in high school, every college was going to convert me to a receiver. Bo wanted me to make the conversion to defensive back. My first thought was, "I'm not good enough, and they're going to get rid of me in some kind of way." But I trusted and believed in Bo. He changed my position and gave me the opportunity to play. We had a great relationship. I love him to death because of all he's done for me, not just as a coach, but as a person.

I had no idea I'd play defensive back. I never played defense in high school. Lloyd Carr was my position coach at the time. He spent a lot of time getting me ready to play. Going through the season, I thought I was never going to see the field. Then the opportunity came to play as a true freshman. Tony Gantt broke his leg. Tony's injury was the start of my Michigan career.

I'll never forget my first start. I was going back home to play against Indiana. I couldn't remember a play to save my life. I blew every check that could possibly be blown. Lloyd called down from the press box and said, "Look, calm down and just think." After that, I relaxed a little bit and made some plays. I had great players around me, including two All-American corners, one was Brad Cochran. They gave me confidence. But that first game was awful. That was the worst game ever.

Whatever the team needed, I filled in and played that position. I moved to receiver my sophomore year and started in the first game against Notre Dame. Bo had plans for me to play both ways. I practiced all training camp on both sides of the ball. Paul Jokisch and I were the two receivers, and Jim Harbaugh was the quarterback. There was a lot of hype going into that season. In that first game, Harbaugh ran a reverse and I got hurt. I ended up only returning kicks for most of that year.

When I came back my junior year, I started back at corner. We wound up having a good year and ended up going to the Rose Bowl. My biggest memory of that year was the last game against Ohio State. Going into Columbus, we had to win that game. The Big Ten title and the Rose Bowl berth were on the line. On their last offensive play of the game, Ohio State threw a one-on-one to Cris Carter. I wound up making the stop, forcing a game-winning

Erik Campbell makes a stop on a Notre Dame player during the 1987 season. Campbell, a tailback and track star in high school in Indiana, played receiver and defensive back for the Wolverines.

field-goal try. You know the history of that one . . . they missed it! We won 26–24.

You never forget getting dressed for the last time. It was an unbelievable feeling—the last game I played at Michigan, the last time I put on that uniform. That's the biggest memory I have. We played Alabama in the Hall of Fame Bowl, which is now the Outback Bowl down in Tampa. We weren't favored, and we didn't have Bo. Bo had had a heart attack and was in the hospital. It was a scary moment as a team. We were like, "Wow. Bo's not here!" Going on that bowl trip without Bo, you felt totally different. Gary Moeller took over as head coach for that game. We had to play our butts off. We knew that Bo would be watching back home from his hospital bed.

The game against Alabama was my greatest game as a player. I broke up plays and made key tackles at the end. Bobby Humphrey was their great tailback. I made a couple of big hits and big stops on him. The team erupted because they'd never seen that side of me. There was a two-point conversion that I stopped by making a solo tackle. For me that was the best game I had, and it was the last game I had.

After the game was over, we were so exhausted. I don't know how many plays we were out there, but we were hot and we were tired. We played our butts off. Demetrius Brown hit John Kolesar late in the game for the winning score. That feeling going into the locker room, it's tough to put into words. Doug Mallory and I were teammates. We were safeties and played in the secondary together. We looked at each other, and we knew it was our last game. Neither one of us wanted to take off that uniform because we'd never put it on again.

Everybody in the country knows Michigan. The first thing people ask you is, "What was it like to wear the winged helmet?" Everyone knows our helmet is a unique fixture in college football. They also want to know what it is like to play in the Big House. Any city in the country you play in, everybody asks about playing in the Big House.

You become a man at Michigan. That's a unique opportunity some young men have—to become a Michigan Man. By becoming a Michigan Man, you're going to be well rounded in all phases of life. It will teach you how to go out into the real world and be a productive citizen and be a great representative of the university.

Erik Campbell is the only player in Michigan football history to start at all four secondary positions in one year. He is currently Michigan's assistant head coach and receivers coach.

JAMIE MORRIS

TAILBACK

1984–1987

I ALWAYS WANTED TO GO TO MICHIGAN. I think at age eight I watched my first Michigan–Ohio State game. Being from the East Coast, you didn't really get a lot of the Michigan games. They showed Michigan–Ohio State, Notre Dame games, and Boston College games, that's basically what you got. I fell in love with the helmets, the pageantry of the crowd, and the fight song was a nice little ditty that you could hum. I just fell in love with Michigan. So I asked my brothers about Michigan and who the little guy on the sideline was.

When Michigan went to the Rose Bowl and played USC, they could've won the national championship. But I felt that the referees stole it from them because of the Charles White mystery touchdown/fumble play. I remember taking a shower that night, getting ready to go to bed—I was crying in the shower because Michigan had lost, and it was just something that stuck with me.

I never thought I would go to Michigan. But as fortune would have it, my brother Joe played in an all-star game and had told Bo a lot about me. He had a good all-star game and Bo was interested. That's how I got recruited by Michigan.

Now I know the rest of the story. I think B. J. Dickey had a job out in the Boston area. He came and got some film of me and sent it back to Michigan for the coaches to look at. The way my recruiting coach, Bob Thornbladh,

Jamie Morris sprints past a Wisconsin defender during the 1987 game against the Badgers. Morris was the school's leading rusher when he left after the 1987 season (he's since been passed), and like his brother Joe, went on to play in the NFL.

put it, Michigan had one extra scholarship, and they were looking at two players, me and someone else. I guess they flipped a coin and I won.

I wanted to see the University of Michigan, and I got an opportunity to go on a recruiting visit. The biggest thrill was meeting Bo Schembechler. I got to go to a Michigan-Indiana game, a big recruiting weekend—Chris Spielman was on that weekend, too.

No one really knows this story: it was the Indiana game—Bill Frieder's coaching [Michigan], and Bobby Knight's coaching [Indiana]. It was the year that Knight got thrown out of the game, and I think Frieder put the referees up to it. "Throw 'em out, throw 'em out," he kept saying, and Knight got ejected. Well, at Frieder's press conference, Knight busted in the door, tore things up, and called Frieder names. He was going nuts. And Bo said, "This is why you want to come to Michigan." I was like, "Wow, I do!"

Every player on his visit has a chance to meet with the head coach, to sit down and find out what he's looking for and everything like that. Well, I think I was the next player up. I was going behind the Wheaties' box guy, Chris Spielman, and all of a sudden, all interviews were done. Bo wasn't going to see anybody after he met Spielman. Well, over time I found out what that story was all about.

243

I guess Spielman came in dressed in the fashion of the day, where he had all the holes in his jeans and T-shirt and he had chew in his mouth. Bo said, "Son, you look like a slob." And Spielman said, "You know what, Bo? Earle Bruce was fine with what I had on, and as a matter of fact, I'm gonna go to Ohio State." Bo came from behind his desk and jeered, "You go there, goddamnit, and every year we play you, we're gonna kick your ass." I guess they got into a heated match; they had to break them up. So it was pretty wild. Of course, I didn't get a chance to see Bo that day. It was a good thing I didn't see him, I guess.

So that next morning, Sunday, I met with him down at the Campus Inn, and we had a 15- to 30-minute meeting. We talked, and he said, "I want to offer you a scholarship." That was a great thing.

When a player's on a recruiting visit, everyone's nice to him. They tell him all the good things he wants to hear. When he gets out there on that field for the first time, they're screaming and yelling at the top of their lungs. He can't believe those are the same men who recruited him, screaming and yelling, calling him an SOB, calling him every name he could imagine.

My dad was in the military, so I was OK with it, I could handle it. But I mean they could break a guy down. They'd build him back up, but they'll break him down. And all of that high school All-American stuff is out the window. Just remember this: you become meat to them.

There was one particular incident for me. We were trying to run the counter trey, and we kept trying, but I couldn't figure the damn play out. In high school, they used to give me the ball, and I'd just outrun everybody and score touchdowns. It was just the way it was. But not in college football—you had to learn the plays. And it took some time for me to get it down. We kept on trying to run this play, and I remember Bo saying, "Son, I don't think you're ever going to play at Michigan." He told me, "The next time I ever try to recruit a 5'7" tailback, please shoot me, just shoot me." So, I thought I was destined to be gone soon.

But it takes time. You study your playbook and get with your individual coaches. Tirrel Burton really brought me through the years—he brought me through that season. By the end of my sophomore year, I started to get it. When they said the hole was going to be there, I saw the hole. It was starting to come to me. The playbook was making sense. I just didn't take the ball and run up in there, looking for daylight.

This time I ran, let the blockers do their job, and I became an astronaut—"ass-tronaut"—reading asses. I was a player reading asses. If the ass swung my way, that meant get up inside. If it swung the other way, that means get outside. You just read the asses of the blockers. Coach Burton taught me that you read the ass of your block. "Shoot," I thought, "I can do that. I'm gonna read the asses."

For me to leave Michigan as the all-time leading rusher, I have to say it wasn't just my record. That record represents the guys who were in front of me and the guys who came before me. Michigan was "three yards and a cloud of dust," and I got an opportunity to be the leading rusher on a team that is known for running the ball. We're going to run the ball. You can put 11 men on the line of scrimmage—we're still going to run the ball. That should tell you something right there. That's the Michigan type of mentality. To be included in that, that's the greatest thrill.

It's an accomplishment, but that's a team thing. I remember the guys who blocked in front of me: John Vitale, John Elliot, Mike Husar, Dean Dingman, Tom Dohring, Jeff Brown, and Derrick Walker; the wide receivers Paul

Jokisch, John Kolesar, Greg McMurtry, and Kenny Higgins; and quarterback Jim Harbaugh. I didn't do these things by myself. I'm not the tallest and I'm not the biggest guy out there. So for me to accomplish the things that I accomplished, I had to have those guys in front of me doing their job. You've got to have 11 guys all doing the same thing for one to accomplish something.

The thing I remember most about being at Michigan is my first game, running out onto the field and touching the banner. That's a moment that's unforgettable. If you ask any Michigan player, they'll remember the first and the last time they touched the banner. The first time you do it, you're playing before the largest crowd in the history of college football. You're hearing "Hail to the Victors" being played and you're coming out with the guys who you eat, sleep, and bleed with. Those are the moments that you cherish.

In his last game for the Wolverines, the 1988 Hall of Fame Bowl, Jamie Morris rushed for 234 yards, which at that time was a Hall of Fame Bowl and Michigan bowl record.

MONTE ROBBINS
PUNTER
1984–1987

It's been almost two decades since my days as a Michigan punter, and yet my former coach, Bo Schembechler, and I chuckle about a particular play from my career as if it had occurred yesterday.

When Bo and I meet, he gives me the crooked grin and the shake of his head.

"What were you thinking?" he asks.

We both laugh at the memory of the decision I made during a game against Illinois in 1985.

On the punter's to-do list, running for a long gain is not usually high on the list. But in this particular game, my legs helped the team even beyond my punting.

During my sophomore year, we were in a real dogfight against Illinois. It was fourth-and-22. For some reason, I felt like I had the ability to run around left end and make the first down. It wasn't very smart. You don't see a lot of punters running on fourth-and-long. But I had felt plenty of pressure from the left end. On every punt, he was consistently strong on the rush. I knew that if I took a step forward and let him go by, I had an open lane to run.

That's what I did. I stepped up, pulled the ball back as he brushed by me, and off I went. I passed the first-down marker by a good yard, but still had to dive forward for it. As I said, it wasn't smart.

"If you wouldn't have made that first down, you better have kept running," Bo said as I came back to the bench.

I would have kept running, too. I wouldn't have wanted him to catch up with me.

My crazy jaunt turned out to be important. It resulted in a field goal. Those were the only points we managed that day as we tied Illinois 3–3.

My decision to attend Michigan was not quite as dramatic. I came from a small farm town in Kansas, and our football team was composed of a ragtag group of guys. For example, I became the punter because I could kick the ball farther than any of my teammates. It was my sophomore year when I took over the full-time punting duties, and yet I was still playing both sides of the ball because our team was so small. When I was 16, a buddy of mine wanted to attend a kicking camp and asked me to join him. Our fathers accompanied us to this camp, held at TCU. Ray Pelfrey was the instructor, and it was his personal camp we attended, which is still popular today. We received an outstanding education on kicking, and the lessons

Monte Robbins punted his way into the Michigan record books a number of different ways during the mideighties, including with an 82-yard boot against Hawaii.

learned helped me perfect my craft for the rest of high school and eventually into college.

Michigan was a school I saw weekly on national television in Kansas. Little did I know Ray was very close with several recruiters throughout the nation. One of those recruiters happened to be from the University of Michigan.

He made contact with Fritz Seifert, who was the recruiting director at the time, and told him about me. Fritz and the other Michigan recruiters took a look at me, and it went from there. Ohio State, both Kansas and Kansas State, and Louisville were very interested in me, as well. But it was a very simple decision for me. I was absolutely wowed by Michigan. Being away from the Kansas element and seeing the unique opportunity Michigan presented was amazing. The education was incredible, and I knew that historically, and traditionally, it was definitely one of the best schools I could have ever been involved with. It didn't take me more than five minutes to know where I wanted to be.

After all the games I'd watched of Michigan and seeing guys like Anthony Carter, John Wangler, Butch Woolfolk, and Bo on the field, I never would have thought in my wildest dreams that I would be a part of that. And yet, here I was with a scholarship to the school I watched every Saturday afternoon from my home in Kansas.

248

I was very lucky during my tenure there to be a part of some amazing stories. I was a member of a Rose Bowl team that, although we lost, was an incredible milestone in my life. Besides my "legendary" dash that would have incurred Bo's wrath had I not gotten the first down, I had a few moments on the field that still stand out.

The Rose Bowl was a tremendous experience. The national championship was at the back of everyone's mind, but the issue at the forefront was winning the Big Ten and playing in the Rose Bowl. I was lucky to be a member of a Rose Bowl team. I wish the turnout of the game had been different, but I wouldn't have traded the experience for anything.

To go and experience the rich tradition of the Rose Bowl is an awesome feeling. I was only able to go once, but it was a wonderful time. They put on a really good show in Pasadena. They treated everyone first-class. That includes family, friends, and players. We had wonderful accommodations, and the activities, the dinners, and all the recognition were second to none.

But stepping on the field was amazing. You'd been through so much during the season, and then all of the events that led up to the game. This game is high-profile and absolutely center-stage. There's a lot of attention on that game. And there rightly should be. Because of the stature of that game, it makes you feel pretty important.

One moment that really stands out on the field, though, is a booming punt I had against the University of Hawaii. It was the last game of the season in early December, and I'd had a great year statistically. On that particular day, however, it felt like I was just short-stepping everything. As soon as the ball would leave my foot, the ball would travel too high and just too short. To say the least, I was disappointed. After a few of those punts, I took a different approach and went in relaxed on another fourth down. Their special teams had been rushing me all afternoon, and it was no different on this particular play. My goal was to blast it over a guy rushing in on me, and I had fully extended my leg on the kick. It took a great roll, and was downed on the 2. When all was said and done, I was credited with an 82-yard punt, which still stands today as a Michigan record. To see that I still hold a record at an institution that has produced the likes of Woolfolk, Carter, Desmond Howard, and Charles Woodson is a very humbling feat. I'm lucky enough to still be in the record books, and even though most people don't remember me, I have a lot of fond memories of being there.

I still stand back and have to pinch myself to really comprehend that I was and still am a part of the University of Michigan's football history. I am very fortunate to have my path end up there. Had I not run into Ray Pelfrey, I don't know what my chances would have been of ending up at a program like Michigan.

I credit Ray for getting me there. I worked on the farm in the summertimes, but in the autumn, I was a Michigan Wolverine.

249

Monte Robbins' career punting average of 42.8 yards per punt is a Michigan record. He also holds the season mark of 43.62.

KEN HIGGINS
WIDE RECEIVER
1985–1986

WHEN I GRADUATED FROM HIGH SCHOOL, I moved to Ann Arbor for the summer. My older brother was in medical school at Michigan. I lived in his apartment and worked at the golf course during the day. In the afternoons and evenings, I worked out with the guys on the team. I couldn't even bench press 135 pounds. Mike Gittleson, the strength coach, informed me that Michigan had never had a recruit who wasn't able to bench 135 pounds. I had the distinction of being the weakest football player ever recruited to Michigan, maybe excluding a kicker or two.

During that summer, I almost never ran into Bo. It was all the strength and conditioning guys and the wide receivers coach, but there wasn't a lot of coaching going on, it was mostly player workouts. Three days into the start of the season, Bo called on me during a meeting as "Pinky" Higgins. My first impression was—"What the hell was that?" Was he questioning my manhood, my toughness? Bo was all about, "You've got to be tough enough to play at Michigan and in the Big Ten." So I was thinking, "He thinks I'm a pansy or I'm just this guy who was benching 135 pounds six weeks ago. I went up and asked him, "What's with the nickname?" Bo just got this smug grin on his face and said, "You're going to have to go figure that out."

"Just great," I thought.

Bo was always giving guys nicknames, just not usually ones like "Pinky." It turns out Pinky Higgins was an All-Star shortstop for the Tigers and the

Receiver Ken Higgins, shown here hauling in a pass against Purdue in 1985, played two seasons at Michigan, where he also excelled in the classroom.

Red Sox back when Bo grew up. Bo's a huge baseball fan. He claimed that that was the source of the nickname. I still don't know whether he was sending me a message or not. Maybe he wanted me to prove I was tough enough to play for Michigan, but he'll never tell me. I was Pinky to Bo for the rest of my time at Michigan. It was an abusive nickname at first from the other guys on the team, but after I showed I belonged there, it was just another nickname.

The transition academically to Michigan was the easier part for me. The classes weren't easy by any means, but that was where I was more in my comfort zone. You had to be pretty disciplined; you would practice, go straight to dinner, and then you had to go straight to the library as a freshman. You had to be disciplined about getting your work done. I made the mistake of signing up for 8:00 A.M. classes—which in high school was doable, but in college was impossible. If Bo knew this at the time, I would have gotten into a lot of trouble, but I missed a lot of classes as a freshman. I figured out which classes you had to go to and which classes you didn't.

My academic career wasn't that big of an issue with the guys on the team. They were all aware of it, and it was not a problem. The bigger issue was when you would run into a T.A. or a professor who had a preconceived notion that all football players were as dumb as a box of rocks. I had an incident in a psychology class my freshman year. The first assignment of the semester was a paper. I wrote what I thought was a pretty good paper and got a B-, which for me was very disappointing. I talked to the professor and got a very unsatisfactory answer as to what was wrong with the paper.

The next assignment was the midterm, a multiple-choice test where I got the highest grade in the class by far. In handing back the papers, he gave a little speech about how "this one really, really surprised me. In fact I was kind of stunned." He then handed the paper to me and said that I had the highest score. I realize, looking back, that the reason I got a poor grade on the paper was that he read it through the lens of, "This guy is a football player, it can't be any good." You would run into that from time to time, so I felt that sometimes the people outside the football program had more issues with my good classwork than they did inside the program.

252

I was redshirted my sophomore year. I played in one game my freshman year against Michigan State because two of the flankers got suspended for a curfew violation. I actually started that Michigan State game, although we ran two tight ends and one wide receiver for 98 percent of the game. I didn't really play in 1984, played a fair amount in 1985, and then played a lot in 1986.

My junior year I transferred into the business school at Michigan. That year we were 6–6 and played in the Holiday Bowl, which was a pre-Christmas bowl game. I had a couple of conflicts due to our schedule and needed to move some finals around. One was my economics final. I met with my professor and told her, "I'm going out to the Holiday Bowl. The game's at this time, and we're leaving on this date. I can't take the final when it's scheduled. Can I take it early?" She said no problem and told me to come to her office to take the test. It was the same test as the rest of the students were going to take, so I had to promise that I wasn't going to talk to anybody about it. I appreciated her flexibility and said fine, thanks. As I was getting ready to leave, she turned to me and said, "By the way, what instrument do you play?" I said, "No, no, no—I'm not in the band." I had been redshirted that year, so she didn't know me. But it was just classic.

I took a lot of razzing because I never scored a touchdown, and then I finally got one. But I only got one my whole career. My senior year, at

Indiana, I scored my only touchdown, toward the end of the first half. I was the third receiver on the play—we ran a route where I ran a 10-yard out on the short side of the field. The play was designed to go to the wide side. Indiana got pressure on Harbaugh, so Harbaugh scrambled. When that happened, part of the drill was for me to run deep. The other receivers were supposed to run horizontally with Harbaugh and just get open. I ran deep, nobody saw me, and I was a mile behind the defense waving my arms.

Harbaugh did a few spin moves, finally freed up, saw me, and winged it as far as he could. I was back there waiting for it to come down, just hoping that the defensive back couldn't recover fast enough. I ended up catching it right on the goal line and scoring. It wasn't that impressive. It wasn't like I caught the ball and beat anybody. I was just behind everybody, but those are the hardest catches—when you have time to think. I always thought that the harder catches were easier to make because you had to concentrate. It's the ones where you are all alone and the ball is coming right in your breadbasket that you struggle with. It's all about focus, right?

I was so excited to be at Michigan. I still remember, in my freshman year, Bo would give this big pep talk on Thursdays after practice. Pep talks weren't given on Saturdays because it was all business before the games. Bo's philosophy was that you were either prepared or not by that point. But on Thursdays he would give those great, and often inspiring, talks. I remember sitting in on those the first couple of weeks of my freshman season and thinking, "This is great. This is the most fun I am ever going to have." Just putting on the helmet and running out of the tunnel is a part of all that tradition that is at Michigan, and I was very aware of that growing up a Michigan fan in the family I did. I always felt like I belonged there, the challenge was to prove it—and that took a while.

253

Ken Higgins was a first-team Academic All-American, Academic All–Big Ten, and a recipient of the Big Ten Medal of Honor, awarded to the student demonstrating proficiency in scholarship and academics.

MARK MESSNER

Defensive Tackle

1985–1988

When I made a recruiting visit to UCLA during my senior year at Detroit Catholic Central, the weather, Venice Beach, and coach Terry Donahue were enticing inducements.

Remember, I was attending an all-male high school. It was December. It was cold and snowy in Detroit. I got off the plane in Southern California, meeting immediately with coach Donahue. Then it was off to the beach for lunch. It was sunny and 75 degrees. There were bathing suits and roller skates. When we walked the campus, it looked like a botanical garden.

It was like nothing I'd ever seen before. My thinking was, "If I have an opportunity to live this lifestyle, why wouldn't I take that?" I convinced myself that I was going to put myself first and come to California to have a good time.

When I got off the plane in Detroit, I told my parents, "I'm a Bruin."

My parents, Del and Sharon Priddy, went to bed thinking I was going to UCLA. But I went to bed reconsidering. I started to think that maybe I should stay home so my stepdad could see my games. He had cancer. That night I lay in bed and thought long and hard about going out there for myself versus being able to play college football in my backyard. I knew that if I went to UCLA, there was only an off-chance my stepdad would see any of my games.

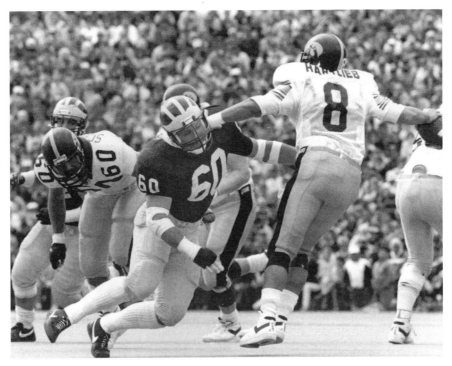

Defensive tackle Mark Messner (No. 60) pressures Iowa quarterback Chuck Hartlieb during a game in 1987. Messner earned first-team All–Big Ten Conference honors four times, becoming just the third Big Ten player in history to do so.

The next morning, I crawled into bed with my parents and blurted, "I'm a Wolverine." By then, I had already called Donahue to say I wasn't coming, and called Michigan to say I was.

The comical part of the story is that when I returned from my UCLA visit, there was either a Buick LeSabre or an Olds 98 in the driveway. As we parked, out of the car popped Bo Schembechler and his assistant, Gary Moeller. They didn't come into the house. Bo just handed me a Michigan highlight tape.

"Remember this," Bo said to me. "You are a Michigan man and you belong at Michigan."

Bo had intensity in his voice. "You don't know what you are doing, son, because you haven't been there," he added. "But I have been there, and you belong here."

It's impossible to put Bo's presence into words. He simply gets into your heart and your head. For such a non-imposing person, he has phenomenal impact. He turns boys into men, and men into family men. To me, everything about Michigan is Bo.

You didn't fear Bo, you feared his disapproval. He's not going to hurt you or knock you on your keister. But you can't imagine disappointing him. You were concerned that he might not yell at you, because the day Bo stopped yelling your name was the day he wrote you off. He wasn't in a tower watching. He was walking around with that ruler, smacking you on the back of the leg, just to let you know he was there.

I have one story about Bo that rips out my heart, and another that swells me with pride.

After Bo's bypass surgery in December 1987, I was among three players who visited him at his home. It was just before the Hall of Fame Bowl. Jamie Morris, Jumbo Elliott, and myself saw him just after he had been discharged from the hospital. It was difficult to see our Rock of Gibraltar lying on the couch, struggling with every breath. His strong voice, with his short, searing words, was reduced to a whisper. He told us he couldn't coach at the bowl game. He gave his message to take back to the team. To see our mentor that frail was difficult. I was used to the Bo-is-going-to-be-here-forever Bo. Now I had to recognize that he was human. He felt pain. He had emotions.

A year later, we were in Columbus, and we had just beaten Ohio State 34–31 with everything on the table. We were going to the Rose Bowl, and Bo's history in the Rose Bowl wasn't very good. In the locker room, Bo stood up, his hair disheveled. He looked more excited than we had ever seen him. In my opinion, Bo knew that this was his team. He knew the character and resolve of that team. He knew he was going to win that Rose Bowl.

We always sang "Hail to the Victors," but I never saw Bo put as much emotion into a rendition as he did this day. He sang the song with his teeth clenched and his lips tight. Emotion poured from him. He had complete confidence in our team. To be captain of that team meant the world to me.

Going into the Rose Bowl against USC, I felt pressure. I believed I needed to have a great game to live up to the expectations that Bo had for me. If I didn't play well, I was worried that we could let this game slip away. Statistically, I didn't have one of my better games, but in the huddle it was "confidence, confidence, confidence." And we won 22–14.

It was one of my most memorable games because it was one of two Rose Bowls that Bo won. And it was a nice finish to a season that started badly. We were really just three points from an undefeated season—we should have been undefeated. My roommate, Mike Gillette, a phenomenal kicker, missed a chip shot to beat Notre Dame. Instead, we lost in South Bend. Then in our home opener, up by 16 points with four minutes to go, we lost to Miami. Being a captain of an 0–2 start, in your senior year, isn't palatable. To turn it around and win everything and finish No. 4 in the polls showed the team's character.

In my Michigan career, I did have two experiences that haunt me from a comedic sense.

In my rookie start against Notre Dame, I was hoping we would get the ball first so I would have a chance to absorb some of the game action. Instead, we kicked off. I ran out onto the field and got down in my stance. Steve Beurlein was at quarterback, barking out cadence. I was so nervous, I puked on the offensive lineman's hands. He couldn't move. The ball was snapped while he was still looking at the mess on his hands. I flew through the line and hit Allen Pinkett for a two-yard loss to start my career.

I purposely blank out who the Notre Dame lineman was. But I'm sure he remembers my name.

The other funny moment came when we were playing in Hawaii. I was so fired up about being in Hawaii that I vowed to catch a marlin. Paul Jokisch, Jim Harbaugh, a few others, and I chartered a boat for the entire day. The plan was to be out there eight hours. We went out there with our skin the color of mayonnaise. And I refused to get out of that fighting chair. I was in there six and one-half hours. I was fried like a piece of bacon. Finally, I decided I had better go inside to rest for a few minutes to get out of the sun. I wasn't in there five minutes, and the line started screaming off the pole that I had left behind. All the guys started yelling for me because I was the one guy who was so insistent that I was going to land a fish.

Finally, I settled into the chair, and I wondered why my teammates weren't there cheering me on. Instead, they were in the back laughing. I fought that fish for 45 minutes. Sure enough, when I hauled in my catch, I discovered that the guys had hooked a five-pound bucket on the end of my line. I had fought a bucket for 45 minutes. All the way home on the plane, reporters were asking, "How was that bucket fish? We hear it was quite an experience."

Running out of the tunnel before a game is certainly a Michigan moment. What people don't realize is that that banner is 10 feet high. And I don't have a vertical jump. When I was coming out of that tunnel for the first time, I was worried I would jump and not hit that banner. Finally, I went down the tunnel. And the energy I felt was incredible. The crowd was loud. I didn't hear it. I felt it. There's a very narrow opening at the end. When I emerged, the feeling was indescribable.

Bo didn't celebrate individual performances. It was all about the team. But we would look at film history so Bo could prove his belief that "it's not the size of the dog in the fight, it's the size of the fight in the dog" that mattered. On film, we would see guys, like middle guard Al Sincich and linebacker Paul Girgash, who were too small to accomplish what they did at Michigan. Bo would tell us to look at their technique and how they played with pride and inspiration.

That was important to me because people thought I was too small. I thought I was too small. I went to Michigan thinking I wouldn't play until I was junior or senior. I figured Michigan had All-Americans three-deep. But I wanted my dad to see me play. If I had not been in Michigan's program, I might not have been able to play like I did. Michigan's style of play allowed an agile, quick player to have an opportunity. At 245 to 250 pounds, I was not a prototypical defensive tackle. I was giving up 30 to 50 pounds to everybody.

My Michigan experience has influenced my life in countless ways. Where do I want to live? Where do I work? Where do I want to raise my family? After my NFL days, I couldn't wait to get home. I wanted to raise my children around the University of Michigan and this program. When I started working, my mandate was to come back to Michigan before my oldest child started school. I was willing to start over if I had to. It was that important to me.

Obviously, I made the right decision to attend Michigan. My dad was able to see my entire career. He died in 1989. Here's the irony: I was drafted by the Los Angeles Rams and still got to go to Southern California. I lived out there 12 years, but now I'm back in Michigan where I belong.

Mark Messner holds the Michigan record of 36 sacks in a career. He had five against Northwestern on October 31, 1987.

KEITH MITCHELL

DEFENSIVE END

1985–1988

WE WERE IN HAWAII FOR OUR FINAL GAME, and my head was not in the game. Prior to the game, I'd found out my dad had disappeared on the family. No one knew where he was. At that point, I could have cared less about a football game. During Bo's pregame speech, my head was down. We went out and played the game and then following the game, we started our bowl conditioning for the Rose Bowl back in Ann Arbor. I was off by myself when out of nowhere [then defensive coordinator] Lloyd Carr came and grabbed me by the shirt. Lloyd recruited me because Downriver [southeastern Michigan] was his recruiting area. "I don't know what the hell is going on with you," he yelled. "In Hawaii, when Bo was giving his speech, he saw your head down on the ground."

This speaks volumes as to how in-touch our coaches were with the players. Keep in mind, I was not an All-American. I was a nobody. I couldn't believe these guys were paying attention to me. I just broke down. I let him in on the story. Both he and Bo had met my father. My father had been very active in the recruiting process, and even more amazing, my father was only 35 years old when I was recruited to play at Michigan. He made an impression on these recruiting trips and was a fun, gregarious guy. But at this point, it didn't matter. I told coach Carr that I planned on quitting the team and returning home to work and help out my mother. Coach Carr jumped up.

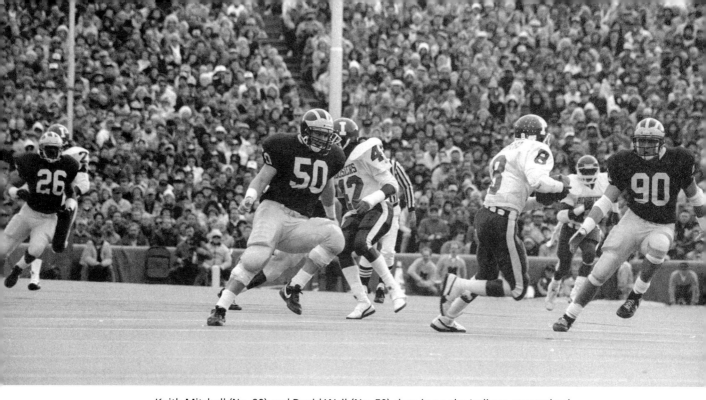

Keith Mitchell (No. 90) and David Weil (No. 50) close in on the Indiana quarterback during the 1988 season. Mitchell almost left the team and the university at one point in his career but was convinced to stick it out by coaches Carr and Schembechler.

"You're coming with me right now," he bellowed. He grabbed me by the shirt and yanked me into Bo's office. Bo, of course, was busy and just about ready to leave his office.

"I'm in a hurry, Lloyd," Bo said.

"Bo, I need you now," Lloyd said in raised voice.

"Damn it, Lloyd, this better be good," he replied. Lloyd told Bo the whole story, and I repeated my intentions to drop out at the end of the semester and go home to work. Bo, I swear to God, responded in classic Bo fashion.

"Goddamnit, Mitchell, you're not going anywhere!" he yelled. "You're staying right here at this school."

He knew damn well that if I quit, I would never come back and probably end up working at the nearest Ford plant. Both he and coach Carr called my mother on the spot and explained the situation. They had a great conversation and wouldn't hear of me leaving. So I stayed. They would not allow me to pay for my father's sins.

I ended up living in California because of their persistence. When we traveled to the Rose Bowl, I absolutely fell in love with California. Later on, I ended up going on *The Price is Right* and winning a car. I made up my mind that I would go to California following graduation. If the conversation had never taken place with Bo and Lloyd, I know for sure I would be in Downriver. I look back at those days and know those two guys changed my life. I don't know if they did that all the time, but without a doubt, I am absolutely grateful to them. To this day, they still ask me about my father, who did come back.

I originally committed to Colorado, and when I was coming off the plane back in Michigan, I saw Bo and Lloyd standing to the left of my parents. It's when [former Michigan assistant] Bill McCartney was still coaching Colorado, and I guess he called Bo and let him know he had "one of his boys." Bo and Lloyd took us to a bar in the airport and talked me into going to Michigan. The Downriver area has some great athletes but not terrific athletes. I guess I stood out more than others, but I always told people I just looked good because everyone else sucked.

Putting the Michigan helmet on for the first time is awesome, but keep in mind, it's terrifying, too. You're thinking, "Holy shit, what did I get myself into?"

261

It's indescribable when you come running out of the tunnel at Michigan Stadium. The hairs on the back of your neck stand up when you're hitting the "M Go Blue" banner on the field. There are a lot of moments in my life I've forgotten, but there are many that are ingrained. Running into the stadium is one of those moments. To this day, walking through that tunnel still gives me chills.

It was in February of my freshman year that we went to Indiana. We attended a dinner where Bobby Knight actually came in and spoke to us. After the dinner, my roommate, Derrick Walker, and I were in our room taking it easy when we smelled some cigar smoke. Neither one of us knew where it was coming from, so we went to check it out. The room connected to ours was the coaches' room, and inside were Bo smoking a pipe and Bobby smoking a cigar. We could hear everything they were saying, and this was only a week after Bobby threw the chair onto the court during a game against Purdue. Bobby was lamenting about coaching and some of the kids on the team. Just as Bo was about to go off about our team, both Derrick and I backed away. Neither one of us wanted to know what Bo was going to say. After all, it could be about us. Of course, there were moments on the field that stood out, too.

We were playing Iowa during my senior year and we had a running back named Tracy Williams. It was first-and-goal on the 2-yard line, and there were about 40 seconds left. This drive was for the Big Ten championship, and Tracy ended up fumbling the ball. The Hawkeyes recovered. We found out at practice on Monday that Tracy was so devastated, he packed his bags and quit. I felt so bad for him. It's something I'll never forget.

Ohio State is an unbelievable place to play. It's pretty loud and pretty scary. But another scary place is up in Wisconsin. When you come out of the visitor's tunnel, there is literally chicken wire on the sides, and they also tell you to keep your helmet on because the fans like to burn marshmallows and throw them into your hair. They're even crazier because they are right on top of the field. But Ohio State is really a nutty place. I will never go there to watch a game. My buddy just went there last year and took his 62-year-old father and his 60-year-old mother. They're walking out of the stadium and this much older woman walks up to them and says, "Michigan sucks! Screw you!" I would never go back there again. It's fun to play in, but horrible to watch.

The Rose Bowl is just an event behind all the pageantry. It supersedes the game itself. It's almost as if the game is anticlimactic. I still think it's the reason Bo had the record he did at the Rose Bowl. We were doing something every night we were there. By the time the game hit, we were tired. But it's still a great experience, and the atmosphere is what convinced me to come out to California.

We were playing in the Hall of Fame Bowl right after Bo had his heart attack, and he obviously couldn't coach. In the first half, we were just going through the motions against Alabama. We headed to the locker room behind. But at the half, Bo was put on the speaker phone. It riled us up, and we went out there and kicked their ass. I don't remember what he said, but I do remember him booming, "Gentlemen, are you there?" It sounded like he'd just gotten off the operating table. Just hearing his voice was enough to motivate you. You knew the old man was always watching no matter where he was.

I've told my little sisters, who are twins and 13 years younger than me, that it's important to pick a school with a good football team or a good sports program. When you're out of college, no matter where you are, you'll find people who will become friends because of the school you chose. There is no way of counting how many people I didn't know at school, but know now and consider friends because we went to the same school at one point in time. It's an instant connection.

Michigan is one big family. I've met a lot of guys who played at different schools, and they did not have the same experience. I had a buddy who played at Oklahoma and told me how the locker rooms were segregated with blacks on one side and whites on the other. They never hung out with each other. But that wasn't the case in Ann Arbor. I still think that when Michigan recruits, they recruit guys who they know will get along with one another. But I've always felt Michigan recruits for character and it shows with how the Michigan family helps one another.

Keith Mitchell is currently a screenwriter in California. He recently wrote the screenplay for the film *Mr. 3000,* starring Bernie Mac.

JOHN DUERR

LINEBACKER

1985–1987

I WAS A ROLE PLAYER AT BEST—though it turns out my role was Monday through Friday. I never held a grudge about that. It never bothered me that this was my role. I had a lot of guys, mostly scholarship guys, who would ask me, "Why are you doing this? You get your ass kicked every day, you're not going to start, and you have to pay for the whole thing on top of it! If I was you, I'd be gone."

That was the difference. I came to Michigan under a difference premise than they did. I was happy with my situation. I knew I wasn't fast enough. I knew I wasn't strong enough. I knew there were a hundred guys at Michigan, and more than 50 percent of them were all-state, 25 percent were All-America. I was just a guy from a small Catholic school in Dearborn, who by the grace of God, Lloyd Carr, and Fritz Seyferth, got the chance to play for Michigan. They were the ones who said, "Hey, we know what kind of guy you are. We like you a lot and we want you to come walk on." I couldn't have asked for more than that.

I remember walking into the locker room the first time. We were getting ready for summer camp physicals, and I saw my name on a locker. I couldn't believe it; I was going to Michigan! No one else I knew could believe it either. Everyone in my high school knew what kind of team we had and the kind of production I had my senior year. My team and I laid an egg my senior year. Everyone was stunned. It was a shocker but a fortunate break for me.

Walk-on linebacker John Duerr was credited with one tackle during his career at Michigan, but his contributions to the Wolverines program go far beyond statistics.

My first two years at Michigan, I did not make any impression at all. I'd be surprised if Bo even knew my name. My junior year, I can't explain what happened, but I went to the summer camp, ran, went to the passing drills. I was there every single day and I started making a contribution as best as I could. I started to catch some people's eyes where they started to see that I had a value to the team. Our first game was against Notre Dame, and I was named scout team champion against the Irish. Finally, after the first two years, I had made a name for myself—again Monday through Friday.

You develop friendships with the guys you go up against in practice. If you put up a good fight, they can't do anything but respect you. If you're no challenge at all, they might as well throw a plastic bag onto the field.

I remember one time in either my junior or sophomore year, we were running goal line. It was late in the season, dark and cold; Bo never wanted to use the indoor practice facility. We were headed south on the practice field. The coaches had a new package called the Jumbo Package. They took two tackles, Jumbo Elliott and Clay Miller, and put them on the left side of the offensive line. I was playing the right side of the defensive line on the demonstration team. Those two fat bastards double-teamed me from the 5-yard line, and I swear to God, they didn't stop blocking me until I was through the end zone. Then they dove on me in the back of the end zone. It was a painful play. They got up and high-fived each other right on top of me. I mean, holy cow! That's 600 to 700 pounds of beef on top of me, and I weighed 230 pounds. That's how you earn your respect.

At the time, I thought the coaches, fans, and media made a bigger designation between a walk-on and a scholarship guy than the players did. Players are players. They're all out there sweating together. They're all out there getting yelled at together. They're all going to go win together. At the end of the day they all go to the same party together. There was no designation between a walk-on and a scholarship guy between the players.

A walk-on conjures up a lot of different images for a lot of guys, players, coaches, even my family. There is not a cattle call for walk-ons. It's not like Michigan says, "Student body, on August 15 we're going to have a walk-on tryout and will pick three or four guys." That's not how it goes. Every guy that walked on at Michigan was asked to walk on. They were handpicked guys who could have got scholarships to a lot of other schools, but decided that the opportunity to play at Michigan was greater than the opportunity to play at a smaller school.

266

That's one thing I don't think a lot of people know. For some reason a "walk-on" is seen as almost a plague—like he was able to overcome two broken legs or polio or something. I can't believe how many times I'm asked, "You could have gone and played at Grand Valley State, Dayton, or even Eastern Michigan. You had a chance to earn a scholarship to one of those schools, why would you choose to walk on at Michigan?"

To which I say, "You tell me." It depends on what you want to get out of the college experience. I'd rather test myself against All-Americans in the best program in the country than go to a school that finishes 3–6 or 4–5 every year. I got a chance to go up against John Elliot every single day for the last two years of my career. That guy was an All-American twice and became an All-Pro in the NFL for 10 or 12 years. I had a chance, some people may not call it a great chance because you're going to get your ass beat quite a bit, but I had a chance to prove myself against some of the best in the country. I'll take that chance.

If you Google me, you'll find out I was credited with one tackle, but it was about Monday through Friday. A hundred and some guys are working year-round. It's not like we'd show up from 8 to 10 on Saturdays in the fall and become a great team. There's a lot of work that goes with it! Everybody has a job in it; walk-ons like me had a job. Without those guys—I don't care what anybody says—without those guys you don't have the same success.

One word that a lot of Wolverines would use to sum up their time at Michigan would be "pride." It will be with me for the rest of my life. Some people introduce me that way. When I golf with my uncle, an attorney in Detroit; he'll introduce me as, "Here's my nephew, he played football at the University of Michigan." It's a great tag. I'm part of an elite fraternity. I don't care if I was a walk-on, or if I started and I'm Jim Harbaugh. I'm still part of that elite fraternity.

I've got a Big Ten championship and an "M" ring that I'll take with me to my grave and pass onto my kids. I really feel like I was the luckiest guy on earth! What more can you want?

On September 28, 1985, John Duerr played in his first game for Michigan, a 20–0 shut-out of Maryland.

BOB AND RICK STITES
LINEBACKERS
1987

GROWING UP IN ANN ARBOR, IT WAS OUR DREAM to go to Michigan. As kids, we used to jump over snow banks delivering papers, acting like we were Rob Lytle. And then during our senior year at Ann Arbor Pioneer, we got a letter in the mailbox inviting us to walk on and contribute to the team. It was truly our dream come true.

We grew up across the street from Michigan Stadium, watching the maize and blue in those winged helmets. When we were eight or nine years old, we went with our grandpa to all the games. We remember seeing people lift up the yellow fence around the stadium and sneaking in. This was before they sold out all the seats, and we couldn't believe how cheap people were.

When you put on the winged helmet for the first time, you actually feel it to make sure it's really there. You don't think of it as a helmet, you think of it as something special. It doesn't feel like a helmet. It feels lighter; it's just an amazing feeling to have it finally on your head. You run your fingers over the stripes because you can't believe that you're really part of the greatest tradition in college football.

When you really feel like you're at Michigan is when you touch the banner running out of the tunnel as a freshman. You realize that that banner is not as high as people think it is. You can always tell a freshman in their first games of the year because the freshmen jump a lot higher than the seniors.

The seniors know that they can't jump that high because they'll hit their facemasks on the banner, but the freshmen always jump too high.

Bo Schembechler was a true father figure; there were really a lot of guys on the team who didn't have fathers, so he had that role. Bo was very fair. There's an image of him being hard-nosed, but that's just a myth. Once in a while he was like that, but he would treat you with respect unless you lost it. Then he would come down on you, which is what should happen with anybody.

During meeting hall with Bo, your hats would be off, two feet would be on the floor, and your hands would be on the desk. Bo would always tell us, "I'll treat you like a man, until you show me you're a boy." He put the fear of God in you, whether you were going to church every Sunday or you were running the streets on Saturdays. Everybody knew they had to act correctly around Bo. While we were playing, there was always something in the back of our minds saying, "I better not do this," or, "I better live the right way and do the right thing," because coach Bo would find out.

On a Saturday night after Bo's worst year, the 6–6 season when we were freshmen; we came back as sophomores and learned about the tradition where you "creep the Quad" on Saturday nights during two-a-days. All the players stayed at South Quad during two-a-days. There was no practice on Sundays. Twenty guys left that Saturday night. Some of the guys left to go back to their apartments for air-conditioning, which we did. Some guys left for other reasons. Bed checks were done twice that night at 10:30 P.M. and 3:30 A.M. by Cam Cameron. During the second bed check, Cam discovered 20 guys missing.

269

We were the only walk-ons who had left that night. Bo, after his worst year ever, decided the scholarship players who left could not be captains. They also had to run on dawn patrol before practice until he stopped them. As for the walk-ons, he tolerated nothing—he kicked both of us off the team. He said he would not discipline walk-ons.

There was a big hush in the room because people were shocked that we had been kicked off the team. We were shocked as well. It stunned us for three days. Gary Moeller was our position coach. Mo said it wasn't the coaches' decision or the captain's decision; it was definitely coach Bo's decision. If we wanted to change it, we had to see Bo at 7:00 the next morning. Bob went down to where Bo parked and talked to him. He said for us to come to his office, which we did. Bo put us back on the team. Some guys

Bob and Rick Stites learned about the "creep the Quad" tradition during two-a-days at the start of their sophomore season, and because they were walk-ons were thrown off the team by coach Schembechler until they managed to talk their way back on.

made up a song for us called "The Stites Boys Are Back." They sang it in front of everybody; it was sung to the tune of "The Fat Boys Are Back," which was a popular song at the time.

The whole team had been on Bo, begging him to put us back on the team. The captains were begging him; it was all the team was talking about during practice. Players actually thought that we were going to climb the brick wall that surrounds the practice field to get back on the team. Our teammates were scared that we would attack the team during practice when we were gone. It was a tough experience because everybody remembers us, but they don't remember the other 18 guys that left that night too.

It was a humbling feeling to know the guys were thinking those things about us when we were kicked off. It is refreshing to know that they were thinking about us as much as we were thinking about them. We know that those guys probably wouldn't have done that for everybody.

A lot of players got kicked off by Bo: Harbaugh, Jumbo, and Moeller. They say you weren't anyone unless you got kicked off.

During two-a-days we always looked at the schedule, we had red-letter games and we had green-letter games. We would always talk about what happened last year and mark some games as red and others as green. Ohio State and Michigan State were always going to be red-letter games.

We would write out personal goals and our team goals on two little sheets of paper that said "M Football." One sheet was yellow and one was blue. You'd write down your personal goals and what you would want to do for the team on one sheet of paper, and on the other sheet would be the team goals. Bo would give you a little cardholder for it and asked you to keep the sheets of paper with you. Bo took these goals seriously.

He would also give us a saying that Fielding H. Yost would use, asking kids to do the right thing: "To come clean, to live clean. To be a better student and better person." When you talk about Michigan, those are the things you bring to your life today: to be a better father, a better spouse, and a better person.

We would like to recognize John Vitale, who was in our class and played four or five years with us. He passed away from cancer a few years back and many of his teammates came back for his funeral. John was a wonderful player and a wonderful man who stayed in Detroit helping kids out. John Vitale was the essence of what Michigan football is about. He was a special, special guy.

271

During their first week as Wolverines, identical twins Bob and Rick Stites were named Scout Team Champions of the Week because the coaching staff couldn't tell them apart.

CHRIS CALLOWAY
WIDE RECEIVER
1987–1989

IT WAS A CHOICE BETWEEN NEBRASKA, ILLINOIS, PURDUE, AND Michigan. I had a good recruiting trip at Michigan. I gained a best friend, Derrick Walker. He was my host and he showed me around. I had a really good time; that played a lot into my decision.

I came from a fairly decent high school, Mount Carmel, in Chicago, and Michigan was big in Chicago. The school had a good reputation around the city, and I felt like Michigan was the best opportunity for me. It had the best of both worlds in football and academics. So I chose Michigan over Illinois. But Illinois recruited me pretty hard. They said they had the No. 1 jersey for me. But Michigan had the better coach.

Bo Schembechler was honest. I would have a scholarship. But with Greg McMurtry coming in, he told me I would have my opportunity to play down the line. That's all I wanted—a scholarship. And a scholarship from Michigan is a big deal.

The transition from high school to college was difficult academically, but on the field it was smooth. I kind of struggled my first year because I wasn't buckling down and studying like I was supposed to. Bo called me out. I remember that speech distinctly. It was in a team meeting. The entire team was present and he told me if I didn't get my act together and pull my grades up he was going to send me back across the water to Chicago.

When you're that young, you know that Bo is a great coach. But you don't fully realize it until you're grown up. My last season was his last season. Today I can't help but think, "Wow, Bo is a college icon and I was a part of his tenure at Michigan. When he went out, I went out." Back then it wasn't as huge of a deal to me as it is now.

The highlight of my career came when I scored a touchdown in the Rose Bowl. I was a junior, and the play was called my way—a short slant route in the red zone. When the ball was thrown, the defensive back, I think it was Mark Carrier, interfered with me. I'm still grateful that the coaches had enough guts to call the same play. I told them I could beat him with the same play. We ended up scoring. It was a big thrill scoring a touchdown and beating USC 22–14

Chris Calloway celebrates a touchdown catch against Illinois in 1988. Calloway played three seasons for Michigan, highlighted by a touchdown in the 1989 Rose Bowl victory over USC, and then went on to play for more than a decade in the NFL.

Coming to Michigan means every day you have to compete. From freshmen to seniors, you have plenty of talented players with whom you're competing. Despite the competition, you have great relationships with all those guys. My fellow receivers were Paul Jokisch, John Kolesar, and Desmond Howard, who was coming up when I was on my way out. That's just what college football is and should be about—that camaraderie, friendship, and bond the players share.

In the NFL it's that hard competition; where you're trying to beat this guy out for a job, or you might not have a job next season. Playing big time football in front of 100,000-plus fans at the University of Michigan prepares you for the NFL. You have a superior coach in Bo Schembechler and first-rate assistant coaches; that prepared me for my whole NFL career. Top quality coaches and a top quality program; when you can take those scenarios and carry them over to the NFL, it makes it a lot easier. You can deal with the competition better than if you were coming from a smaller school.

My four years at Michigan were the best four years of my life. I received a chance to live in Ann Arbor, attend the University of Michigan, and play football. It was a great opportunity to play at a great institution, receive a quality education, and be able to play in front of some of the greatest fans in college football. You can't put it into words. It's indescribable. I feel blessed to have had that opportunity; to have the skills to play football at that level in front of those fans, it was great.

Chris Calloway played in the NFL for 11 years with the Steelers, Giants, Falcons, and Patriots.

DEAN DINGMAN

GUARD

1987–1990

I WAS RECRUITED EVERYWHERE IN THE COUNTRY. I was a state champion wrestler in Wisconsin and received a lot of national recognition. I grew up in southern Wisconsin and came from a close-knit family. It was very important to me that my family could see my games. Back then, the only true football was in the Big Ten. I looked at several schools: Notre Dame, Minnesota, Iowa, and Michigan. After my trips to each school, I could figure out where I really fit in. But at Michigan, playing for a consistent winner and playing for a legend like Bo Schembechler, it just sealed the deal. I knew that, at the time, no person had ever gone to Michigan and not gone to a Rose Bowl in a five-year period. It definitely felt like the right place to be.

It was an amazing experience, how one person like Bo could encourage so many people, from his coaches and his players, to his sports staff as well. This man commanded respect, but it was never through intimidation. Bo was a workaholic. He would sleep in his office at times. But it was inspiring, and I know it's why he was so successful. He took a lot of average players and made them play as a team and fit in. He always had outstanding players, but he had the key role players. Bo was able to make those role players compete at a higher level.

One other thing about Bo was that his mood dictated the mood of his players. It's one of those things I really learned and took into the business world. As a leader in business, you always need to be pumped up to keep your

Dean Dingman sets up on the offensive line during a game with Illinois in 1989. Dingman played in Bo Schembechler's final game, the 1990 Rose Bowl, and then achieved All-American status the following season under new coach Gary Moeller.

workers going at a high level. In football, you could have played the best game of your life, but if you lost, none of it mattered. If it were a bad practice on Tuesday, you wouldn't come in and be joking around on Wednesday. Your mood was definitely dictated by Bo's.

The transition to coach Moeller was very smooth. He had been the offensive coordinator for three years, so it was very similar to what we ran with Bo. Coach Moeller had the same discipline, the same scheduling, and really mirrored a lot of what Bo used to do. It was seamless during that year. I enjoyed the transition on offense when coach Moeller, Cam Cameron, and Les Miles took the reigns and ran the no-huddle offense that was popularized at the time by the Cincinnati Bengals and Boomer Esiason. At Michigan we pride ourselves on conditioning. With Mike Gittleson and the excruciating workouts we went through during the summer, running that no-huddle offense was fun as an offensive lineman. It's usually the defensive linemen that are in better shape, running around all the time. But we turned the tables that year and were able to push the defense all over the field.

Our offense in 1990 was a culmination of the seniors dominating the offensive line and a lot of guys who had been in the program for a long time.

We prided ourselves on dominating people, not just blocking and pushing people around. It was our goal at the beginning of the season to see who could get the most knock-downs and really intimidate the opposing defenses. We really pushed our will on people. You can look at the 1991 Gator Bowl as an example. Mississippi had a first-round draft choice playing defensive line. But against us, he was nowhere to be found.

I was able to see Desmond Howard emerge before his breakout year in 1991. Desmond always showed the ability to make the big play. He was an extremely hard worker, and I really appreciated how hard he played. If you needed anyone to rise up and make a big play, it was Desmond. In 1991 after I left, had Desmond not come out as big as he did against Boston College in the opening game, I would bet that Michigan would have lost the game. That's where you really saw his impact on the big plays. He definitely showed that earlier in his career, when he was running back punts and kickoffs. You also can't discount the great coaching, either. The great Cam Cameron was a coach who told the receivers to get up there and go for the ball. A lot of players wouldn't buy into the system, but Desmond wasn't like that. It was great watching him and seeing him experience all the good that resulted from his hard work.

277

Hard work helped me achieve a lot at Michigan, including some awards. But to be honest, All-American status is expected at Michigan. For me, playing football was never about the honors, it was the journey getting there. It was the workouts, running stairs, and trying to be the strongest guy on the team. There was more honor in Bo Schembechler or Gary Moeller saying something about you in front of the team. It's more important to set goals as a player and a team. At Michigan, the coaches were very vocal about setting goals. Even as a true freshman, there were goals to be set. Being named as an All-American, I think, was a bigger deal to my family. To me, it was another goal to be topped.

Two-a-days during my freshman year definitely stand out in my mind. There were three highly touted recruits coming in that year. I was one, playing strong guard, Greg Skrepenak at strong tackle, and Dave Diebolt at tight end. We were all highly recruited and running two deep together at two-a-days. We all three jumped offside on a play, and Bo screamed at us.

The games that really stand out most to me are the losses. I can remember the Notre Dame game during my senior year because we absolutely dominated them, and it was very disappointing to lose the game. The Rose Bowl loss against USC in Bo's final game was another tough one. Any great athlete really feels the losses more than the wins. I think it's something Bo taught us.

Of course, it was a big deal to play Ohio State. Even in Wisconsin, we always watched the Ohio State–Michigan game. The history between Bo and Woody was great, and it was an absolute honor to play in such a rivalry. I still feel that the Michigan State game was a more intense game to play in than the Ohio State game. MSU played a tougher brand of football, and Michigan State absolutely hates Michigan. There is a respect factor between Ohio State and Michigan with the players and coaches. But I still felt the Michigan State–Michigan game was a more intense and heated game.

Playing for a legend like Bo Schembechler is an unbelievable feeling. It teaches you to do the right things. No one was doing steroids. There wasn't anyone getting in trouble. They taught you at Michigan that if you really want something in life, you have to be prepared to work for it. The feeling at Michigan is that we can always outwork our opponents. Anything I do in life, I know that if I work hard, I can find the answer.

Accountability was a big deal at Michigan, as well. You were not allowed to be late to a meeting, where in life, it seems everyone has an excuse. It was set up at Michigan that you wouldn't live more than a few miles away from the stadium. So if you had a flat tire on your way to practice, you walked to get there on time. You could not get away with excuses. My coach, Les Miles, told me something great: "At Michigan, you don't blame anyone else. You look at the man in the mirror, and see how you could have improved to change the end result."

It's an honor to be a Wolverine. I take pride in the history of Michigan, the former stars who helped build the program, and the incredible academics program represented at Michigan. There's a sophistication and a bit of arrogance at Michigan. At Michigan, you immediately take away that they are better than everyone else, and I truly feel they are. Michigan is the epitome of class.

Dean Dingman was a co-MVP of the 1991 Gator Bowl against Mississippi, blocking for an offense that gained a record 715 total yards. Michigan won the game 35–3.

YALE VAN DYNE
WIDE RECEIVER
1987–1991

I WAS IN A FILM CLASS WITH DAVE DIEBOLT, Greg Skrepenak, and Erick Anderson. Our attendance was less than extraordinary, and our respective coaches received a call from our professor, letting them know we had not been attending. Each coach let his player know such behavior wasn't acceptable and he had better make some corrections. My coach, Cam Cameron, wasn't understanding. I went into his office, and he let me know I was off the team.

"I'm going to give you a life lesson by dismissing you," he explained. "You're going to go out in the business world and get your ass kicked. You're not getting the basic tenants of being successful in life. You're not doing the small things to succeed."

So I went out to China on the Run restaurant with a girl I was dating. After the ordeal, I was practically crying in my beer. I lamented about how it was unfair. At the time, an up-and-coming player on the team had actually been arrested for a stolen credit card. But for whatever reason, he was promoted into my position on the depth chart. I was upset that I was booted off the team for missing a few classes and he was arrested and actually promoted! At the end of the meal, we opened up our fortune cookies. She opened hers and it was nice and cute. And then I read mine aloud: "Those who don't play by the rules shouldn't complain." I was later allowed back onto the team, but I never forgot that lesson.

I walked on at Michigan. My uncle [Rudd Van Dyne] played there under Bennie Oosterbaan and Bump Elliott. My great-grandfather and my aunt also went to Michigan. I had a bit of a legacy there. I wrote letters to about 30 college coaches after being highly recruited at one point. When they dropped off, I sent out letters to the coaches at schools I wanted to play for, and the only one who wrote back was Bo Schembechler. He set me up on a recruiting trip, and I ended up walking on.

I can still remember my first game against Notre Dame in Michigan Stadium. It's a surreal feeling. I knew full well going into that game that I wouldn't sniff the field, but just running out and jumping to touch the "M Club Supports You" banner is unreal. It's almost like an out-of-body experience. It's amazing. It's the same through all of the years. Whether it is first or fifth year, it's always the same surreal feeling, running out of that tunnel and onto the field.

I was not a big contributor for Bo. I was mostly a mop-up guy on the field. But playing for Bo, it was like a father-son relationship. I always felt compelled to do the right things and make him proud.

Bo has an iconic stature with people. He has the integrity that every good coach has. I have a great story about Bo that exemplifies the kind of human being that he is. I was working for a Fortune 500 company, and a guy I worked with closely approached me.

"Hey, do you know Bo Schembechler?" he asked.

"Well, sure."

"We have a guy who has adrenal cancer," he explained. "I wanted to know if you could call Bo." Bo is very active with the Millie Schembechler Foundation, which was founded because of her battle with cancer. I agreed to call Bo for this guy, and not even two minutes after I'd hung up the phone to leave a message with Bo, I heard a familiar voice.

"Harvard!" he boomed. "How are you doing? What can I do for ya?" We shot the bull for a bit, and then I explained my reason for calling. I asked if he would call this man and talk with him.

"Hell, Harvard, I'm no doctor, I don't know anything about the disease. I just raise money for the foundation!"

"I know, Coach," I replied. "But you'll really make this guy's day. He has four daughters and it might make his day to hear from you." Bo didn't even think twice.

Yale Van Dyne runs for some extra yardage after a reception against Notre Dame in 1991. Van Dyne walked on at Michigan and was a member of two Rose Bowl teams, winning one and losing one.

"Of course I'll do it," he said. After that conversation, I heard nothing more. It was about seven months later, and I was in Scottsdale, Arizona, for a sales meeting. While I was unpacking my suitcase, my roommate and I began to talk and find out about one another. The guy asked me out of the blue if I went to Michigan. I told him yes.

"Oh my God," he yelled. "You're not going to believe this. I was in my office and I got a call from Bo Schembechler, and it was the greatest phone call I've ever gotten in my life. I spent an hour on the phone with him, and he was just a super guy." That story proves to me the type of guy Bo really is. He's always true to his word and would never let anyone down.

My name is an interesting story with a Michigan connection. When my dad was only a kid, he sent out 40 to 50 letters to various ballplayers, and only two wrote back: Tobin Rote, a quarterback for the Detroit Lions, and Yale Lary, a Lions cornerback. As a young nine-year-old, he declared that he would name his boys Tobin and Yale, and although he ended up having five boys, he has one named Tobin and another Yale.

Bo always called me Harvard Van Dyne. Always. You can only guess as to why. During my first freshman semester, I had a real tough time. One day Bo came up to me and asked how I was doing.

282

"Harvard, you didn't do very well last semester," he said. "What are you going to show me for second semester?"

"Well, Coach, I think I'm going to get a 3.0 this semester."

"Well, you better," he replied. "Or else I'm going to stop calling you Harvard and start calling you Washtenaw Community College."

My grades improved, but my first time playing was another story. We went to Wisconsin, and I was rooming with Desmond Howard. I was a sophomore and he was a freshman. The coaches came in for lights out to see if we were ready for the game on the following day. I was excited because I knew I was going to play. Wisconsin was down that year, and I knew I would actually see the field. Gary Moeller came in and looked at Desmond the whole time, asking him the questions. Keep in mind, I'm the one who's supposed to play and Desmond is a redshirt freshman. On top of it, walk-ons are insecure as it is because you're held to a different standard than the guys on scholarship. So I'm thinking, God, he's not even looking at me and I'm the one who's playing. I was feeling low.

The next morning when I arrived at the stadium, I walked to my locker and saw No. 34 hanging in my locker. Prior to this moment, I'd always worn double 25, since senior Rick Hassel wore the "real" 25. As I look at the new jersey hanging in my locker, I though to myself, "Thirty-four, that's Walter Payton or Earl Campbell." I didn't know any receivers with that number. And even worse, there was no name on the back of the jersey. I opened up the game program that was always put in our lockers and sure enough, my name wasn't to be found.

After warm-ups, Bo gave us a little talk before our second round of warm-ups and told us he wanted us to wear our wet turfs, which is an extended nub on your turf shoes. I hadn't packed mine, so I went to Bob Bland, one of [Michigan equipment manager] Jon Falk's cronies. I whispered low because Jon Falk couldn't stand walk-ons. I asked Bob for a size 11, and he reached into a bucket and handed me a pair. As I threw the shoes over my shoulder, Falk walks by and says:

"Hey Van Dyne, what the hell are you doing?"

"I was getting my wet turfs." I replied.

"Shit, son, you don't need them. You won't be playing anyway." It was a rough morning for me.

283

But in the second series of the third quarter, I finally saw some time. I was subbed in for Chris Calloway at "A" receiver. The problem was I'd never practiced at "A" receiver. They called for an "A" post, and our quarterback Demetrius Brown threw a perfect pass to me. I was wide open. But my confidence was ebbing at an all-time low, I second-guessed as to how I should catch the ball. The ball hit the ground and I was lit up by the safety. He sent me sliding across the omni-turf full of water and sand. Demetrius screamed at me, and I could see Bo shaking his head on the sideline. After the game, when Bo was in front of a TV monitor watching game film, he looked up and said to me: "Harvard, you disappointed me." You live and die for those moments to play, even when you have a day like mine.

Game day is totally different than any other day of the week. A great example of this is Johnny Kolesar. Both Johnny and I are good buds and were back then, as well. Johnny was the worst practice player in the history of college football. I think Bo, Cam Cameron, and even Johnny would tell you that. He was a total goof-off. He would run around and grab ass and even spank you. He would horse around and have footballs bouncing off of his head, prompting Bo to yell, "Johnny, come on, son, you're better than that!"

But come game day, he was dead serious. He didn't speak, and it was like he was in a vegetative state. Here I was all week not playing and not even anticipating playing, watching Johnny horse around all week. So on game day during receiving drills, I ran around and pinched his butt. Johnny just erupted.

"Goddamnit! It's freaking game day for crying out loud!" I was just a freshman, as green as they come. I thought, "Holy Cow, there's a guy with a different attitude on game day."

During my sophomore year, we beat USC in the Rose Bowl. Just being out there with all the pageantry in California and in that stadium is amazing. It was also my first trip to California. The next year, though, we lost, and it was Bo's last game. Everyone wanted so badly to send him off the right way with a win in the Rose Bowl. It was really disappointing that we lost that game. Right before that game, though, something strange happened. As Bo started to give his pregame speech, the Air Force planes flew over the stadium. Coming into our locker room was this gigantic pipe, and the whoosh that came over the stadium because of the planes somehow went to a deafening level because of that pipe. Everyone almost dove to the floor like it was an earthquake or something.

It's pretty cool to be a member of the Michigan family. You take pride in the fact that you are embedded in Michigan tradition. Everyone takes something different away—whether it be the band, the stadium, the atmosphere, or even the educational aspect. But those factors, along with many others, are what make Michigan what it is, nationally and worldwide.

Yale's longest pass reception was a 60-yard catch against Iowa during his senior year at Michigan.

ERICK ANDERSON
LINEBACKER
1988–1991

As my senior year wound down, I knew I wanted to go to a school that was going to challenge me. I wasn't interested in going to a program that was going to promise me early playing time. I talked to my dad and he said I had a couple of choices: I could go someplace that is promising me early playing time. They may be right or they may be wrong. Would I be happy if they take football away from me at that school? Or I could look at a place like Michigan. If I go there, I may not step on the field until my fifth year, if I'm given a fifth year. Am I willing to wait that long to play?

I thought about it and decided, if I think I am the best, I wanted to play against the best week in, week out, day in, day out.

When Bo Schembechler came for a home visit, the one thing that stands out in my mind is that he was honest with me. Bo told me, "Erick, I can't guarantee you anything at Michigan except a fair chance. That's the one thing I can promise you, you will get every opportunity to prove yourself." Bo didn't promise me starting, he didn't promise me playing time, and he didn't promise me anything but a fair chance. He got up after saying that, he thanked my mom and dad, thanked me, and he and coach Meter left.

As soon as they closed the door, I told my parents, "That's where I want to play. I want to play for him and I want to play at Michigan."

My parents said, "Are you sure? You still have visits to Notre Dame and Northwestern." I told them, "There's no point in taking those visits because

Linebacker Erick Anderson (No. 37) calls defensive signals against Illinois in 1988 as Alex Marshall (No. 59) and Brent White set themselves on the line. Anderson came in as a fullback and left as the best linebacker in the nation.

this is who I want to play for." That's how I ended up in Michigan, the brutal honesty of not being guaranteed anything but a fair chance.

It was not an easy transition. I went into my freshman year playing fullback. I'm in the same backfield with Jamie Morris, Jarrod Bunch, Leroy Hoard, and Tracy Williams. It was very intimidating. It was hard, and at times I was ready to leave.

Bo liked to scrimmage. Everything revolved around scrimmaging, getting us in game situations as much as possible to see what he had. I was running fullback, going against one of the top defenses in the country, and I was expected to know my plays and execute.

This encounter typified my freshman year: it was early on in preseason, we were in two-a-days, and we were scrimmaging. Going into a scrimmage, I was talking to Jamie and he said, "Erick, whatever you do, don't be ghostin' today." I said, "What do you mean 'ghostin'?" Jamie said, "Don't turn into Casper out there and just disappear and not be seen. You've got to get out there and you got to make a name for yourself. You've got to play and no matter what happens, just keep going and going and going."

My first play in, I just happened to be Jamie's fullback. He was a preseason All-American and I was a freshman coming in trying to block for him. It was an off-tackle play, and I knew it. I had studied my playbook and I had to kick out the end. The ball was snapped, and I shot out and attacked the end. I didn't knock him down, but I still interrupted him enough that he wasn't going to make the play. I had done my job. The whistle blew and Bo started going crazy, "Who's the fullback? Who's my fullback?" I raised my hand and said, "I am, Coach." Bo said, "You went the wrong way! Anderson, get out of here, I don't want you back in here until you know what you're doing. Get out of my huddle. Get the freshman out of here."

I was crushed, so I sat back and Jamie came up and said, "Don't worry about it. We all go through it. The biggest thing is you've got to get back in there. You've got to get back into the game and get after it. It's just a scrimmage. Don't prove to them that you're not going to compete. Yeah, you made a mistake, but get back in there."

Now I understood what Jamie meant by "ghostin" it, I wanted to fade into the background and just get through this scrimmage. I wanted to skip my next turn because I wasn't ready. I didn't want to go in there. Jamie came to me and said, "You can't do that. Get in there."

I jumped back into the scrimmage with Jamie the tailback again. It was an isolation play. I knew this play and was ready. The snap count came and I made contact with the linebacker. I drove him back. My feet were still pumping, driving him backwards, when the whistle blew. I turned around to come back, and as soon as I did, I realized I had done something wrong. Bo was standing there picking Jamie up off the turf in the backfield. He turned and saw I was the fullback. He said, "Anderson, I thought I told you not to get back in. Just start running. Get on State Street and keep running until you hit 94, take a right, and don't stop until you hit Chicago. You're the worst player we have ever recruited; I don't know why we're wasting our money on you."

I thought, "Here's Michigan football."

I made the transition in the spring from fullback to outside linebacker. I hated it, I felt like I was on an island lining up over a tight end. I didn't feel I could compete at that position, but that's where the coaches wanted me to play. It wasn't until my sophomore year that I was switched to inside linebacker and I felt comfortable. I had always envisioned playing inside linebacker at Michigan.

I talked to Bo when I made the switch from fullback to outside linebacker and then to inside linebacker. I wanted to find out if he was looking for a place where I could contribute, or was he trying to find a place to hide me. I needed to know his reasoning. Bo told me, "No, we feel we're trying to find you a place where you can help this team out." Bo's explanation calmed me down. I was very excited. Lloyd was the linebackers coach and Jim Herrmann was a volunteer coach. I connected with both of those guys.

John Milligan and J. J. Grant were our starting linebackers. John's only a year older than me, and J.J.'s two years older. I thought if I could get myself into nickel situations, I could establish myself there, even though I may have had to wait, like my dad had said, until my fourth or fifth year to actually start. John and J.J. were good linebackers and they were young. Unfortunately for John, he broke his ankle. I had an opportunity. I played well enough that they couldn't get me out of the lineup. It was hard work, but I was very fortunate to be in that situation.

I won the Butkus Award, I was All-America, and I played some in the pros. But truly, the biggest honor I've ever had athletically was being elected captain at Michigan. Being a captain of the team with the greatest football tradition ever was incredible. I was humbled to be one of the leaders that year, but it was the senior class' team. Greg Skrepenak and I were just representing our senior class and our team.

Michigan football is the one experience I consistently draw upon to compare things in my life to. Whether it is in companies I have worked for, with organizations I have been a part of, or as part of my family, I am constantly going back to lessons learned and the philosophies of Michigan football. It was where I learned the lessons of treating people the right way, doing things the right way, giving it everything I have, and leaving it out there. Unfortunately, most experiences fail in comparison to Michigan's program. Most experiences cannot measure up to what we had at Michigan, but it's a great gauge to constantly return to.

Erick Anderson won the Butkus Award in 1991 as the nation's best collegiate linebacker. He's the only Wolverine to ever win the Butkus Award.

J. D. CARLSON

KICKER

1988–1991

MANY PEOPLE DON'T KNOW THIS, BUT BO SCHEMBECHLER really has a great sense of humor. He had nicknames for all the kickers. The theory was that he really didn't know our names. You couldn't figure out why you had the nickname you did. For instance, my nickname was "Herb." There was, of course, speculation as to why this was. Maybe it centered around me being a serious student. Perhaps Herb sounds geeky and I reminded Bo of a geek. Or maybe it was because of a television character named Herb Tarlek from *WKRP*. I have no idea, and I never asked him why. My buddy [and backup kicker] Gulam Khan's nickname was "Peanut." Now, he calls us by name, so I've confirmed that he really did know our names as players. It was just one of those things that really endeared him to all of the players. He made it fun. If something funny happened in the meeting unintended, people would be rolling on the floor, Bo included. It made it a lot more enjoyable, and it made us want to win more. Not that we needed any more incentive, but Bo's the type of person who gets the best out of you.

I grew up in Tallahassee, Florida, where Florida State is located. I was a very good student with a 3.8 grade-point average and was also the science student of the year. I also won a college scholarship to study Latin. My criteria for college was to find a school that was not only a dominant football program, but would also provide top-notch academics. My high school not

J. D. Carlson kicks one through the uprights during the Purdue game in 1991. While his 1989 debut as a starter against Notre Dame was forgettable, he had one of his most memorable outings the following week against UCLA.

only excelled in academics, but it also happened to be the winningest football program in Florida.

I knew what I was looking for in a college. So I took the top 25 teams in football and matched them up with the top academic institutions. The only school on that list was Michigan. I worked with my high school football coach to put together a video from his weekly television show. That's how big football was for our high school, my coach had his own TV program. We took clips of me from that show and sent them to Michigan.

Bobby Morrison was actually the guy who recruited me from Michigan. Being a kicker back in those days, they didn't throw scholarships around like they do today for kickers. I was actually in *Street and Smith*'s top seniors to watch, one of the top 15 kickers in the nation. I was all-state both junior and senior year and actually booted a 50-yard field goal. I ended up getting one scholarship offer, and that was from Tulane University. They were 0–11. I knew I wasn't going there.

I received other offers from Illinois and Michigan to walk on. I was accepted into Yale and met all of their coaches and toured the facilities. But at the same time, Michigan had dug out my video and gave me a hard look. Around April of my senior year, Michigan contacted me and I visited and met with Bo. Meeting Bo and seeing the facilities sealed the deal.

Bobby Bowden was a reason I understood the "big time" coach. I'd met with Florida State and also watched some games. Although I wasn't offered a scholarship, I still had a good understanding of how impressive a coach can be at a major program. But when I met Bo, he exuded the sense of tradition that I really wanted. Florida State was a good program but they had little tradition. Everything at Michigan with Bo felt it had always been and would always be. It was something you immediately wanted to be a part of.

I can remember my first game as a starter like it was yesterday. It was 1989, and we opened our season against Notre Dame. I had been battling for the starting job with another former walk-on, and he was a good friend of mine by the name of Gulam Khan. They didn't tell us who would be the starter until the day before. All I focused on was making my kicks in practice because I knew missing them would hurt my chances of starting. Following practice, the coaches pulled me aside and told me I'd start.

Although I prepared like I always had before high school games, I really hadn't considered what it was like to kick in front of one hundred thousand people. I'd been on the team for several years but being on the team and practicing are two different things. When people are actually rushing you and really trying to block your kick, that's an entirely different experience.

So I went out against Notre Dame and lined up to kick the extra point. It clanged off the left upright. Then, on the opening kickoff of the second half, Rocket Ismail returned it for a touchdown. The coaches took me out of the game and put my buddy Gulam in. My immediate thought was, "Hey, there were 10 other guys out there who should have gotten him!" But their thought was my placement of the kick was the reason for the return.

So when my buddy kicked off his first time, and Ismael ran back another touchdown, I admit I felt a little vindication. But Gulam ended up breaking his arm on the play, being absolutely pancaked by Notre Dame's fullback Anthony Johnson. So it was almost by default that I got back into the game.

The game ended pretty badly, too. On an onside kick, I literally hit the guy next to me. Usually, it's supposed to go downfield. I literally kicked it down the 30-yard line and hit the guy next to me. I'll never forget my position coach Jerry Hanlon getting me on the phone after I botched the onside kick and telling me something pretty compelling.

"You've got to decide that you want to play for this university," he bellowed. He was exactly right. I had all this time endeavored for this outcome. But I really didn't prepare myself. All I'd ever thought about doing was getting on the field. I never adequately considered what it all meant. The next game I proved to be properly vindicated.

I nailed four field goals against UCLA the next week and even kicked the game-winner. I'm almost thankful my buddy Gulam broke his arm and gave me the opportunity to start against UCLA. I hit the first field goal pretty early in the first quarter, and we took the lead. Something that really helped was hitting a kick at the end of the half. UCLA called a timeout as I lined up in an attempt to ice me. Obviously, they'd watched the Notre Dame game a week before. I made that kick, too, and I felt great going into the half. Although we were down, we battled back and forth and needed a drive and a two-point conversion to tie in the fourth quarter.

Elvis Grbac was the quarterback and he drove us down for the touchdown, but the two-point conversion failed. So here I was, going out to try another onside kick. As bad as the one was a week earlier, this one was absolutely perfect. It literally bounced 20 feet in the air, and Vada Murray caught it in stride, giving us the recovery. The guys drove down the field, and I had the opportunity to hit a chip shot. I converted the kick, and we won the game.

Another great experience was kicking the game-winner against Ohio State on the road. There were three seconds left, and the crowd was going nuts. I'll never forget kicking the field goal and the place going silent, except for the Michigan fans in our corner. You could hear the dull roar coming from another side of the stadium. Every now and then they show the game on ESPN Classic. All of my coworkers and friends will laugh because I literally jumped seven feet off the ground. It's unbelievable because if you knew me, you'd know how poor of an athlete I really am.

You can't really play it down. You're beating a significant rival, it gave us a share of the Big Ten championship, and kept them out of the Rose Bowl. We all ended up getting rings because we earned the share of the Big Ten.

You can't beat it. There is a lot of animosity against Ohio State. I was thankful because my brother was there and so was my family. My brother had come up to the team as a walk-on and a kicker. He traveled as my backup. It was a great feeling, and I was definitely lucky to have so many great memories.

When you play at Michigan, you're on a big stage. I think Michigan has worked very hard to develop a very special tradition. When I was a freshman, guys like Mark Messner and Jamie Morris made it very evident to us to uphold that tradition. It's not something that everybody who shows up there just becomes a part of it. The success is something you have to work hard to perpetuate. You need to lead by example. The people that aren't willing to pay the price either don't amount to anything or get cast aside early. It's not so much being a part of the tradition as it is doing everything you can to make a contribution to enhance that tradition.

J. D. Carlson was a three-time All–Big Ten selection as a kicker. His five field goals against Illinois in 1990 notched the win for Michigan.

BRIAN TOWNSEND
LINEBACKER
1988–1991

WHEN BO SCHEMBECHLER CAME IN TO RECRUIT ME, he told me that every kid who had played for him had won a Big Ten championship and played in the Rose Bowl. Every kid that played for him had had that experience. That was probably the number one factor that made me pick Michigan. I was a big fish in a small pond at my high school, Northwest High School in Cincinnati. We were second place in our league in football, basketball, and track. I wanted to win championships. I wanted a place where I would be challenged.

My father worked at Ford, was a blue-collar man, and always said, "You have to work for what you get." That was important to me. I liked that coach Schembechler wasn't a person who was going to promise anything. A lot of different coaches came in and tried to promise this and that.

Never winning a championship in high school and wanting to be challenged made me a little different than everyone else. I wanted to see what it was like to be on the other end; to be on the bench and have to work to get what you earned. I thought Michigan presented me with that challenge and opportunity, both educationally and athletically.

The philosophy never changed between Bo and coach Moeller. When Bo retired, I remember sitting at the press conference thinking, "Why me? I came to Michigan for you." In retrospect, I didn't realize that it was the

Michigan philosophy that made the program great. I looked at it as, "Bo was the man and if we lost Bo, we're going to lose everything." Bo implemented it, but every other coach made sure the culture stayed there.

Coach Moeller, coach Carr, and all the rest of the coaches let us know that nothing would change. There was a new head man, but the successful environment was still the same. The characteristics of Michigan would remain intact, and those who didn't adhere to it would be pushed aside.

As a young guy who had to prove himself, my relationship with Bo was mostly fearful. You had to earn Bo's respect. We really didn't have much of a relationship except for, if you did it right, you didn't hear anything. If you did it wrong, he was there and he would challenge you. I didn't feel that way with Mo because I was starting to play more as a junior and senior. Under Bo's leadership, the guy that trumped everybody was Bo. You would talk to the assistants, but you knew that in the end, Bo made the call.

Mo put a lot more power into his assistants. Bo was so domineering that I wonder if when Mo became the head coach he thought, "When I was an assistant, I didn't have enough power to get things done, so I'm going to give my assistants more power." You would deal with your assistant coaches. You could go in and talk to Mo, but he would put it back on the assistants. Mo would say, "This is what your assistant coach has said." He felt your assistant coach has watched you every day, watched the film on you, so he had the muscle. My relationship with either one wasn't as sound as it should have been. My real relationship was with the defensive coordinator, Lloyd Carr.

Lloyd was a guy that knew your potential. What I liked about Lloyd was that he would try different methods. He would challenge you by "pushing a player" to get it done. He would pull you aside to talk to you. You would get what I call "Lloyded," where you would get hit and hugged at the same time. I didn't understand it because you would think you were doing well, and he was hitting you, so you felt down. Then the next day he would be talking to you and hugging you.

I didn't think I was going to come back for my fifth year. The coaches wanted me to play two positions, switching between the "rover" and the "fox." Lloyd felt like I could do both. I went in to talk to him about it, and he said, "I think you can be an excellent player, but if you don't want to play . . ." I told him it wasn't that, I just didn't feel like I was getting it done.

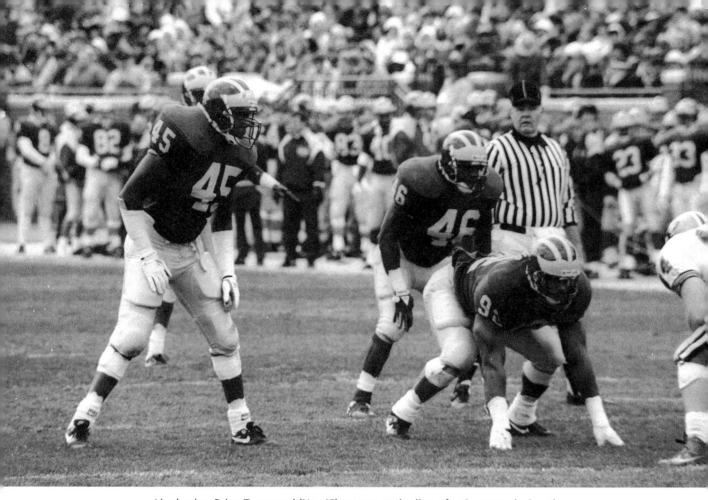

Linebacker Brian Townsend (No. 45) sets up at the line of scrimmage during the Purdue game in 1991. Townsend went to three Rose Bowls and played two seasons in the NFL before going into basketball coaching.

I felt like my tires were spinning. Lloyd said to me, "I will meet with you once a week in the summer. We will look at film and get a chance to look at how you play." I went from third to second on the depth chart.

Lloyd taught me that summer why coaches call specific offenses and defenses, how the defensive backs rotate, how the defensive linemen rotate, what my faults were, and how to correct them. In his summer tutelage I went on to become a drafted NFL player. It was all because he took an hour once a week during the summer to say, "Watch this film, look for this, and tell me what you think." He got into my mind and allowed me to grow mentally and understand the game of football from a better perspective. So that when I got on the field, I was like a coach.

If it weren't for Lloyd that summer, giving me confidence and intelligence, I don't think I would have had the senior season that I had. I have so much respect for Lloyd Carr that it's ridiculous. He taught me how to think the game. He said, "You don't have to be the fastest or the strongest or the quickest because mentally you can think faster and be stronger, and it will allow you to make plays."

After my wife, Rachel, passed away, my life totally changed. There were many days that I sobbed, wanting my life to be back to the way it was. You go through a great deal of depression and think, again, "How could this happen to me?" But what playing at Michigan did for me was allow me to be optimistic and see something in the worst, and make it the best.

One of the greatest things that helped me through Rachel's passing was something that Michigan taught me called "sudden change." When you're on defense, you're fighting to get stops. All of the sudden you get the stop and your offense gets the ball. Maybe they get the ball at the 20-yard line, or it was downed at the 5 or the 10. You come to the sidelines and you want that break. But what if the Wolverine offense fumbles the ball inside the 20-yard line? That's the worse-case scenario; it's in the red zone. All of the momentum is for the other team, and that's called "sudden change." You have to go through the sudden change of relaxation to the highest intensity level in the toughest situation in all of football.

297

If you came onto the field and said, "How could the offense put us in this situation? I'm so tired, I was just out here. Man, they've got a great opportunity to score." You would be doomed. But if you came on the field and said, "I accept this challenge. I'm glad I'm in this tough situation. I will find a way to get out of it with a field goal or no score at all."

That is what occurred in my life after a month of sobbing and feeling sorry for myself. I just said, "This is a matter of sudden change. I've got to adapt and look at this as a challenge. I've got to look at this as an optimistic situation and see how I can make this better." With the help of the Michigan family and the Ann Arbor community, I was able to put together some scholarship programs back in Ann Arbor in Rachel's name. That is what Michigan football has done for me. I don't think I would have got that from any other institution, organization, or culture. Michigan teaches you character. It makes you be a better father, husband, and community leader.

If I see another guy with an "M" ring, I know he has character, class, and a work ethic. Wolverines had to have perseverance, poise, and leadership. You had to have a desire to be the best, but at the same time, you had to be compatible with different situations for when you went through the worst. Being through the worst, you had to have pride, confidence, and optimism.

Brain Townsend is an assistant coach of men's basketball at Ohio University.

CORWIN BROWN

Defensive Back

1989–1992

IT WAS DEFINITELY THE HELMETS, THEY DRAW YOU IN and then, once you experience everything else, you're done. Growing up watching college football, I always noticed the team with the different helmets and I thought, "What is it about those guys? They're jumping all around, they're crazy, and they're always on TV." I would see them all the time, so there was a lot of interest on my part. The funky helmets and Bo Schembechler; it was a no-brainer to me. Michigan was where I wanted to play.

When I went on my official visit, Lance Dottin was my host. Lance was the greatest dude. We're still best friends to this day. He was so nice. I thought he was the most unselfish guy in the world. Lance tried to take me everywhere, show me everything, and told me all about the school. He had only been there a year, but it was the way he was describing the whole experience at Michigan. Honestly, I couldn't even fathom it. When he was telling me about it and how everyone was supporting the program, I wanted to sign up right then and there.

The recruiting trip was nice because we were hanging out with the basketball players and the football players. All of a sudden I was meeting guys whom I had been watching the past few years, like Chris Calloway and Derrick Walker, who are Chicago guys like me.

My senior year, there was this function at the Palmer House in Chicago, where some of the recruits would come and talk to Bo. Michigan wasn't sure if they were going to take me, but I knew I wanted to go there. I was sitting in this room with my parents. We didn't have anything to say to Bo because, first of all, we were all in awe. All we wanted to hear him say was, "We want you to come to Michigan." At the time, Bo wasn't ready to say that, so I was just looking at him, thinking, "Man, I can't believe I'm sitting here with this dude!"

Bo was something else. Once I got to Michigan, we developed a pretty cool relationship. I was a young guy, so he didn't pay too much attention to me, except for this one incident. Chris Calloway was Bo's favorite guy of all time. Chris and I would fight in spring practice every single day. One day, toward the end of practice while we were fighting, Bo came up to me and yelled, "You keep your hands off of him; you haven't done anything around here yet." He grabbed me, and I thought, "I guess he likes me, at least he knows who I am." Bo was so cool.

The last time I saw Bo outside of Ann Arbor was at the airport. I was in line, and Bo and his wife were about to go to Europe. I saw him and said, "Hey, coach Bo." He started talking to me, saying, "Corwin Brown, you're a clown," which he always said. Bo left and then came back two seconds later. He handed me his mail and said, "We're going out of the country, can you make sure you mail this?" I said, "OK, Coach, I'll mail it." After he left, all the people around me were asking, "How do you know Bo?" I was the man of the hour at the airport because I knew Bo.

When Gary Moeller took over for Bo, the offense became more wide open. We used a no-huddle and we were passing all over the place. On defense, though, we were pretty much the same. What Mo and Bo stood for, believed in, and what they preached was still Michigan football. That part didn't change at all. The only difference was the offensive strategy and the scheme. Other than that, it was the same. It was sad when Bo left, I can still remember that day.

I didn't feel cheated about Bo leaving. I felt only sadness, because it was a health issue for Bo. When he spoke to us he was in tears, which in turn put a lot of us in tears. We just wanted Bo to be all right. You still knew that Michigan football was Bo Schembechler, whether he was coaching or not didn't make a whole lot of difference.

Safety Corwin Brown flashes a signal at the line of scrimmage during the Florida State game in 1991. Brown was named a team captain his senior season and finished his career with a Rose Bowl win before being selected in the 1993 NFL draft.

I didn't know Mo really well until my senior year, when I was elected captain. After that honor, I had a lot of conversations with him. Mo was cool. You could always go to his office and talk to him. Mo always wanted to know the pulse of the team. He'd ask about each guy, what their mood was like, and how they felt about the game.

In the beginning, everybody wants to leave because they think they should be playing. Then halfway through the freshman season, they love the school and they're thinking, "How could I even think about leaving?"

At Michigan, during training camp, our seniors addressed the team. Halfway through camp, senior speeches began. The offense went first, followed by the defense. Guys got up and talked about their experiences at Michigan; what it was like and what it meant to them. It was amazing. It broke me down. Ninety-five percent of the seniors said that when they were freshman, they hated it and wanted to transfer. It was during the senior speeches that I learned about the guys. Players really grew, and I bonded with my teammates. The speeches pulled me in, and everyone takes care of one another. Not every school is like that.

Bobby Abrams gave the one speech I'll never forget. It was one of the most incredible speeches I've ever heard. Hearing Abrams talk about his experience, and what it meant to him, and what it made him do, I thought, "This is Michigan football."

I redshirted one year; so I had two senior speeches. In 1991, my speech was a poem called, "Fuel for a Dream." It was about the emotions and the energy that made you go on no matter what. I just talked about being 100 percent, always trying hard, whom I played for, and how much I loved the guys I played with. You could say it was about a number of things, but it was mostly about why I chose Michigan and what drove me, because I was really driven. That was the only way I was going to make it. I wanted everyone to buy into what I had.

Holding the Rose Bowl trophy after we had won in 1993 was my full-circle moment. I had a crappy game. It was the worst game that I ever played at Michigan. But at the same time, we won. Nobody will remember the game that I played, but everybody will remember that we won. For my class, that was our biggest accomplishment. Washington had put it to us the year before and they were talking stuff. Our senior class was determined to go out with a win.

My class was a part of five Big Ten championship teams. It meant a lot to us, but the way Washington destroyed us the year before, if we didn't win that last game, it wouldn't have been as special. We wanted that game. I remember holding that Rose Bowl trophy; Dwayne Ware and I were taking pictures. It was right at that moment that I thought, "This is what I came to Michigan for."

What it means to be a Wolverine is doing it the hardest way, the best way, and not even thinking about taking a shortcut. It's giving everything you've got to the task at hand. It sounds like a cliché, but unless you've been there, you wouldn't understand.

Corwin Brown was named All–Big Ten in 1992. He played in the NFL for nine seasons with the New England Patriots, New York Jets, and the Detroit Lions. As a member of the Patriots, he played in Super Bowl XXXI.

DERRICK ALEXANDER
WIDE RECEIVER
1989–1993

I NEVER LOST A SINGLE GAME TO OHIO STATE in my five years at Michigan. I loved to beat the Buckeyes. That rivalry is unlike any other. That game usually determines who the champion of the Big Ten will be. I remember during my senior season, Ohio State was undefeated. The week before they came to Ann Arbor, they were holding up their roses on TV, expecting to coast their way to the Rose Bowl. We ended up shutting them out 28–0. It also prevented them from going to the Rose Bowl. The Ohio State games were the best games I ever played in. Nothing else compares. I used to take visits to Ohio State when I was in high school and knew how important it was for the school to beat Michigan. When Ohio State beat Michigan, the players get gold pants. None of the guys who played against me ever received any gold pants. The most memorable Ohio State games were when we went there. Their fans are wild and loud. I remember one year Elvis [Grbac] complaining to the refs that he couldn't hear anything because of how loud it was.

I always liked Michigan. I loved watching the Wolverines on TV. I definitely liked watching them more than Michigan State. When it came down to choosing a school, I was hesitant to go to Michigan because they were predominantly a rushing school. But I was talking to Gary Moeller, and he promised me the offense would have more of a passing game.

I did everything in high school. I played running back, receiver, defense, and I returned punts. I was used to getting the ball a lot. Michigan guaranteed me that I would see the ball a lot, and it was time for their game plan to change. I couldn't help but agree to be a Wolverine.

Gary was the guy who persuaded me to come to Michigan. When he took over for Bo, I reminded him of the promise he made about getting me the ball as a receiver, especially since he was now the head coach.

Bo Schembechler's an impressive guy. He was a great motivator and really got you ready to play a game. You saw him on TV for so long, and I was thrilled to get one year with him. Bo is always associated with winners. When I was a freshman, the new football facility wasn't ready yet. We were having our meetings at Crisler Arena. After one of our meetings, coach Moeller was leaving the room and was coming down the steps and just fell down. I think he broke his ankle because of the fall. Before we left for the day, Bo went out and really made fun of Moeller.

"Now, this is the way you walk down the steps," he announced, tiptoeing slowly down each step. It was pretty funny.

Coming out of high school, you know about the Michigan tunnel and the Michigan helmet. I even liked the black turf shoes Michigan wore because of the turf they had at the time. It's something you dream about. But when it actually happens, it's unbelievable. You're running into the biggest stadium in the country, and all of these people are watching you. It's difficult to put into words. When you actually play, that's a whole different experience.

We always had a weekly press conference before the games and I made a prediction during the 1992 season that we would beat Michigan State. George Perles, Michigan State's head coach, responded. "Who's this guy?" he asked. "I've never heard of him and he hasn't done anything special." His comments fired me up and I ended up having a big game. I returned the ball for a touchdown off of a punt and also had 108 return yards. We won the game 35–10.

It was a great game against Illinois back in 1993, and we were really in control of that game. I had a 90-yard touchdown in that game and I felt we really were going to win that game. We had the ball, running the clock out, and we ended up fumbling it. Illinois recovered and scored, winning the game as time expired. Even though it was one of my best games, losing to Illinois hurt a lot more.

I can remember the season Penn State came into the Big Ten [1993] as well. The Nittany Lions were supposed to be the toughest team to ever grace the Big Ten, and everyone was worried that they would just dominate the conference. We ended up going there for the game and we had to take two little planes to get there, the offense being on one and the defense on another. It was a tough game, and we were losing in the first half. But I ran a punt back at the end of the half, and it seemed to fire us up. We ended up winning the game, and it was by far one of the more memorable games I ever played in.

Derrick Alexander finds a way into the end zone after a catch against Minnesota in 1992. Alexander also returned punts for the Wolverines, including a 79-yarder for a touchdown in the 1994 Outback Bowl, an Outback Bowl record that still stands.

The Rose Bowl is the best bowl game I'd ever been to. We went to the Rose Bowl three times in my five years at Michigan. When you go somewhere else for a bowl game, you realize just how special the Rose Bowl is. It's an unbelievable experience. The Rose Bowl is the granddaddy of them all, and other bowl games are just games to play. If you go to the Rose Bowl, you know you've done something special.

Playing with the guys I had the opportunity to was amazing. I played alongside Ty Law, Amani Toomer, Tim Biakabutuka, Steve Everitt, Leroy Hoard, and there were so many guys who went on to the pros. If you look back at the seasons I played, it's amazing to see how many great guys I played with. It makes you feel good that you were able to call them teammates.

Michigan is all about tradition. It's something that cannot be explained. You have to be a part of it to truly understand it. Michigan is long-standing tradition, and to keep up that tradition for as many years as Michigan has is difficult. But it's a dream to help keep that tradition alive. You go up there and expect to win and it happens. Playing hard, winning games, and playing in Rose Bowls is part of the experience. The difference is at Michigan, it's expected.

Derrick Alexander still holds the Michigan record for the longest reception when he had a 90-yard touchdown against Illinois. Derrick spent time with the Cleveland Browns, Baltimore Ravens, Kansas City Chiefs, and Minnesota Vikings in the NFL.

The
NINETIES

MERCURY HAYES
WIDE RECEIVER
1992–1995

ISTILL RECEIVE FAN MAIL FROM PEOPLE WHO REMEMBER that game against Virginia in 1995, where I made the last-second, game-winning catch. I didn't want to lose that game. I told myself that I would catch every pass thrown to me in the Pigskin Classic. It was the first game of my senior year. And it came with a national audience. It was the only college football game on TV. Even though we were losing in the fourth quarter, I was mentally focused. I was trying to perform, not only for Michigan, but also for the NFL scouts. I was given the opportunity and hooked up with Scott Dreisbach in the end zone at the end of the game. Dragging my foot in the end zone was planned. It was one of those moves that you practice. It's one of those things as an athlete that you want to be practicing. As an athlete, you're always thinking of the last play. You always have to be mentally prepared for it. Whether it is the first catch or the last one, you're always mentally prepared to make that kind of a catch. But it was definitely one of the games I'll never forget, and neither have many of the fans.

I ended up at Michigan because of the fantastic opportunities the school presented. Many schools recruited me, but no school offered everything that Michigan could. It was Gary Moeller who brought me to Ann Arbor.

Gary was a Michigan guy. He was well-rounded and gave every guy the opportunity to be the best he could be. He was definitely a Michigan guy

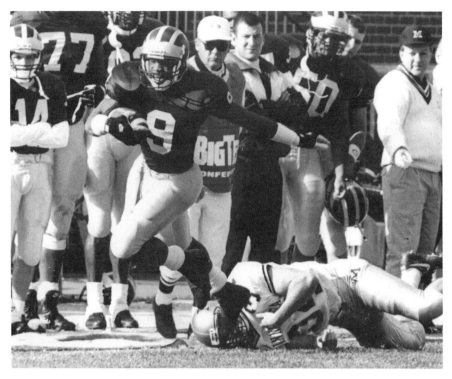

Mercury Hayes slips a tackle and heads down the sideline against Minnesota in 1992. This play was similar to his first career touchdown at Michigan when the University of Houston traveled north from his hometown for a 1993 game in Ann Arbor.

and a hell of a coach. It was very disappointing when Gary was dismissed. [Moeller was fired after allegedly exhibiting unprofessional behavior at a restaurant.] It was rough to see him go. But he bounced back and ended up coaching again in the NFL. It was definitely an eye-opener. Although you're a Michigan Man, we learned a valuable lesson from him that he constantly taught us: no one man is bigger than the team. It's the outlook we took from that day forward. I was very disappointed as a Michigan member to see a Michigan Man like Gary go through something like he did. By being on the staff prior to Gary's dismissal, Lloyd Carr was the ideal guy to succeed Gary. Lloyd picked up and kept going. We didn't miss a beat and the records show that. Michigan does a thorough background check with not only its athletes but also their entire Michigan family. Lloyd took what he learned from Mo and already had been the defensive coordinator. He took over and allowed us to follow in his footsteps.

During the 1995 season, Lloyd let both Dreisbach and Griese go at it and let the best man win. It raised the competition level between the two. It was a great opportunity to have the ability to compete with guys like that every week. But it's Michigan. You're surrounded by guys like Derrick Alexander, Amani Toomer, Tim Biakabutuka, Ty Law—I could just keep going on and on with names. It was like any given Saturday, it was on. It was great to be around guys like that and it was what it's all about it.

You could already see how good Charles Woodson was going to be, as a freshman. Coming into camp, he was a very confident guy, and I don't think even he knew how good he was. He was making plays as a young fellow coming in. He took the initiative from coach Carr and was obviously one of the best cornerbacks to come out of Michigan. To play both ways and make the phenomenal plays he could make in Division I football was great to see. When you see another young cat coming in and performing to the level he was as a freshman was exciting. He had a confidence and a swagger coming into Michigan, and he stepped right in for Ty Law, who graduated the season before.

312

Todd Collins and I had a connection as quarterback and receiver. It always seemed as if he knew where I would be, and I always knew where to be at the right place and right time. Griese and Dreisbach were two different styles of quarterback, and it would throw you off. I caught a few passes from Tom Brady, although he was only a freshman when I was a senior. He was just a young fellow.

From day one, you're on an absolute high when you run out of the tunnel into Michigan Stadium and jump to touch that banner. It's like you never come down. It's unbelievably exciting. When you come back home after the season, it's all anyone wants to talk about. It's a beautiful feeling to be experiencing that.

During my sophomore year, I made an acrobatic catch against Ohio State, and that play stands out. Todd Collins threw it over my right shoulder, and I had to turn my hands the other way to make the catch.

It definitely gets no better than the Rose Bowl. It's unbelievable. It's more of a statement to little kids and society that Michigan is continuously playing in the Rose Bowl, the granddaddy of them all. Being in the Rose Bowl is quite an experience because of the hype behind it. The Big Ten schools always go to that game, and for that particular game you are representing the Big Ten.

Playing the University of Houston during my sophomore year was exciting since I was from Houston. U of H was coming into Ann Arbor, and coach Cam Cameron pulled me aside before the game.

"Son, let me tell you something," he said. "If you catch this out route, and you run the right route, you'll end up scoring a touchdown." It was amazing to me that Houston came to the Big House and I would end up scoring my first touchdown—a 43-yard touchdown pass—against them. It's something I'll never forget because Cam told me specifically that I would score.

"You'll get the ball because you're the first read," he explained. "The way they play, they isolate on the side. If you catch the ball, you will score." True to his word, I caught the ball, and their lead cornerback slid right off my leg. I ran in for the score.

A Michigan Wolverine is a man with dignity and a man with pride. If you give it your all at Michigan, you get everything out of it. As you're taught when you're younger, you always need to seize the opportunity. Being a Wolverine is being that man who seizes the moment.

Mercury Hayes recorded 180 yards and 2 touchdowns, including the game-winner, against Virginia in the 1995 Pigskin Classic. After college, Hayes played in the NFL and Canadian Football League.

ROD PAYNE

CENTER

1993–1996

I WAS LOOKING TO DO SOMETHING DIFFERENT when I went to Michigan. I'm from South Florida, and everyone thinks it's a paradise. For me, growing up was an experience of looking to get out. In South Florida, all you heard about was Florida, Florida State, and Miami; they were the powerhouse schools. During my official visit to Michigan, I fell in love with the school. Michigan was what college should be. If you were going to take all the characteristics of what college is, and what a storied program is, the only school that would come up would be Michigan.

Growing up that far south, you don't have any reason to go to Detroit. I had never ventured north of Georgia before coming up to visit Michigan. Over the years, I've heard many Michiganders complain about the weather and ask how I could have left Florida. But that's more of a condition of them growing up in Michigan. Everything that seemed negative to them seemed new and different to me.

When you first get to Michigan, it's football, it's not the cookie cutter story that people think it is. It's getting handed your pads, your helmet, your boots and rifle and told to stand in line. You were busy working; busy building the inner blocks and gears to Michigan football, as opposed to what everybody else is seeing as the story—all the wins. When you show up as a football player, it's after all the recruiting and stroking of the egos. It's where the rubber meets the road when you get handed that first playbook.

Rod Payne prepares to snap the football to quarterback Brian Griese during a 1995 game. Payne was the 12th center from Michigan to become an All-American, and David Baas recently became the 13th.

You don't really have time to consider what it is to be a Michigan football player. That's a good thing, because at the end of your career, you hold it so much dearer to you. As you start to come up for air, you realize the inevitability of not being a Michigan football player any longer, which makes you pay attention to what it was about.

People always talk about recruits, but there are a lot of recruits who were told a lot of big things and then never played a down. They may not have made it past two-a-days, but when the reporters were writing about them they were the going to be the greatest players ever at Michigan. They were going to be the next so-and-so and then they never even made it to the first game of the season. It's what you do, and that's where Bo left the legacy in "Those Who Stay Will Be Champions"—it's not "those who arrive."

The transition from coach Moeller to coach Carr was a weird deal. It was tough because the seniors who were coming back—Jarrett Irons, Steve King, Chuck Winters, and I—felt that if anybody else comes in here who's not a Michigan guy, we're history! A lot of people didn't understand that. It was a tough time when we lost Gary over what we thought was BS, and we still do. We let it be known: "If you guys are looking for a coach, you better look close by." It was great that Michigan gave Lloyd that interim title for a period of time. The seniors on the team rallied behind him to the point where he had a successful season, and the rest is history.

Make no bones about it, Michigan is a corporation. It's big, and unfortunately there are many variables now that are different than when our fathers were watching Michigan football. It was the worst moment to see Gary thrown to the wolves. We felt the university really didn't back him. They didn't say, "Screw this, this is not an issue." At first players felt, "Let bygones be bygones." When that wasn't going to be the case, our attitude was, "the hell with this." We were pissed. We weren't pissed at the university, so to speak, but more at the way the fans and the media reacted.

Michigan has a bunch of codes we live by, and one of them is about the critic. It's not the critic that counts; it's not the man who points out where the strong man stumbles, or how the doer of deeds could have done them better. It was at that point we realized who the critics were and who was part of the team. Coach Moeller's downfall was an unfortunate event where we recognized a lot of critics. But it built a closer and stronger team.

Another code that we live by at Michigan is the expectation for the position. What that means is you take out the individual—the person who wears the helmet, wears the position, wears the crown is held to the same standard as everyone else before him. I was the 12th All-American center at Michigan. David Baas just became the 13th. Michigan Men really do play at a special place that, for all intents and purposes, has everything intact.

When you start talking about tradition and what it means to do something, for a very brief time, a very significant part of a continuation of tradition is in your hands. At least for the guys I was with—they worked, they were just like the other guys; they didn't want to be the ones who didn't perpetuate.

Football is not the glorified story people think it is. It can be, but only after hard work and sacrifice. That's the reality of when you show up with your pads. My coaches loved me, but if I wasn't the player I was, I wouldn't have been MVP or team captain. My coaches wouldn't have good things to say about me.

The hallmark of any Michigan Man's career is when he gets that senior ring, that senior pinky ring. The "M" ring is a campaign, a rite of passage, rather than just a moment. You have your moments where you realize you're hot, you're going to start, your moments of big losses like the Colorado game, and big wins like the Remy Hamilton kick against Notre Dame. You have all those memories, but it comes down to what you're going to take with you— it's the friendships and the journey of that struggle with those guys who were just like you.

When we came in as freshmen, we had guys from all over the place— Texas, Florida, Georgia, Michigan. All these personalities of different people, we were all young kids coming in as 17- and 18-year-old knuckleheads. Most of us hadn't smoked it, drunk it, screwed it, or done anything yet. But under the guise of the team for the next four or five years, we would go through all of those things together. You really do cherish that.

317

A two-time first-team All–Big Ten selection at center, Rod Payne was a co-captain and a first-team All-American his senior year. Payne could snap the ball with either hand.

CHRIS FLOYD

FULLBACK

1994–1997

I REMEMBER DURING THE 1997 SEASON I GOT INTO an argument with Ben Huff over a seat in the team meeting room. When you go into the team meeting room, all the seniors sit in the front and everyone else sits in the back. There was a seat available in the front, but I didn't know he'd claimed the seat. So I sat down because his name wasn't on it. Ben Huff came in and told me to get out of the seat. Well, we went back and forth for a while, and the guys in the room were saying, "C'mon, Floyd, just give the seat up for Huff." Now, we're supposed to be dead quiet when Lloyd comes in. I told Ben just to find another seat, but he was intent on getting this one. When Lloyd walked in and saw us arguing over the seat, he sent us both home for the day. Nevertheless, we met up at Schembechler Hall, headed to my apartment, and killed a six-pack. Despite both of our competitive natures, we put our differences aside. First and foremost, we were teammates.

When I was going through the recruiting process, I was leaning toward Notre Dame and Colorado. What set Michigan apart was when my parents came to Ann Arbor with me. Ann Arbor was also close to home. Coming to Michigan made my mom happy, and I was glad I made the decision to attend Michigan as well. When Notre Dame came up here, we beat the Fighting Irish pretty badly. And Colorado's program fell apart over the years. It all worked out for me.

Chris Floyd finds an opening during a 1997 game against Colorado. Floyd was a senior fullback on the 1997 team that won the Big Ten title, the Rose Bowl, and a national championship.

Coach Carr was still the defensive coordinator when I was in high school. But he also recruited me, since Detroit was in his area. He influenced my parents on Michigan and he would call every day when I was still in high school. He didn't call to talk to me. He called to talk to my parents. I guess he figured if he could convince my parents to like Michigan, he could get me to like it, too. Coach Carr always let us go out and play. He was a great leader for us. I enjoyed every moment playing for him, and I was thrilled when he was named the head coach after being the interim.

The first start I ever had was against Virginia in 1995. The Cavaliers were a very beefy opponent. Looking back, they out-muscled us, out-hustled us, and out played us. To be in that game after four quarters was amazing. You would have thought we should have been blown out. But it was a big time game. It taught me a lot about playing in the tough times. Many times during that game I thought we would lose. But I learned that it takes more than one guy to get it all to turn your way.

The mediocre years at Michigan were rough. After we won the national championship, we saw just how close we were to winning games during those other seasons. We should have been competing for national championships then, too. During the summer of 1997, I remember talking with [teammate] Eric Mayes and telling him how there was no reason we shouldn't win every game. I can remember it like it was yesterday. I told him Iowa was the toughest team to beat, and it turned out that way during 1997. It was one of those things where our team spirit was so high. It turned out where we would actually look forward to practices, where in the past we wouldn't be so happy about it. That year was definitely an awesome trip.

My best personal game was against Notre Dame in 1997. It was the game I showed the coaches I could be a complete player. I was absolutely flawless in that game. I scored a touchdown, and can distinctly remember punishing guys who tried to sack Griese. I remember pancaking a guy on a blitz and wondering what Greg Mattison [Notre Dame's defensive coordinator] was thinking as he watched that. Back when he was coaching at Michigan, he didn't always see my best at practice. I really wanted to know his reaction after I put a hit like that on their linebacker.

I watched the Iowa game during that year from the sideline because of an ankle injury, but that game was scary. It was like everything we had worked so hard for was going to be lost because of this one game.

When Tim Dwight ran back a 61-yard punt for a touchdown at the end of the first half, we couldn't believe it. We ended up pulling it out at the end. When Marcus Ray picked off the pass in the fourth quarter, we were relieved. I could have had a heart attack after that game.

One of the best moments during 1997 was beating Northwestern. They'd beaten us two years in a row, and it just sucked. To finally get some sweet revenge against them was the best. I can speak for the others guys who played in saying that Northwestern had been lucky. It was time to put that all to an end. I was glad to beat them.

The Penn State game was one of the best of all time. That team had our number for years. Let me tell you about playing at Penn State. We would get phone calls all night before the game, [the callers] talk so much garbage to you. It gets you fired up. We ended up unplugging the phones because they were ringing so much. To go in there as underdogs took pressure off of us. Penn State was sitting at the top of the mountain in the Big Ten, but I knew the whole time that we'd beat the Nittany Lions. Even though they had Curtis Enis, I knew he wouldn't get anything done against our defense.

Even sweeter was going into a hostile environment like that and walking out with the stadium silent. You could hear a pin drop at the end of the game. I remember going around and thanking our fans who showed up. It's a tough place to play. I remember one year, a snowstorm hit before the game. It had an effect on the game. Mercury Hayes was running up the field wide open and would have surely caught a touchdown pass. While he's looking for the ball, a snowball comes out of the stands and blasts him in the face. Their fans would also pelt us with snowballs on the sidelines. We dealt with a lot of that from Penn State fans, and to go up there and do to them what we did was the best feeling.

I remember the Charles Woodson and Marcus Ray battle with David Boston during the game against Ohio State in 1997. But there were a lot of other battles going on, too. Andy Katzenmoyer and Antoine Whitfield were just two of the weapons they had that year. But we prevailed. I look back at the game and just say, "Wow." Every year, it seemed Ohio State was supposed to beat us, but we always rose to the occasion. It's easy to be an underdog because the pressure is off.

321

Playing in the Rose Bowl meant a lot to me. It was great to get our first Big Ten championship and our first Big Ten outright title in a long while. For us to finally get in that position was great, especially for me. I remember at the Senior Bowl after the 1997 season, I met Florida's defensive back Fred Weary, and he was showing off his national championship rings. I remember thinking, "Wow, I have one of those coming." For years and years, I wanted to go to Pasadena, and it was the icing on the cake for my final year at Michigan.

It was a big relief to finally win a national championship at Michigan. I had a Big Ten ring and a national championship ring all in the same year. It was a relief walking around with some big metal on my hand. That ring means the most to me. The guys I help out with now have fire in their eyes when they talk about a national championship. [Michigan wide receiver]

Jason Avant still walks around, talking about, with some changes here or there, we could have won the last two bowl games. That ring still speaks for itself, and the guys playing now want one, too. They know how close they have come in the past to having perfect seasons and now they want it more than ever.

Being a part of this program is like a family. Everyone loves one another here, and it's the honest-to-God truth. Currently, I work at the University of Michigan, and I earned this job because of Lloyd Carr. He helped me when I needed it. I know that if he couldn't have helped me, he would have found someone who could. You cherish being a Wolverine for life because you know there will always be a Wolverine ready to help you.

Chris Floyd played in the NFL for the Cleveland Browns and New England Patriots before coming back to work at the University of Michigan.

BEN HUFF

DEFENSIVE TACKLE

1994–1997

I WAS ALWAYS "THE LEGACY" BECAUSE MY DAD PLAYED for Michigan. That's why the Wolverines recruited me. My parents met at Michigan, and I grew up in Charlotte, North Carolina, as a Michigan fan. As a little kid, I remember running from sports bar to sports bar trying to find the Michigan game on TV. From an early age I had the maize and blue in me.

When I got into football, my dad never really pushed Michigan on me too much; he did let me know about the school's tradition. We had relatives up there; so when we visited I always went to the stadium and into the locker room. Seeing the program from the inside made it much more important for me to go there. Going to Michigan was a really big deal for my family and me.

I was a big fan of coach Gary Moeller; he was an old-school coach. He obviously knew my dad. He actually called me "Marty" a few times, which I didn't appreciate. We used to joke around about that. When he was let go, we were surprised by the whole situation. Coach Moeller was a good leader. At Michigan, no one spends a whole lot of time dwelling on things because the next season is coming. Everything moves along pretty quick.

The transition to coach Carr was pretty easy because I was a defensive player and he had been my defensive coordinator. I wanted coach Carr to have the same success as every previous Michigan coach. They always talk about the team, and I don't think there's a coach who's bigger than the team. Once we switched to Lloyd, everybody backed him 100 percent.

Ben Huff (53) joins in on a tackle of an Indiana ball carrier with teammate Sam Sword (93) during their 1996 Big Ten match-up.

My dad was a linebacker, and I came to Michigan as a linebacker. But early on the defense changed. Coaches started moving faster guys, running backs, to linebacker. I was on the traveling team as a freshman and sophomore, but I wasn't playing. I could see the other guys they were putting in, and I asked the coaches in spring ball if I could play scout team defensive line. I did well, and they said, "If you get bigger, maybe you can play this."

In the off-season I conditioned and put on weight. It ended up being a good fit for me. I went from being an average linebacker to being a faster D-lineman and defensive tackle. I took it upon myself to make the switch. I was just a guy who had to find a spot. Playing was the most important thing to me. I was willing to do whatever.

It was tough early in 1997. I tore my anterior cruciate ligament (ACL) in camp. Once I returned to the team, besides doing rehab and going to class, I became almost like a coach. Brady Hoke was the defensive line coach, and he had a lot of confidence in me. He would have me help out with some of the younger guys. We had Josh Williams, Rob Renes, and one of my good buddies, Glen Steele, who was in my class. That's how I made it through the season.

I was happy to be a part of it. I was happy to be around. I was happy for the whole situation. It was a difficult time; being a fifth-year senior, thinking you may get another year due to a medical redshirt and then all of a sudden you're denied. I addressed the team and let them know that I didn't have any regrets as far as the season, being injured. I just didn't know if I was going to play football again.

Injuries are part of the game. It's all about perseverance. I see guys get hurt all the time, and they just don't think they can come back from it. I'm not one of those guys. When the injury happened, I didn't doubt that I was going to play again. That was my thought. Some people doubted me, and I used that as fuel for the fire. I worked hard. I've torn that ACL again. I've done it twice now. I've had a number of surgeries, and each time something happens I think about that—I think about leaving on my own terms and I work harder. And here I am still playing.

During our first four years our class lost four games each season. There were only five of us, scholarship-wise, who stayed for our fifth year: Steele, Brian Griese, Zach Adami, Rob Swett, and me. It was a testament to us that we had some mediocre years and then topped it off with a national championship. It was pretty special. That class, and the guys in that class, are my best memories.

I lost to Ohio State once in five years. If you ever see guys who played for Ohio State or played in the Big Ten, those are the kind of memories you keep—Old Bragging Rights. My fourth year, they were undefeated and going to the Rose Bowl. They were ranked No. 2, and we went into Columbus and beat them 13–9. I remember being on the field with them, thinking, "They don't think they can win." It was just an odd feeling because at Michigan winning is everything. They instill that in you from early in your career. To have the sense that another team on the field just doesn't feel they can beat you is a weird feeling, especially a team with the caliber of players and coaches of Ohio State and the record they had had during the nineties. They had some great players, Orlando Pace and all those guys. I could just tell that they didn't think they could beat us. I felt that a lot throughout my career when we played them.

Anywhere you go, people ask, "Where did you go to school? Where did you play college ball?" When I say, "Michigan," I get the same response, "Wow! That must have been pretty special." It's the elite of college football and a big part of my life. It's unique. Some people will call it arrogance. Some people will call it cocky. It is what it is. People have their opinions. But pretty much universally Michigan's going to be at the top of everything: tradition, the uniform, the fight song, and the stadium.

The fact that I could become a Michigan Wolverine was very special for my dad; he'd been through the summers, the training, and the practice. He knew more than anybody what I was going through. It was fun for him. I would take six or seven guys to see him on weekends and we would barbecue. It was a very fun time for us.

Ben Huff played in the NFL for the Atlanta Falcons and is currently a member of the Arena Football League's Dallas Desperados.

KRAIG BAKER

KICKER

1995–1998

LAST FALL I WAS TOLD BEFORE ATTENDING A FRIEND'S WEDDING that I'd bet-ter not forget my national championship ring. The groom happened to be an enormous Michigan fan, and the first thing he asked to see was my ring. By the end of the evening, his father nudged me, and said, "The wedding ring ranks pretty high. But it's one notch below his chance to wear your championship ring. This is the biggest day of his life and he's happier about wearing your ring."

In this small little world, Michigan is everything. It's like that all over. My sister has told me stories of where she would get off the plane in a foreign country, and random people would come to her and say, "Go Blue," because she was wearing a shirt with a Michigan helmet on it. Even in third world countries, Michigan is known.

I didn't start kicking in football until my freshman year in high school. Since the age of five, I was always on the soccer field. I went out to our high school football game and watched the guy kick that night. On Saturday morning, I set out to see how I could kick. After a few broken windows, I decided there was something else I wanted to do. After three years of kicking in high school, I attended a national kicking camp, and after the completion of that camp, I had 20 scholarship offers from schools. I narrowed it to three: Michigan, Michigan State, and Notre Dame.

In Ann Arbor, I seemed to click. Coach Gary Moeller was still the head coach, and we really hit it off. In my heart, I knew I wanted to be a Michigan Wolverine.

The first time I ever played a game in Michigan Stadium I ended up punting. I knew I would get a chance to play the game and I can remember jumping pretty high and touching the banner. Knowing there are 110,000 people out there as you sprint out of the tunnel is a feeling unlike any other.

My four years at Michigan are best described as a roller coaster. But my feelings when I reflect on my experience at Michigan are still very positive. The competition between Jay Feely and me was very intense. There were games where we wouldn't know who was going to kick off. The hardest part of the game was before the game. A lot of adversity was thrown at me. The neat thing about what happened at Michigan was the closeness between Jay and me. Although we were fierce competitors, we would both pray for one another before the games.

Even though I ended up playing behind Jay during my senior season, I knew it wasn't God's will for me. And I was very much at peace with that. It was my strong faith that really helped me through some of the tough spots. But it was several teammates, Jay included, and their similarly strong faith that was very inspiring. It was definitely an up-and-down career, but the 1997 season made the struggles worthwhile. Everyone I talk to when they find out I played for Michigan in the late nineties asks if I played for the national championship team. It's great to be able to smile and say I was a member of that team. And there were some moments and games that stand out from the rest.

There was a lot of talk before that Ohio State game, especially with David Boston talking about the Buckeyes beating us by two or three touchdowns. We were very focused and knew if we went out and played well, in our minds, no one in the country could stop us. Ohio State week is a week of its own. Everything is a little different that week. Going into it, coach Carr was very excited, as were the rest of the coaches. And because of the magnitude of the game, they're a little uptight, too. I remember him smirking about David Boston's comments, saying to us, "We have a chance to go undefeated. You would think Ohio State would realize that and not attempt to pump us up anymore." He knew the team didn't need any more motivation. We only won by six, but even when they had the ball they really never threatened us.

The Rose Bowl was different than anything we experienced as team. But for me, it was similar. Before the game, coach Carr had not settled on his

Kraig Baker in action during the midnineties. Baker was a grade school soccer player who took up placekicking his freshman year of high school. By his senior season he had scholarship offers from 20 schools around the country. *Photo courtesy of Per Kjeldsen*

kicker. As was the case for the season, Jay and I didn't know who would be handling the duties. We both knew how important the moment was. Neither one of us wanted to be a spectator. The importance of the Rose Bowl—now a national championship game—weighed heavily on our minds. We both wanted to kick.

I credit the Lord with the unbelievable strength during the time leading up to the game. I felt stronger as every day progressed, and by New Year's Day, I found myself as the starting place kicker.

The game itself was an unbelievable experience. The media attention was more than any of us were accustomed to. The fishbowl atmosphere is very difficult to put into words. The team really came together and all year we'd talked about climbing Mt. Everest. Whenever you have a goal and you reach it, it's an unbelievable feeling when it's achieved. The moment is one we can all talk about for the rest of our lives.

Obviously, we were disappointed to share the title with Nebraska. At the same time, we felt we would beat them if we played. At the beginning of the season, coach Carr showed us the number of publications that ranked our schedule the toughest in the nation. After he read off the eight publications, he repeated a line from one: "If Michigan goes 8–4 with this schedule, it will be a good year."

Imagine their shock after we went undefeated.

When I went out to kick, there was one simple thing to remember: every kick counts. I grew up playing soccer, and I thrived on the pressure of the game. Whether it was a penalty kick in soccer or a field goal in football, any kicker will tell you the pressure moments are the best. You can usually tell by the smirk on their faces when the camera pans on them as they wait for their opportunity to kick. The kickers also have the oddest role on the team. I can fill a book with all the harassment stories kickers take. But on Saturday afternoons, they'll certainly pat you on the head and get you ready to go. Being a kicker can be a love-hate relationship. But it was definitely worth it when you put on that helmet and represented the maize and blue.

I still have my Michigan helmet back home in Indiana. It's out on display, because whenever people come over, they want to touch it or even try it on. It's quite a sight to see little kids putting this huge helmet over their heads. I don't mind it at all. It's great to see everyone excited about my days at Michigan.

The best story I can possibly share, however, about the aura of Michigan is one that involves my brother. It was in 1995, when Tim Biakabutuka torched Ohio State for 313 yards, and we upset them 31–23. After the game, I walked up to Tim as he sat there unfastening his gloves. He gave them to me. In turn, I ended up giving them to my brother. Instead of putting them away to preserve them, he still wears them nearly 10 years later every time he plays flag football. That's true pride for the University of Michigan.

An Indiana native, Baker booted a career-best four field goals against Indiana University in 1997 with friends and family present.

JAY FEELY
KICKER
1995–1998

GOING INTO MY SENIOR YEAR, I HAD GOTTEN MARRIED in the off-season and so did Jon Jansen. I didn't know this at the time, but I guess we were the first players to have gotten married while we were playing since Bo was there. Coach Carr's concern was that my focus was not going to be on football; it was going to be on my marriage. There were definitely highs and lows in my relationship with coach Carr, but through it all we had a great respect for each other. I think very highly of him to this day. But coming back after I had gotten married was definitely one of the lows. What Lloyd told me was, "Jay, I don't think your focus is on Michigan football. You can keep your scholarship and go to school but I don't think we want you on the team." This was coming after we had just won the national championship, and I was floored! I never questioned my commitment to the team. I was there the whole off-season working out.

Lloyd was testing me; he loved to do that—test people. He loved to push buttons to see if you were going to give in and fold or if you were going to fight back. I told him, "That's not the case. You know how I feel. I want to be on the team. I want to help my team and do whatever I can." He told me to meet him the following morning at 6:00 A.M. before team meetings. I came in and he said he was busy and could I come back the following morning at 6:00 A.M. He did this to me three days in a row. That was his way; he does this a lot, pressing people's buttons.

Jay Feely kicks off against Iowa during a game in Ann Arbor in 1997. Feely played four years at Michigan and has played five seasons in the NFL.

If I would have not shown up the second or third time, I would have been done. Lloyd would have had his answer—that I was not as committed as he wanted me to be. But I kept coming back, and finally he said, "You obviously want to be on the team and what we're going to do is place you at the bottom of the depth chart. You'll have to earn your way back up." Kraig Baker started the first game against Notre Dame kicking. He missed a couple of kicks. Coach Carr put me in, and I kicked the rest of the year.

I don't really know what he was thinking at this time. We were playing Syracuse the second game of the season. The night before the game, we always went to the Campus Inn, ate dinner, and stayed the night there. Dinner was always silent; you didn't talk during dinner. He called me up after the team dinner and said, "Jay, I've got a car outside and I'm sending you home. You were talking during dinner and you're obviously not focused." Again I was floored! I hadn't been talking; I hadn't done anything like that! A couple of the players whom I was with—Tom Brady was one of them—even said I wasn't talking. They didn't know what Lloyd was talking about. My wife had no idea what was going on when I walked in the door. I didn't even know if I was supposed to go to the game the next day.

Bobby Morrison was one of the assistants, he called me at my house when I got home and told me to make sure I was at the game before the rest of the team got there. I showed up, having no idea what was going on or if I was going to dress. The team came in, then Bobby came in, he told me to dress and go out for warm-ups. I went out for warm-ups and started. In fact, in the game, we were in a fake field-goal formation where they threw me a pass. Coach Carr never said anything about that formation; he never addressed it or told me it would be happening.

Two weeks later, we were getting ready to play Michigan State. It was on a Wednesday, and Lloyd called me into his office after practice again. He said, "I saw you staring at me today out on the field. I think you're pissed off at me and I don't think you're focused." This whole time I had never said anything. Whatever he said, I just said, "Yes, sir, Coach, whatever you want me to do." Finally, I just told him exactly how I felt. I said, "Coach, let me tell you where my priorities lie. My priorities are number one to God. Number two is to my wife and being a great husband. Number three is to this team and to help it any way that I can and be the best player I can be."

Then I said, "As far as you, and who you are, and what you think—I don't care what you think! I don't care what you do, or what you say! I'm just going to go out there and be the best I can be and help this team any way I can!" He looked at me and stood up and said, "Jay, maybe we had a misunderstanding." He stuck out his hand and we shook hands. We were then buddies the whole rest of the season.

It changed to the point that, when we went to Hawaii for the last game of that season, they had a big alumni dinner, and Lloyd asked me to give a little speech and do the invocation. It was a crazy year for me; an interesting journey behind the scenes with Lloyd and what he was thinking. I knew that I didn't have any ill intentions ever.

My relationship with coach Carr was unique. We had a deeper relationship than just coach and player. That's my nature; I love to talk to people about things that are much deeper than surface level. I went over to his house a couple of times. One time I was playing golf by his house, and because he told me to stop over whenever, I did. We watched one of the NBA Finals games when the Bulls were playing. We just sat and talked.

I'm very grateful to coach Carr. When I got done playing, he sat down with me to talk about my life after Michigan. He said, "Jay, I really believe that you have the ability to kick in the NFL. More than anything, I think you have the mental makeup to be tough enough to kick in the NFL. I think it may take you a couple of years. You may have to have the fortitude and willingness to keep trying when the door is closed."

That's exactly what happened to me. That always stuck in the back of my mind, I would always think back and listen to what he said. It meant a lot to me that he told me that. It took me two years after I got out of Michigan before I had the opportunity to play for the Falcons. Now I'm going into my fifth year. If coach Carr had not taken the time, and he didn't have to, and been honest with me and tell me something that maybe I didn't want to hear; I might not have had the fortitude to press on.

The biggest adjustment, I think, for any Michigan football player is learning the tradition. It was learning how hard Michigan works and that they do it a certain way with certain required standards. If you weren't willing to exert that amount of effort or you didn't have the character they were looking for, you would move on. They would ask you to leave or kick you out. They want a certain type of player, a certain type of man. Ideally, when you get to play at Michigan, you've molded yourself into that Michigan Man.

Jay Feely was involved with Athletes in Action while at Michigan and credits Bruce Dishnow, the group's leader, for developing his faith. Feely is currently a member of the New York Giants.

JON JANSEN

TACKLE

1995–1998

I WAS GOING TO BE A STAR BASKETBALL PLAYER. In high school, I did really well; I was all-state a couple years in basketball. But when it came down to it, I saw my best opportunity in football. My passion has always been football. It's been that way ever since I was young. There are a lot of things that you can do in football that you can't get away with in basketball. I like the physical contact of football.

My freshman year I was a tight end. Nobody knew who I was. I was just a number. Two great tight ends, Mark Campbell and Jerame Tuman, were in my class. I was just one of a bunch of great players. My body started to develop a little bit more. I began to put on some weight. When spring ball came around, I had a choice to make.

Coach Moeller sat down with me and said, "You could be one of these tight ends, you'll play and do well. But you have the opportunity to be a great offensive tackle. We really like your attitude, your ability, and the way you move. If it's all right with you, we'd like to try you at offensive tackle this spring."

As soon as they put me in there, I loved it! From the moment I played offensive tackle, I knew that was for me! When spring practice was over, the coaches told me, "Going into training camp next year, you're our number one guy. It's your position to keep or lose." I made my mind up that nobody was going to play right tackle while I was at Michigan other than me.

Right after my redshirt year, coach Moeller was dismissed. It was an uneasy time for me. I saw it as the coach who recruited me, knew me, and wanted me, was gone. Another coach was coming in, and I wasn't sure if I was his first choice or if he was going to bring in someone else. It was also tough because coach Moeller was such a good man. The way that he left was disappointing to everybody. We weren't disappointed in coach Moeller; we were just disappointed in the circumstances. I lost an opportunity to know a great man.

Coach Carr stepped in and did a tremendous job of making it an easy transition; making a tough situation OK in a lot of young kids' minds. But Lloyd was just the interim coach. Originally, it was presented to us that coach Carr was part of a national job search. He was going to be given his chance, but there were going to be others, as well.

That entire 1995 season the players felt, "If somebody else comes in, they're going to be watching the films." It was not only an audition for the coaching staff; it was also our audition since we had no idea who was going to be the coach.

Making Lloyd the interim coach was a good move by the university. All the assistant coaches stayed the same. So while there was a transition with the head coach, there really wasn't a big change in our approach during the season. Guys didn't have to learn a new system or prove themselves to new people.

When there's talk about players, it's a reflection on the coaches; and when there's talk about coaches, it's a reflection on the players. Nobody liked what was being talked about going into 1997. In some small part it was our motivation going into that year. We said, "Let's ignore everything that's going on and let's show everybody what this Michigan program is about. What we're all about."

We hadn't won a Big Ten championship, hadn't been to the Rose Bowl, and we were sick and tired of everyone talking about how, "Michigan went to four Rose Bowls in a row and then the program went down." We weren't going to be the guys that let the past guys down. A lot of players on our team believed, "Enough is enough! This is our year, let's go out and do it."

If you ask a lot of guys about the 1997 season, the most memorable moment was not the Rose Bowl victory against Washington State that sealed the national championship. The most special time, the time when we felt the most success and complete elation, was after we beat Ohio State in Michigan Stadium. To be able to celebrate with our fans, with everybody running onto

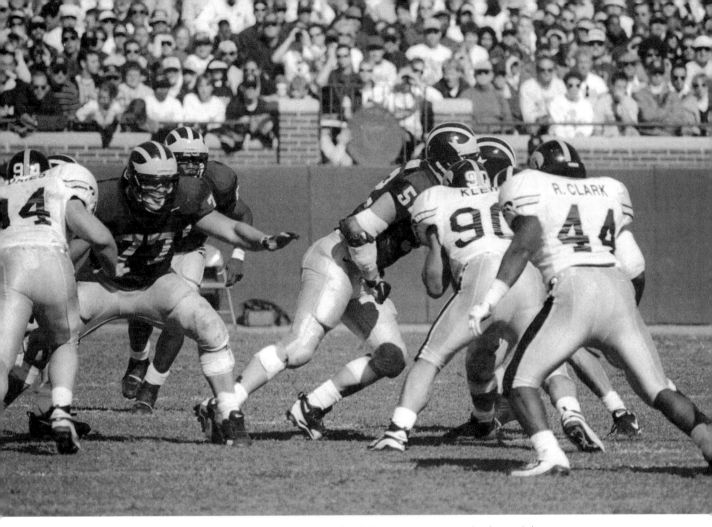

Jon Jansen (No. 77) blocks against Iowa in 1997. Jansen was recruited as a tight end but eventually moved to offensive tackle, where he became the 10th offensive lineman under coach Lloyd Carr to earn All-American status.

the field, knowing that we were the Big Ten champs and going to the Rose Bowl—that was something that is hard to put into words. Singing "Hail to the Victors" in front of everybody, it was amazing. Most guys will say that that was the most special moment of that year.

On a personal level, the best time I had during college, from my freshman year through my senior year, was the time spent with the guys in our offensive line room. The camaraderie we had was great, not just among the players, but with the coaches. Originally, it was with Bobby Morrison, then Mike DeBord, and when Terry Malone came in, he was a perfect fit. You always knew who the bosses were, they were always the coaches. But when we stepped in that offensive line room, it was a group of guys who had one mission—to be the best offensive line, and the best team in the nation that year.

The coaches were, and still are, among my best friends. I still talk to those guys, if not weekly, then monthly. I can't say enough about the way they develop boys who come in at 18 years old and leave as men at age 21 or 22. I had so much fun with the coaches and players; that's what I loved about being at Michigan!

I had such a great time with all the coaches that I hate to single one out, but I really enjoyed being around Bobby Morrison. When I was there, he had gone from a defensive coach to offensive tackle and tight ends coach, and then after that to recruiting coordinator and special teams coach. Bobby was a guy who always had a positive outlook on everything. Bobby was so much fun. I admired him a lot for his perseverance and ability to relate to players.

Michigan means everything to me. You can fill in any adjective you want, but it's about trust, honesty, success, and family. It's caring about your teammates. It's about players coming from all over the country, each with a different background, becoming one family. Every time I get a chance to get back to Michigan, it's like going home. Once you're in the family, you're never excluded.

Jon Jansen set Michigan's school record by starting 50 games during his four-year career. He was elected co-captain of the Wolverines in 1997 and 1998. Jansen is currently a member of the Washington Redskins.

The
NEW MILLENNIUM

DREW HENSON

QUARTERBACK

1998–2000

M Y FAMILY HAD ROOTS IN MICHIGAN, but I had never lived there until we moved when I was 15 years old and in the ninth grade. I had been a Michigan fan, but I didn't really understand how big it was until I was living there. When you see how much people follow it 12 months a year, you realize that Michigan is probably bigger than any professional team in the state. You knew the Wolverines were going to be there year-in and year-out, when you're 10 years old and when you're 50 years old.

I committed to Michigan in November of my junior year; the coaches told me they would not recruit a quarterback in my year or the year ahead of me. It didn't really matter if they brought someone in after me—that was not something I was worried about. If you got the chance, you wanted to line yourself up in a place where you could play. That was the reason I committed early, essentially, they could throw me in the 1997 recruiting class because I would be there, even though I wouldn't arrive for another 12 months.

I would have been crazy not to try and recruit other guys to come to Michigan once I signed. I knew I was going there, since I committed early, and thought, "We need to get the best skill guys on offense to come here with me." I was going to do whatever I could to get these other top players. We would all be the same year and could all go through it together.

With all the recruiting services, it wasn't hard to see who the top recruits were that were left. I knew that Marquise Walker and David Terrell were the

Quarterback Drew Henson gets set to throw during a 1998 game against Eastern Michigan. Henson left football to join the New York Yankees organization but eventually returned and is now playing in the NFL.

top two receivers and Justin Fargas was the number one tailback coming out. Lloyd, Stan Parrish, and Bobby Morrison, the recruiting coordinator, would tell me who they liked most, thought they had the best chance with, and when they were going to come in for their visit. I would give them a phone call and talk with them about what they were going through and what I was going through. I'd tell them why I was going to Michigan and try and put the thought in their head, "If we can get all these guys to come here, we can try and do some special things."

We sent Marquise my highlight video, and I was looking through all of their stuff down at the football office. I was trying to get to know these guys and develop some relationships. The guys that were in my recruiting class are still my best friends in the world. They were the ones I basically lived with on a day-to-day basis for three years. I had already done my research, with my dad being a coach, and was secure in what I wanted to do with my college pick well before anyone else was. I wasn't the only guy who did that. Anyone who has committed before anyone else does that. I had just committed so early that I had more time to talk with other guys coming out.

I was also the national player of the year in baseball as a high school senior. I was an All-American in football, but it was baseball that I set national records and had even more accolades. I was dead set on going to college one way or another. I really did not consider just leaving and playing baseball. I had already committed to Michigan, and the school had changed its recruiting pattern for me. I had gotten one heck of a recruiting class to come in with me and I wanted to be a part of it. From the ages of 18 to 21, I wanted to be a college student and have that experience. My two choices were going to be: sign a baseball contract that allowed me to play football, or go to Michigan and play both sports. I told the baseball teams from day one that they weren't going to get me as a full-time player right out of high school. That scared off 29 teams. The Yankees, Diamondbacks, and the Tigers were the three teams that, when it got to the MLB draft, were willing to work with me in one way or another.

The thing about Michigan that I don't think other programs do as much is really put pressure on their players in practice to prepare them for the game. That was one of the first discussions coaches had with me a freshman, "You've got to be a State Street quarterback before you can be a Michigan Stadium quarterback!" You had to prove it on the practice field. They put so much pressure on you in practice that the games were fun. The games were easy; there wasn't anything I went through on the field that was any more pressure than practice. They weren't going to put you out there in the stadium with America watching and the coaches' jobs on the line, if you hadn't proven that they could trust you with the ball.

The coaches were in a tough spot with me and Tom Brady. They had two quarterbacks who could have played anywhere else who were both in the program. We both really wanted to be "the guy," and believed that we could be and should be "the guy." We competed our asses off all the time for it. When I was a freshman, Lloyd played Tom and I was a back-up. I didn't like it, but I respected it. I never got mad at the coaching staff, that's just the way the situation was, so I had to move forward. They would always say, "Be ready," but that's all I could really do anyway.

I knew that tons of people in the state wanted me to start as a freshman; I would have been blind if I didn't. At the same time, I was 18 years old and there are a lot of things that you don't know when you're 18. As much as I wanted to play, I was also trying to get used to a whole different level of football compared to high school. As a college freshman living in a dorm and getting adjusted to school, there are a lot of things changing in your life on top of your football responsibilities. If I had played as a freshman, I think I would have done fine. It wasn't always easy, but the way things turned out, for Tom and for me, made us better athletes and a lot tougher because of it.

My relationship with Tom Brady was good. I'm still good friends with him and we talk a few times a year. But there is always that feeling out period when anybody new comes into the program. When I came in as a freshman, Tom had been there three years, going into his fourth year. He was 22 years old and I was 18—there were a lot of differences in maturity. The more Tom and I got to know each other, we had a lot in common; he was a baseball player and a big sports fan. If there was anybody I had to be in that situation with, I'm glad it was him. He made it easier on me and I think I made it easier on him because we were both able to handle it and pull for each other. The only two people that know what it's like to go through a situation like we did are the two people in it. Even though you were competing every day against each other, at the same time you're helping the other guy rally. It's a difficult position for two young kids to be in.

Lloyd Carr has been great to me from the day I met him. People always ask me who my hero is, who had the biggest influence on my life, and I say that Lloyd has had more of an impact on my life as an athlete and becoming a man than anyone besides my parents. I saw Lloyd and the coaching staff a lot more than I saw my parents after I finished high school. He takes on the responsibility of 100 kids. Lloyd taught me how to become an adult and a professional athlete. In college you're deciding on the type of person you will become. You're learning about yourself a lot more then than you did before, and probably more than you would after. I'm really glad that Lloyd was there.

I never said I was coming back for my senior year at Michigan. I said I wasn't entering the NFL draft. At that point, after my junior year, I knew I was either going to go play baseball or come back and play my senior year. I wasn't going to go into the NFL draft and that's what I said, people just took it however they wanted.

It wasn't the Yankees offer that blew me away; it was never the contract offer. If I was about money, I would have never gone to college. I would have collected a few million from Arizona or New York right out of high school and played baseball from the start. There was a lot more money available when I was 18 years old than what I signed for.

At 20 years old, I thought I wanted to be a baseball player. I had played baseball every summer, and those were my favorite memories growing up. To have the opportunity to go to the Yankees and play third base for them was something I always dreamed of. That's why I left. It was simply, at that time in my life, I thought I wanted to be a baseball player. The opportunity came and I took it.

I was surprised and hurt by the backlash that seemed to follow my decision. I committed to Michigan in the 11th grade. I took no other visits. I was as much of a Michigan guy, and I am as much of a Michigan guy, as you can find. I love the school. I love tradition. I'm as proud of my Michigan degree as anyone. I didn't understand why people would be that upset about a decision I made.

344

If you look at my best friend, David Terrell, he left Michigan at the same time. Why was there no backlash for him? He went and played in the NFL and I went and played baseball. If I knew that I wanted to be a football player, I probably would have left after my junior year, too. I don't know if there would have been a different reaction if I had gone into the NFL draft. But I had made a career choice. I was a Michigan guy through and through, but your college career is only three or four years. This was a decision that was going to affect the rest of my life.

A lot of Michigan fans don't think there is anything else out there besides Michigan sports, but there is. There are a number of years to live after you leave Michigan, and there are decisions you have to make that will affect that. My decision just happened to come when I had a year left of eligibility. I was a little disappointed in the fans' reaction. I didn't want to come back to Michigan for a while. I knew I had given my heart and soul to the program.

I'm sure even some of the coaches were upset with me, but the one who wasn't was Lloyd Carr.

Lloyd was disappointed I wasn't coming back, I'm sure, but he never treated me any differently. He was the one person who said I was always welcome to come back. That's one of the reasons I respect him even more. When I made this tough decision, I sat in Lloyd's office with my family and said, "Coach, the Yankees traded back for me. They made me a contract offer and I want to play baseball for a living. I feel like I want to do this right now and get it started." I cried when I told him, and it's about the last time I ever cried, because my time at Michigan meant so much to me. It did confuse me a bit, but it was a career choice that I felt like I wanted to make. I was ready to become a professional. I was ready to play baseball. Things have changed since then, obviously, but that's how I felt.

When I left school, I felt confident that I wanted to be a baseball player. Having done that for three seasons full-time, it was the first time I didn't have football. I realized that there was something missing and it took me that long to figure out what it was. I needed to be a quarterback; I needed the ball in my hands. Last year was the first summer since I was four years old that I didn't play baseball. I missed it some, but not as much as I missed game day and being a quarterback when I was playing baseball. It took not having football around for me to appreciate it and realize that my personality fits being a quarterback more than it does being a baseball player. There have been good times, and there have been frustrating times. But I'm a better person and stronger athlete because of it.

Playing for Michigan fulfilled my lifelong dream of being a college athlete at a major school. I'm proud to be a Wolverine. It helped me grow and become a man. I'm happy with the person I am today and I attribute most of that to my time at Michigan. It taught me to grow up and it prepared me for the world.

During his athletic career, Drew Henson has played college football for Michigan, baseball for the New York Yankees, and pro football for the Dallas Cowboys.

DAVID BAAS

OFFENSIVE LINEMAN

2001–2004

I DIDN'T GET INTO FOOTBALL SERIOUSLY UNTIL AROUND NINTH GRADE. I lived in Oklahoma until I was 12. My dad was laid off, so we moved to Sarasota, Florida, because we had vacationed down there. I played in one pee wee football league in sixth grade in Oklahoma and I was a big wuss. My brother would smack me around. I didn't know at that point if I even liked it.

When I began high school, I started off playing in the band, which most people make fun of me for. I played trumpet. John Sprauge, the football coach at Riverview High School, discovered me while I was practicing with the band. He said, "No, no. You come with me." Basically, he introduced me to the whole aspect of football.

My whole career started with Ned Ashton. He was the offensive line coach and he taught me how to be tough, how to play the game, and he kept pushing me until I eventually earned a scholarship. I acquired the taste for football through the way he coached and his passion for the game. Coach Ashton stressed being tough and playing hard. That's been my approach here at Michigan.

I was familiar with Michigan before I came up here for a recruiting trip. My dad was born and raised in Battle Creek, and my grandfather still lives there. My mother was born and raised in Saginaw and Bay City. It's funny looking at photos from the past of me and my siblings, we're wearing

David Baas played every position on the offensive line before being moved to center a couple games into his final season. He became the first Wolverine to win the Remington Trophy as the nation's best center. Baas was the first pick of the second round by the San Francisco 49ers in the 2005 NFL draft. *Photo courtesy of Per Kjeldsen.*

Michigan T-shirts. Back then, I had no idea, but after attending Michigan, I look back now and say, "Wow, I used to wear stuff like that."

On my recruiting visit, I fell in love with the atmosphere and what Michigan was all about. Michigan Stadium overwhelmed me. I loved it the first time I saw it. I thought the coaches and the entire staff were very genuine about what type of people they wanted to bring into the program. They really appreciated me being there, which ultimately led me to make my commitment to Michigan.

Making the transition at Michigan was hard at first. I had hurt my knee at the end of my high school season and tweaked it again during an all-star game. When I arrived at Michigan, the medical staff told me I needed knee surgery. The doctors said I could always risk it and have surgery later, but why risk that? I was going to redshirt anyway. It was tough having surgery right off the bat.

It was disappointing not getting to know Steve Hutchinson, Jeff Backus, Moe Williams, and Dave Brandt. I was lucky to get to know Jonathan Goodwin when I backed him up for a year at left guard. It was difficult because I wanted to be out on the field, learning from such great players as the ones I just mentioned. Mike Gittleson became my best friend. I was in the weight room for most of the year. My teammates didn't know me very well. They didn't have an idea of what I was going to be like. Some of them called me "the Ghost" because they were just skeptical of me.

I felt pressure to perform. Then came another injury, a broken wrist, and I had to play with a cast on. There was just one obstacle after another that I had to overcome to prove myself. I played with a cast and a splint on for most of my redshirt freshman season. I just continued to work hard and do my best because a lot of people saw my ability and what I could do for the team.

Everything turned around for me toward the end of my redshirt freshman year. I was a backup, but I started getting healthier. I got a little playing time. Once that spring hit, right before my redshirt sophomore season, I really started coming out of my shell and produced. Once I got into the season, it was nerve-racking at first.

I had one start against Purdue at left guard. The only thing I can remember was missing a block, then turning around and yelling at John Navarre to duck as he got sacked. On the sidelines, my fellow offensive linemen told me coach Terry Malone was constantly yelling, "If Baas messes up one more time. . . . So-and-so, you're going in and we're moving so-and-so over."

He was just going crazy. Then I'd settle down and do something good. Then I would miss a block and he would go crazy again. Because of that game, I take credit for the gray hair he's got on his head.

It's a hallmark quality for a Michigan offensive lineman to be able to play any position. I actually came in to play tackle. I played tackle for possibly a week. The coaches then moved me to guard. I've been a guard ever since then. After 29 or 30 starts at guard, I got to a point where nobody could beat me in practice or in games.

Situations arose, and I was moved to center, which I had practiced a little bit in spring ball. The coaches were split on whether to move me or not. It was a week before the Iowa game, and the coaches told me, "You have to go in there. We have plenty of confidence in you, you're the captain."

I had never played center before in my life until that Iowa game. I had to learn the last fourth of the playbook. I'm glad I paid attention in meetings because knowing what to do is entirely different than doing it; making the calls while everything's going a million miles an hour in front of you. That's why I respect the center position a lot more than any other position. It's much harder than what people give it credit for. At tackle, you have better athletes going against you, but it's a lot simpler.

Being named All-America at center was very surprising to me. It's that whole scenario where I'm thinking, "Wow, if I do my job and don't care about what is going on around me, then good things happen." I'm very proud to be an All-American and be on the All-American wall at Schembechler Hall.

The biggest surprise of all was receiving the Remington Trophy. I was blown away. I had only played nine games at center and I still won the trophy for the best center in the nation, which was just outstanding. I felt grateful. All the centers at Michigan should feel vindicated because it represents them too. Being the first to win that Remington Trophy sets a new standard for centers at Michigan; I'm glad to start that tradition. It gives more incentive for centers in the future to become what I was.

Jim Fisher was my roommate for two years, and I don't want to say he's a smart-ass, but he is. He's a great person, but he doesn't show any sign of emotion. He seems uptight. He'll go to Burger King, cut out a coupon for a buy-one-get-one-free and still brings his own slice of cheese to put on his Whopper because he doesn't want to pay the extra 25 cents. He's always been that way.

After the Rose Bowl this year, it kind of struck us that we were going our separate ways. It was all over, and it was sad. I'm not sure, but I think I almost saw a tear come out of that man's eye. Jim came over and actually gave me a hug. We were almost speechless. We didn't know how to say good-bye to each other. It was almost like one of those soap opera things in a weird way. It then hit me—everything was over. I had to move on with my life, but I knew that Michigan and the players I have grown to know, and the great friendships I have, will always be there.

David Baas has been All–Big Ten at two different positions. In 2002 and 2003, Baas was All–Big Ten at guard and in 2004 he was All–Big Ten at center.

MARKUS CURRY

SAFETY

2001–2004

WHEN WE LOST TO NOTRE DAME IN 2004, it wasn't a nail in the coffin, but it sure felt like one. We took it personally. We had no business losing to Notre Dame, especially that early in the season. It was a spear in our heart. We had to look in the mirror and ask ourselves how serious we were about this season. Were we really serious about being champions? We could have easily folded, but we stuck together and worked together. We weren't about to throw all our practice and hard work down the drain. We weren't going to listen to the outside sources, and we were going to do whatever it took. We did everything to get our swagger back and to win the rest of our games. When people are talking badly about us, that's when we want to throw it back at them and say, "Take that!" This is Michigan. We take pride in everything we do.

I was always a Michigan fan. My brother Julius graduated from Michigan, and once he went there, I had the opportunity to see everything about Michigan firsthand. Michigan is family-oriented. That's another factor that brought me there. Playing at Michigan is something I'll always cherish. Being in the Big Ten and having the most wins of any college football team in Division I football, you just can't beat that.

Coach Carr is the man. I have the utmost respect for him. He not only wants to see you grow as a football player but he also wants to help you grow from a boy into a man. He always had the door open for you and was always very truthful. He stressed success and the steps it takes to become successful. Coach Carr was always looking out for his players.

During the 2004 season, freshmen Chad Henne and Michael Hart were unbelievable for us. They have passion for football and they knew how to step up and play. Some guys can't handle that pressure, but those two true freshmen definitely stepped up to the plate and took advantage of their situation. The mental toughness they showed all season was unbelievable. They showed how important it is to be prepared for a game.

I truly believe the preparation time for games is more intense than the game itself. This is especially true before the Ohio State game and the Rose Bowl. It's put up or shut up. It really is. You don't want it to seem like a job, but if you're not pulling your weight, it's obvious you're not doing enough to prepare. Getting amped up to play a football game is second nature. Of course you'll go out and be ready to go. But it's all about how much you've really prepared for the game. Playing in the Rose Bowl was fun, but there was still preparation involved. You want to go and relax and have a good time, but it's important to remember you're there to take care of the business of winning a bowl game. You can't just be satisfied playing in California and just playing in the game. You need to be prepared to play those games and win them.

352

Playing in Columbus is like a dogfight, from the bus ride all the way to the stadium. We've had beer cans thrown at us, and I've seen two- or three-year-old kids giving us the middle finger. They don't even know what it means. It just tells you how much of a tradition that game is. The game is crazy. When you walk into that stadium and you come out of the tunnel and see nothing but red, you know it's pretty serious.

My biggest game was at the Rose Bowl during my junior year. Being able to play in that game was unbelievable. Everybody in the world was watching you. You really can't explain how it feels. It was like a chill that never leaves your body. It is remarkable and I'm blessed to have had the opportunity to play in the Rose Bowl. Not just once, but twice.

The Rose Bowl against Texas was where we played Michigan football throughout the game, despite the outcome. I don't care what anyone else says—we played Michigan football in that game. The comeback game against Michigan State last season [2004] and the comeback against Minnesota in 2003 were other examples of Michigan football. Of my four years at Michigan, we

Markus Curry was a *USA Today* All-American defensive back and punt returner coming out of high school in Detroit. At Michigan he compiled 119 tackles and 7 interceptions during his stellar career at cornerback. *Photo courtesy of Per Kjeldsen.*

did our best preparation for the game against Texas. We had everything we needed to succeed in that. It just didn't turn out our way.

Coach Herrmann took a lot of heat for that Texas game, but he is one the best coaches I have ever played for. I don't believe anyone else could have had us better prepared for that game than coach Herrmann. He's on another level as a human being. He always has fire in his eye when he talks about football. He always prepared his players and I will vouch for him on any day. I don't care what anyone else wants to believe or say, coach Herrmann always prepared us to win.

As a senior, I knew I had to step up to the plate. When you're younger, you imitate the people you see. But as you get older, you realize there are a lot of people watching you. We always talked about our legacy, not only in terms of a program but also as a player. You have to look at yourself and ask if you really did lead by example. If you didn't, then you're not only wasting your time, but you're wasting your teammates' and coaches' time as well. They depend on you to make the right decisions. Of course you'll make mistakes. I made many. But the difference is I learned from them and did my best to avoid them again. And there were some stressful moments for me at Michigan.

I definitely believe the incident off campus where I was shot was blown out of proportion. What they read in the newspapers is all they have to go by. I know the type of person I am, and so did my teammates and coaches. I believe that's what kept me focused and grounded when I was suspended. If you feel guilty, you will act guilty. Football is stressful enough. But adding extra issues is even worse. But you need to stay strong, and realize that everything happens for a reason. I didn't complain about it. I knew it happened for a reason and I dealt with it.

I was definitely afraid after I was shot. The doctors told me how lucky I was. The bullet came so close to my spine, and had I been hit there I would have been paralyzed. In my mind, I was blessed. God stopped that bullet from doing any more damage. I could have been paralyzed or worse, I could have died. Knowing my life would not be affected, I then wondered about my football career. Would I be able to play again? Going for a month and not knowing if I would be able to play was pretty stressful. I tried to play it off, but it was tough.

I don't completely remember telling my brother that I would play again only because of the medication I was on. But Julius agreed with me. He reassured me that I would play again. In time, I did get back on the field. My faith in God did help me, and I know without my faith I wouldn't have made it through that situation or Michigan.

I definitely believe Michigan is about tradition. Nothing has changed with the tradition at Michigan. You can look back at the teams in the sixties or seventies up to the present day. It may be different guys, but it's always a similar outcome. Michigan teams do not slump. The atmosphere and attitude are unbelievable within the coaches and the players. We take it very seriously. You will have your ups and downs, but I knew coming to Michigan there was always the chance to be a champion. It's right up on the wall: "Those Who Stay Will Be Champions." You go further by asking how you can apply that to your life. Being a Wolverine means you're mentally tough as you grow from a boy to a man. I don't think it's an experience I'll ever have again. There's nothing else like it. You're always a Wolverine.

Curry made a career-best 10 tackles against USC in the 2004 Rose Bowl. He was signed by the San Diego Chargers of the NFL in 2005.

LLOYD CARR
ASSISTANT COACH
1980–1994
HEAD COACH
1995–Present

THE FIRST TIME I EVER SAW MICHIGAN PLAY IN PERSON was the 1969 Michigan/Michigan State game in East Lansing. A friend of mine was an assistant coach at Michigan State so he got me a place to stand right down in the north end zone. I was there when Duffy Daugherty brought out the Michigan State team and Bo brought out the Michigan team. That was really the beginning of my knowledge of Michigan football as it is today in terms of Bo Schembechler.

When I was a high school coach, Bill McCartney was a high school coach at Divine Child and Bo hired him at Michigan. I came up a couple of times to watch practice and met Bo. I think I was the first coach Bo hired whom he didn't know. I had worked as an assistant at Eastern Michigan University. Alex Agassi, who was a very close friend of Bo's, was the athletic director at Eastern Michigan. From Eastern Michigan, Gary Moeller hired me at Illinois; I was at Illinois with Mo for two years. The job became open at Michigan. Jack Harbaugh had left to take the defensive coordinator job at Stanford. Both Mo and Bill McCartney recommended me for the job. Bo told me that

Head coach since 1995, Lloyd Carr guided the Wolverines to their first national title in nearly 50 years in 1997. Carr trails only Fielding Yost and Bo Schembechler in victories by a Michigan head coach.

the one guy who really sold him on hiring me was Alex Agassi. I'm thankful to all those guys because it certainly was a great opportunity.

I don't think anybody who assisted Bo had an adversarial relationship with him. Bo had a reputation of being a tyrant. It's amazing the number of people who ask me what it was like to work for him! He was demanding, but he was very fair to the coaches and the players. What I loved most about the job were the staff meetings. We had some great staff meetings that would last a long time because Bo would get into politics; he loved to talk about what was going on in the world and in sports. We've had some great arguments through the years. More than anything else, the most fun was in our staff meetings other than coaching the games. We had a great time and a great camaraderie, too. Bo was a fun guy to be around. He was not necessarily a fun guy when we lost, but there was nothing in my experience coaching with Bo that I didn't appreciate.

Looking back on it, I appreciate the tremendous integrity with which Bo ran this program the most. He never cheated or violated the rules in recruiting. He always stressed to us the importance of recruiting kids with good character, kids who could succeed academically here, and who would represent this program in a way that would make everybody proud. Those are really the things that make his legacy so special because he won more championships, I think, than anybody, but he did it the right way, and that is hopefully the way it will always be here at Michigan.

I had the benefit of having great mentors. Bill McCartney and I went to the same high school, so from the time I met Bill at 13 or 14 years old, he played an important role in my life. When I had the opportunity to go to work for Gary Moeller at Illinois, I learned an awful lot about what it took to be a successful coach. Nobody worked harder than Gary Moeller, nobody had more passion toward the game, and nobody had more fun coaching it. When I came here to Michigan, I was prepared from the standpoint of the coaching part of it. Certainly Bo mentored me in the 10 years I was around him, either in the press box or on the sideline beside him.

In 1987 we had a change on the staff, Mo moved to offense and Bo named me the defensive coordinator. I was able to have a leadership role, and that's something that really prepared me. When you're a coordinator, you learn quickly that you have a responsibility, not only to do your job, but you also have a responsibility to everybody else on the team. The greatest lesson I've learned here is that Michigan, first and foremost, is about team. It sounds simple but I really learned that here. I learned it by watching Bo and being around him and great coaches who were selfless, hard-working, dedicated people; who had great passion and love for the game and the guys they coached. I was fortunate to have some leadership opportunities. In the defensive coordinator's job, like any coordinator, you become responsible for calling and making decisions that will impact winning and losing. The standard here is so high that that brings a pressure and expectation. If you can't handle it; you're not going to last long.

There have been a number of times, down through the years, I saw Bo do it, I saw Mo do it, and I've done it; you make a decision not to recruit a certain guy because you don't feel like he can fit into a team-oriented program. This is a program that's based on achieving as a team. That's the beautiful thing about Michigan football, there's a great camaraderie in this program. We are not a star system. We get as many stars as anyone else, but it's not a system based around the star. We don't build a team around a star. You take advantage of the abilities of your players, but it's always based on playing the game as a team. You have to teach and believe that if you get guys working together, playing as hard as they can, and doing what they are asked to do, then you're going to come out as a championship team. I think that is Bo's greatest legacy.

I've made a few mistakes as the head coach at Michigan. The biggest was the comment about people not knowing anything about pressure. I said that because it was such a painful time in my life. I saw a person that I had great respect and love for, Gary Moeller, go through an incredibly difficult time. The way I was able to handle the pressure of my new role as head coach was because I had incredible support from the players and the coaches who stayed in the program. More than anything else, that particular time speaks to what being a team is all about. We certainly did not achieve all of our goals on the field in 1995, but in a very difficult time for all of us, we were able to do some very positive things. It was because we were a team-oriented program; we were a family that pulled together. I give all that credit to the people who were here because what they did, in working through a difficult time, was very special in my mind.

We have had some teams with injuries, and some with bad breaks, but every team goes into the season with the idea of winning the national championship and being the very best. In the 1997 season, I remember vividly one of our team meetings. In training camp in the fall, there is always one meeting that the captains run. In it they decide what their goals are. I can remember Charles Woodson saying, "I'm sick of losing. Let's quit talking and just do it." He was only a junior, but the way he said it sounded like he was a senior. Charles was not a man of many words, so when he said something, it had an impact on everybody in the room.

We also had great captains, and that team just decided that they were going to concentrate on each game as it came. Every team talks about doing that, but the difference is in 1997, that team did it. For 12 straight games they weren't thinking about anything except the game in front of them. Even as the pressure grew late in the season, particularly after a great win at Penn State, and we moved into the No. 1 spot—the pressure was tremendous. Because of the way they approached the previous nine games, they were able to win the last two and finish it. I knew we had a good team that year, if we could play together.

Brian Griese had a sensational year and didn't get the credit he deserved; he was a great quarterback that season. Nobody appreciated all the little things that he did. He was surrounded by a lot of guys who wanted to win, and we had that great defense. It was a team effort with so many guys who played important roles in big games. We did something nobody else expected us to do. The Big Ten writers had predicted us to finish fifth in the conference and we were 17th in prseason polls. I've always tried to tell the teams that have followed that 1997 team: it doesn't matter where you're ranked or what they say about you. Each team will leave its own legacy, which will be based more than anything else on how you play together as a team.

360

What stands out for me is when I stood out there on that podium at the Rose Bowl and the trophy was presented. I can remember looking out at that stadium and knowing that we had just won the national championship. A bunch of guys had taken a lot of criticism and we knew that together we had done something historic. I've had plenty of special moments at Michigan, but that stands out.

If you look at the quarterbacks I've coached, I've learned the most from Brian Griese. There have been a couple of guys in the NFL that I really respect, Dan Henning for one, and we've had some conversations about Brian Griese. One of the media guys here in Detroit said Brian would never play in the NFL, but what Brian Griese taught me was that intelligence, accuracy, and toughness were the most important qualities in a quarterback. He did not have the strongest arm, but I've never been around anybody more accurate.

When Tom Brady succeeded Brian, he was exactly the same kind of guy, neither one had great mobility. When you look at the guys that I've had, they've all won a championship. Brady won a championship, Navarre, Henson, Henne; they have all won a championship. The only one of those guys that had great mobility was Drew Henson. What they did all possess was very good intelligence, toughness, and the ability to throw the ball accurately.

During his second year, Tom Brady came in and he talked about leaving. I thought for sure he was going to leave and I told him, "Wait until the end of this year, finish spring practice and the season and see how it goes." He came back in to see me the next day and I thought he was gone. Tom sat down in a chair right in front of my desk. He leaned forward and said, "Coach, I'm going to stay at Michigan and I'm going to prove to you that I'm a great quarterback." That was a toughness you learned from. Here was a kid who was not going to be denied what he wanted to achieve. I've never been around a greater leader than Tom Brady, and we've had a lot of great leaders and captains here.

I've learned something from every guy I've coached, that's what is beautiful about this job. So many times, you think that you're doing all the teaching, but if you're paying attention, these guys are smart, competitive, and tough. They will teach you, too. That's where I've been fortunate.

There are a lot of issues that go on during recruiting that should be on the periphery. Guys make mistakes. I run into a lot of guys who say, "Coach, I wish I would have done this or that." The guys who don't say that are guys who make a decision to go to school for two reasons. First, what kind of degree do they have the opportunity to receive? That's where any coach at Michigan, in any sport, at any time, is always going to have the benefit of representing one of the greatest universities in the world. Second, what kind of an opportunity does he have in football? What kind of program does he want to play in? What kind of guys does he want to be around? What are his individual goals? If a guy wants to be in a great program, play with great people, and get a great education, that's when I tell them they have to take a look at Michigan.

They may not decide to come here, but I want them to come up and bring their parents to meet everybody in our program and as many people at the university as possible. The truth is, when they get here, our players and the university sell themselves.

I've never been someone who subscribes to the theory that some coaches are great, charismatic recruiters. If you have something as good as we have here, it's about presenting it. We just had a reunion where every living football player who has ever played at Michigan was invited back. To hear the stories of guys that played for Fritz Crisler, Bennie Oosterbaan, and Bump Elliott, you really get a sense of history and tradition and the people who have been here. I had a coach in the NFL tell me one time, "The difference is that the Michigan players I've coached all love their school." That is why this tradition has continued to be so strong. By and large, we've hired great coaches and recruited great people.

I've always understood that it's a game played by human beings. That's why I believe that you don't assign blame when events don't go the way you want them to. You take your lumps, keep working hard, and keep fighting. That way you have a chance to be successful. That's what I have tried to do. When I have made a mistake, I've tried to tell the players. I think the main objective as a coach is be honest and understand that if we all do our best, we can live with the results. It may not be the results we want, but as long as we can say, "We gave it everything we had," to me that is what athletics are about.

What it means to be a Wolverine . . . it's been everything.

Lloyd Carr's Michigan coaching career began in 1980. Since 1995, he's been the Wolverines head coach and has compiled an overall record of 95–29–0 and a Big Ten record of 63–17–0. Carr's teams have won five Big Ten championships and one national championship in 1997.